Essays on Indian Writing in English

Dieter Riemenschneider

Essays on Indian Writing in English

Twice-Born or Cosmopolitan Literature?

RAWAT PUBLICATIONS

Jaipur • New Delhi • Bangalore • Guwahati • Kolkata

ISBN 978-81-316-0814-2

This edition published in arrangement with Tranzlit GbR
Bahnhofstr.16a, D-61476 Kronberg im Taunus, Germany.
www.tranzlit.de.

Published by
Prem Rawat for **Rawat Publications**
Satyam Apts., Sector 3, Jawahar Nagar, Jaipur 302 004 (India)
Phone: 0141 265 1748/7006 Fax: 0141 265 1748
E-mail: info@rawatbooks.com
Website: www.rawatbooks.com

New Delhi Office
4858/24, Ansari Road, Daryaganj, New Delhi 110 002
Phone: 011 2326 3290

Also at *Bangalore, Hyderabad, Guwahati* and *Kolkata*

Designed and typeset by John Denny,
Puriri Press, Auckland, New Zealand

Typeset in Adobe Minion Pro

Printed and bound in India.

Contents

vii *Foreword*

xi *Preface*

1 **Early Critics of Indo-English Novelists**
Meenakshi Mukherjee and M.K. Naik

6 **Human Labour and Alienation**
Mulk Raj Anand's Novels

26 **The *New Poets Manifesto***
P. Lal and Contemporary Indian English Poetry

37 **History and the Individual**
Salman Rushdie's *Midnight's Children* and Anita Desai's *Clear Light of Day*

51 **Indian Women Writing in English**
A Brief Look at Short Stories of the 1970s and Early 1980s

59 **Marginalizing the Centre — Centring the Periphery**
The Critical Debate on 'Indian' Literature in English

76 **'In the Days When the Love Laws Were Made'**
Arundhati Roy's *The God of Small Things*

92 **Global Fantasy — Glocal Imagination**
The New Literatures in English and their Fantastic ImagiNations

106 **Crossing National Borders**
The Indian English Novel since the 1990s

114 **Nature and Landscape**
An Evolutionary Psychological Analysis of Raja Rao's Writing

125 **'The Train Has Moved On'**
R.K. Narayan's *The Guide* and Literary History

139 **Glocality and its (Dis)contents**
The Future of English Language Literatures Studies

154 **The Persistence and Creation of Internal Borders**
India in Aotearoa New Zealand

167 **Translating Cultures**
Pictorial and Literary Representations of India in William Hodges's Paintings and Travel Book

180 **Retrieving Human Rights**
Indra Sinha's Novel *Animal's People* and Critical Cosmopolitanism

195 *Sources*

196 *Photo Credits*

197 *Author's Publications*

Foreword

One of the notable moments of the triennial conference of the Association for Commonwealth Literature and Language Studies held at Hyderabad in 2004 — and perhaps a no less notable moment in Professor Dieter Riemenschneider's long and distinguished career — came at the book-launch at that conference of his newly published work titled *Postcolonial Theory: The Emergence of a Critical Discourse: A Selected and Annotated Bibliography from the Beginnings to 1990* (Tübingen: Stauffenburg Verlag, 2004). It was in a sense the compendium of his life's work, it carried a Preface by Homi Bhabha, and Bhabha himself came to a crowded room that evening to launch the book with a gracious speech.

Now no two critics can be more unlike than Homi Bhabha, the arch theorist, and Dieter Riemenschneider, the arch archivist, and yet, by bringing both these persons together, that happy occasion demonstrated how these two seemingly contrasted critical pursuits are necessary for each other. The value of Dieter's book was affirmed in two further incidents that followed. When the evening had concluded and the guests had all departed, it was found that besides the copies sold, four copies of the expensively priced book were missing. As Dieter cheerfully enough put it, "They grew feet and walked off!" Obviously, it was a volume worth begging, borrowing or stealing — to say nothing of buying. The other incident concerns a young lady in India who had once published an article on R.K. Narayan and then drifted away from research and academics, but when it was found that her singular contribution to scholarship had been canonized in a 'foreign' book, it was an occasion for her proud husband, a senior police officer, to give a grand party to all their friends. Dieter had ensured that she had her moment of internationally acknowledged fame.

In a book that followed, *The Indian Novel in English: Its Critical Discourse 1934–2004* (Jaipur: Rawat Publications, 2005), Dieter provided a long historical introduction to the genre and then a discussion of the trends in the evolving criticism of each of the three novelists whose works he focused on, Mulk Raj Anand, R.K. Narayan, and Raja Rao. I am the proud owner of a (feetless and therefore perfectly legitimate) copy of this work too, and in his inscription, Dieter modestly describes the book as "my attempts at mapping archival material; the reader as cartographer?"

This self-description appears quite apt, especially when we read of his efforts, ever since he first arrived in India in 1963 to teach German at the University of Panjab at Chandigarh and subsequently at the University of Delhi, to discover and buy copies of "stored away, dusty and yellowed copies of Indian novels [to be found in] far-flung places."(vii) His own personal store now of hundreds of Indian novels in English and thousands upon thousands of the reviews and critical articles and books that they generated must be difficult to match not only in India but anywhere in the world.

But Dieter is not only an archivist, a cartographer and a collector of the Indian novel in English; he is also a tough and discriminating critic of this corpus in his own right. The present book offers ample evidence of his critical bent. He is as assiduous a close reader of the texts as he is a bibliographer, and there is a quiet, undemonstrative firmness about his literary judgments. He does not bow to what the majority of Indian critics may have said, and such sturdy independence gives his own evaluations contrasting and added worth. He is widely read — and over a longer period than some young Indian critics who readily make what Dieter calls "sweeping generalizations" (73), and he does not hesitate to take to task even older Indian critics whom he finds to be either too "formalist" or "ideological", or "ethnocentric" and "narrow-minded." (1–5)

There is a special historical value to the earlier essays in this volume for they are focused on writers who were thought to be colossal giants in their own day but are a bit like desolate grand monuments now. Dieter also includes in his sweep some authors who were minor then and are all but forgotten now, such as Mary Erulkar or Meher Pestonji. He compares and contrasts authors who may be thought to be poles apart, such as Anita Desai and Salman Rushdie. He notes that William Hodges, the celebrated British painter of Indian landscapes, had earlier painted New Zealand landscapes as a fellow voyager with Captain James Cook. He breaks what for many of us is new ground when he surveys the Indian presence in Aotearoa New Zealand, a discovery apparently facilitated by the fact that his wife, the poet Jan Kemp who makes a fleeting appearance here (165), is from New Zealand. And he brings us up to date when he discusses in his last chapter a novel, *Animal's People*, which was published in 2008, and also refers to writers from the Indian languages whom he has read in translation, including Daya Pawar, Omprakash Valmiki and Uday Prakash.

Dieter Riemenschneider's engagement personally with India and professionally with the Indian novel in English is now more than 50 years old, a landmark which was recognized when the Indian Association for

Commonwealth Literature and Language Studies invited him to deliver the keynote address at its annual conference of 2014 held in Chandigarh, the new university where Dieter's India connection began in 1963. His has been a journey of slow and steady labour, quiet accumulation, and unflagging dedication. The present volume is a rich and ripe representation of the range of his erudition, and a fitting finale of his scholarly endeavour if that is what he means it to be.

Harish Trivedi
Delhi, April 2016

Former Professor of English, University of Delhi
Former Chair, Indian Association for Commonwealth
Literature and Language Studies

SURYASAMUDRA AFFAIR

The wicker chair neatly positioned
next to the glass-top wicker table
between two ancient stone-carved pillars
protected by Lord Vishnu and Lord Shiva
in the Octagonal House
Suryasamudra Kerala

no wonder the mosquitoes are perplexed
about the place and undecided
where to settle for their food
nor do the palm-fronds undisturbed
by cawing crows care for this brood

yes, this arrangement pleases me
and so I ask to have my tea
while wondering
should I leave
would I grieve
for what must stay behind

and yet somehow I know
I'm not the one
who'll grow
sitting in wicker chairs
having tea affairs

Trivandrum
14 January 1994

Preface

When the idea crossed my mind to put together a selection of my essays on Indian literature written in English, I was not really aware of questions that might arise during the process of sifting these texts and deciding which ones to choose and include. How should I proceed? Would it be worthwhile to return to the 1960s and my very first responses to novels, poems and stories I had read while teaching German to Indian students at Punjab University in Chandigarh and later at Delhi University? Should I go back to the 1970s and early 1980s when I considered setting up a course on Commonwealth Literature at Frankfurt's Goethe-University? I also asked myself whether these early essays wouldn't merely reflect a sense of time long past, a period when I had paid attention mainly to novels and stories about colonized people written between the mid-1930s and the mid-1950s. And what about my comments on poems composed in the 1960s and 1970s by a generation of poets who felt that they had to break away from their older colleagues' allegedly outdated poetic practices, revered public figures like Manmohan Ghose, Sri Aurobindo, Rabindranath Tagore or Sarojini Naidu?[1] An almost forgotten episode after national and international publishers had brought out comprehensive poetry anthologies as well as the collected work of single poets like Nissim Ezekiel. Finally, wouldn't my remarks on women short stories of the 1970s and 1980s, texts that had challenged Hindu and Muslim ideas and practices of social roles forced upon them, be totally outdated now with the Women's Movement and its campaign for women's emancipation and liberation?

1 Cf. V.K. Gokak, ed. & sel., *The Golden Treasury of Indo-Anglian Poetry*, New Delhi: Sahitya Akademi, 14th ed. 2005

By contrast: which criteria could I cite in favour of my idea of republishing essays written during the last two decades? Wouldn't they — at least some of them — have found their way into libraries, an academic's study or her and his computer? And after all, hadn't the international publishing industry, the media and academia 'discovered' Postcolonial Literatures, including their Indo-English variant, and promoted their study during the last two to three decades? And weren't students and researchers already paying a lot of attention to both its texts and its critical scene?

In spite of my reluctance I have selected a small number of publications which I feel could be read (again) for a number of reasons. A sequence of chronologically arranged essays written over a period of half a century reflects my outside observer's growing familiarity with Indian English writing. It permits insight into its thematic, formal and stylistic shifts and changes as much as into its growth in scope and quality. Besides, it also throws light on the course of a critical literary debate that has focused — and continues to do so — on the pros and cons of Indians writing their novels and poems in English as well as it does on the controversial issue of their 'Indianness'. Finally, the chronology of my essays points out the difficulties critics have faced with a corpus of texts that resisted easy categorization, particularly from a Eurocentric perspective with its claims on the universal validity of critical formulas: a critical reception that has moved towards analytical methods which encompass cultural-historical, multi-, inter- and transcultural approaches as much as post-structural, post-modern, eco-critical, or evolutionary-psychological ones.

A final remark to round off these considerations. Till the end of the 1980s readers of Indian writing in English experienced not a few difficulties that would often affect the quality of early scholarship, among them the lack of a critical tradition and the inaccessibility of an author's work and critical commentaries. For example, by the time my first essay appeared in 1967[2] you would not find more than three dozen entries each on the Indian English novel or on R.K. Narayan's works, just about twenty on Mulk Raj Anand and merely a dozen on Raja Rao[3]: all novelists whose first books had appeared in the 1930s. The place of comments, perhaps even essays, could have been located in a bibliography — if these had been compiled.[4]

2 "An Ideal of Man in Mulk Raj Anand's Novels", *Indian Literature* X, 1 (1967), 29–51

3 See Dieter Riemenschneider, *The Indian Novel in English: Its Critical Discourse 1934–2004*, Jaipur: Rawat Publications 2005, 50–52; 128–131; 230–236; 346–347

4 K.R. Srinivasa Iyengar's *Indian Writing in English* (Bombay: Asia Publishing House 1962), the most comprehensive study available at the time, does not deal with the novel genre and contains no notes on or references to critical studies of the three leading novelists, Anand, Narayan and Rao

Nor was it easy to get hold of novels, short story or poetry collections in book stores even in Delhi, Bombay, Calcutta or Madras, let alone in London. More often than not I was dependent on information obtained from authors[5] who would assist me in contacting their publishers, or from Indian academics like M.K. Naik in Dharwar, C.D. Narasimhaiah and Anniah Gowda in Mysore or P. Lal in Calcutta who had taken an interest in a body of texts totally shunned outside their own university departments.

I was told, the most promising place to find critical material on English writing in India was the National Library in Calcutta, which I visited in 1966. But though I came across a number of entries in several journals, and these mainly on Indian English novels, I could have saved the tedious train journey from Delhi and back and experiencing the little advice I received from the library staff. To my great fortune I met P. Lal at his home, learned a lot from him about his *writers workshop*, acquired a number of poetry collections of hitherto unknown authors he had published, picked up issues of the *miscellany*, a very informative and lively two-monthly — and was introduced to David McCutchion, an English scholar teaching at Jadavpur University, who had taken an interest in the Indian-English novel, and especially in Raja Rao's *The Serpent and the Rope*. I still cherish the lively and encouraging talks I had with both of them and Lal's generosity and hospitality. Nonetheless, even in India such contacts were few and far between and could only be kept alive by postal correspondence after I had returned to Germany in the autumn of 1966: a place not only geographically but also intellectually far removed from the concerns of Indian novelists and their controversies with a public that was little inclined to take them seriously — which I had experienced first-hand after a lecture on Anand's novels the Max Mueller Bhavan, or the Goethe-Institut, had arranged for me in New Delhi in late 1965.

Why then did I continue my research in this field? My answer is simply, intellectual curiosity. I just wanted to learn more about the culture of a country I had chosen as my temporary abode as a Lecturer in German, and once I had discovered that Indian writers had composed stories, novels and poems in English. Besides, English translations of literary works from Sanskrit, Hindi, Bengali or Malayalam as well as historical, social-political and philosophical background studies had bolstered my decision not to

5 Mulk Raj Anand connected me with Kutub Popular, his Bombay publisher, and G.V. Desani advised me to contact a friend in Bombay from whom I bought a copy of *All About H Hatter* that he had stored in his flat

discard my fascination with Indian culture simply because I had left the country. India's long-lasting colonial dependence on Great Britain and the role English had played — and continues to play — had opened my eyes to a very different and exciting dimension of 'English' Studies from the one I had been aware of as a past student of English literature at Frankfurt University.

Over the next few years my PhD thesis, book reviews and essays as well as papers read at conferences kept me busy, as did my plan of introducing a syllabus of Indian English literature at Frankfurt University. Eventually, I was even more successful by setting up **N**eue **E**nglischsprachige **L**iteraturen und **K**ulturen — NELK for short, or New English Literatures and Cultures: a syllabus and a study centre — in the Department of English and American Studies at my university, with Indian English literature being part of it. But let me now turn to the present collection.

From amongst my nearly 200 publications, which include my thesis, monographs, edited works, book reviews, lexical entries, short notes, reports and articles, I have selected fifteen essays published between 1974 and 2015. They range from my almost slap-dash remarks on early Indian critical studies of the novel to the question of the genre's most recent engagement with critical cosmopolitanism. As regards one of my main interests, the development of the novel since Anand's work of the 1930s right up to Sinha's *Animal's People* (2006), I could not miss noticing that many authors critique the social inequalities in their society, a most significant thematic characteristic that has bearing on a critic's approach. As a student of English who had been profoundly influenced by the school of New Criticism and close reading, I realized from the beginning that it would be unforgivable not to contextualize these works historically and culturally the better to understand them.

And what about my students and readers outside India? Wouldn't it by my task to combine textual analysis with information on content? Not to shirk from talking about plots and to include poems or passages from short stories in my essays that would not just substantiate my arguments but simply inform students and readers about unknown texts? And hopefully encourage them to acquire their own copies. Methodological considerations such as these that informed my writing between the 1970s and the 1990s do not any longer carry the same weight since the globalization of the publishing and electronic industry has eased access to creative and critical texts worldwide. It is a development from which my engagement with the history of the critical discourse on Indian English literature, the reception of the novel and the debate on 'Indianness', has benefitted as well.

The diversification of the New English Language Literatures since the last decades of the 20th century has not stopped short of the writing from the Indian homeland and its diasporas. One of its most recent contributions hails from Aotearoa New Zealand. As yet it may not have rooted itself firmly in the country's literary scene but it offers a unique feature in that among its authors we come across Indian immigrants and their descendants from different parts of India, from Malaysia and Fiji whose mother tongues differ widely, but all of who write in English. What an exciting prospect for indigenous critics on their search for 'Indianness'! As also for readers of Indian English literature.

Dieter Riemenschneider
March 2016

Early Critics of Indo-English Novelists

Meenakshi Mukherjee and M.K. Naik

MEENAKSHI MUKHERJEE'S *The Twice Born Fiction: Themes and Techniques of the Indian Novel in English* (1971) is the first study by an Indian critic dealing with the Indo-English novel of the 20th century. Differing from M.E. Derrett who combined a social and historical approach with a critical evaluation of works under scrutiny in her book *The Modern Indian Novel in English* (1966), Mukherjee's methodical approach, she says, is based on "strict international standards of literary criticism" (12); standards that include such categories as 'technique', 'point of view', 'consistency', 'structure', 'character' and 'plot'. References to the novels' historical context would be limited to short reflections upon trends in 20th century world literary history. Arguing that "any novel is best read as the novelist's reaction to his material" (38), the question remains to be answered what precisely is meant by "the novelist's reaction" and how 'literary value' can be accorded to those works that deserve to be called representative among the one hundred and fifty novels that were published during the last sixty to seventy years.

As her main criteria Mukherjee selects 'technique' and 'theme' in the sense Mark Schorer discussed them in his essay "Technique as Discovery" (1948). While I have no objection to Mukherjee's grouping of novels under topics such as 'The Making of a Nation' or 'East-West Encounter', her use of 'technique', which includes analytical categories like 'point of view', 'plot' and 'character', reduces her procedure to a formalist consideration of a literary work that neglects important contextual aspects like historical and cultural conditions of producing a novel, as well as possible influences from the Indian literary tradition. Also, the criterion 'point of view' may underplay the individual character of a particular work and mislead the critic to judge it more or less exclusively in terms of its technical competence and excellence. Further, categories like 'character' and 'plot' applied irrespective of the novels' Indian social and cultural context may lead to erroneous judgements since their meaning derives from Western perceptions.

Finally, Mukherjee's methodical approach is no less relativistic than Derrett's (which she had complained about). While formal criteria are applied to establish whether M.R. Anand succeeds with his characters (which according to Mukherjee he does not), 'character' is given a different meaning when applied to Raja Rao' s novels. Here historical and cultural considerations are included in order to appreciate Rao's achievement. Such procedure does not merely reflect methodological inconsistency but also an ideological bias, since the critic's negative verdict of Anand's works relates to her doubt, if not rejection of this writer's philosophical and social stance of a Western influenced humanist, while the positive judgement of Rao's works suggests her closeness to Rao's idealistic philosophy based on the school of Advaita Vedanta.

M.K. Naik's *Raja Rao* (1972) is the first monograph on a writer who has, over forty years of literary activity, published three novels, a collection of short stories and several essays and sets out to explore why these few works have been acclaimed so highly. Suggesting that Rao is perhaps the most 'Indian' of all Indo-English writers, Naik examines what is meant by it. Two approaches can be distinguished. The first chapter deals with the biographical circumstances of Rao's life and includes a discussion of probable or certain influences on the writer, while the main part of the book is devoted to a detailed analysis of his works according to their years of publication. Naik's analysis is formalistic and informed by close reading. Categories such as 'plot', 'narrative strategy', 'technique', 'blend of forms' reveal the influence of Western critical scholarship, and though he also explores the author's life, factors of influence and possible models, it remains unanswered whether 'Indianness' serves Naik as an historical or a literary category, even if historical and social aspects play a minor role. Thus, the relevance of the Advaita-Vedanta philosophy for Rao is only considered in the context of the structural and formal consequences it has on Rao's works; the fact that it must be seen at the same time as the ideology of a small élite in India does not bear on the critical evaluation of the author's novels. Compared with other Indian critics, Naik does not subscribe to the universality of literary norms and standards but prefers an ethnocentric point of view; yet he remains unaware of the fact that 'Indianness' also signifies an historical category, which in turn disables him to recognize the 'ideological' character of Rao's writings. Rather, it seems to be more important to answer the question whether the author succeeded in synthesizing Western and Indian narrative elements and thereby established the genuine Indo-English novel.

Two examples illustrate the questionable assumptions of this view. Comparing Rao's *Kanthapura* with Ignazio Silone's *Fontamara* (1933), Naik points out their distinct differences — although there are thematic similarities — to demonstrate the 'Indian' character of the former novel, the message of which is defined as spiritual and cultural, while Silone's work is dismissed as being purely political. A second example is Naik's discussion of historical influences on Rao and their function in his novels. Mainly those influences are mentioned that have affected the 'Indian' side of Rao's character and psyche, for instance, the author's own strong interest in philosophical speculation and his fascination for women; in other words, the 'Indianness' of Rao's works is explained by the extraordinary 'Indianness' of the writer's psyche, proof of which can be seen in the way Indian culture has influenced him.

M.K. Naik's *Mulk Raj Anand* (1973) is the first comprehensive Indian study of the most productive and versatile Indo-English author. During a career spanning forty years he has written a dozen novels, about forty short stories, numerous essays, books on Indian history, art, and even cooking. This wealth of material, however, is not the only problem facing a critic of Anand's writings. No other Indo-English author has been dealt with more often and more narrow-mindedly by Indian critics because of his strong political and social convictions. Thus, Naik faces a double task. He has to assess Anand's achievement, and he has to deal with the premises of other critics, that is, among others, with methodological and epistemological aspects of literary criticism. Does Naik answer these questions by merely repeating often raised accusations against Anand as a propagandist and as a failed artist? Or does he tackle the problem of art and propaganda in a more basic manner?

Naik uses the same methodical and structural approach as he does in his *Raja Rao*. He starts with the thesis that Anand's writings are governed by the modern Indian writer's central theme: modernity versus tradition. The author's works will be investigated as to "the extent to which he [Anand] comprehends the nature of both and that of the confrontation." (7) No indication is given as to the premises a judgement will be based on, viz. whether Naik will apply only aesthetic criteria or also socio-literary or perhaps even psycho-literary ones. Rather unexpectedly and fairly early in his assessment, he concludes that Anand's works are of an ambivalent nature — less so in his 'better' novels, but prominent in his weaker ones —, and proof of this, Naik argues, can be found both, in their content and form. The writer, a champion of modernity, is charged with professing an often one-sided view of Indian tradition and of playing down or even overlooking its more positive aspects. Formally speaking, he is criticised for his lack of artistic control due to his reformist zeal. This is noticeable when he interferes in his stories either by way of preaching or by sentimentalizing them. (24)

Naik takes great care to prove his point and, conceding the tenability of his conceptual premises, he presents a convincing and detailed study. For instance, he proceeds more painstakingly in his analyses of plot, character, narrative form and language than Meenakshi Mukherjee does in her book, and his approach is more comprehensive. By contrast with others critics, he arrives at discriminating judgements, for example in the chapters "Two Untouchables: Bakha and Bikhu" and "The Indian Peasant Goes West: The Lal Singh Trilogy". Besides, he follows Anand's dictum that the novel must have a "form which has its own integral pattern." (18) Critic and author also agree that philosophy has to be implicit in a novel while doctrinaire opinions must not be imposed upon it. (18)

Within the frame of reference applied by the critic and keeping in mind that Anand's artistic achievement is being measured by his own categories of the artistically successful novel, Naik's final judgement that the writer's works are characterized by a peculiar ambivalence (23) cannot altogether be refuted. Rather, it is suggested that the problems of Anand's socially committed novels should not be discussed exclusively from an aesthetic perspective but also as to their social function within the context of present day Indian society. This suggests that the meaning of 'tradition' and 'modernity', and exactly what these words stand for, should be examined more closely — which Naik, unfortunately, does not do. On the whole, he is content with referring to those institutionalized forms, patterns of behaviour and thinking that Anand employs to represent tradition and modernity, while the author's own thoughts about them are dealt with only marginally. Naik might argue that he discusses the writer's philosophy in the first chapter of his book calling it humanistic, even if it is eclectically presented. (16) Besides, he accepts the author's view that man's attempts to come close to the ideal of a humanism are faced with numerous barriers, stating that "forces that come in the way [...] are [...] the numerous forms of exploitation of man by man, such as capitalism, colonialism, fascism, feudalism, communalism, communism etc." (17) Still, apart from the fact that communism is never called a form of exploitation in any of the novels, the barriers cited by Naik are not understood by him as interrelated historical stages. Though Anand may concentrate his stories on colonialism (*Two Leaves and a Bud*) or communalism (*Death of a Hero*), he relates these "forms of exploitation of man by man" to specific historical periods, economic conditions and political systems. Neglecting this point, Naik's illustrations of modernity and tradition do not altogether convince. Had he understood them as shaping and determining Anand's writings, his analysis of a single novel would have led him to a more precise understanding of tradition and modernity. To mention just one example. When Naik reproaches Anand for not showing "the inner development" of Munoo in *The Coolie* (45), he overlooks Anand's intention to demonstrate how ruthlessly Indian caste-society destroys the sensitive psyche and the vitality of a 'low-caste' character by not offering him a chance to "develop."

Naik's method of treating social conflicts more or less formalistically stands in the way of his dealing overall fairly with Anand's presentations of historically evolved patterns of social, economic and political suppression and exploitation that affect an individual's life. Had he taken account of this aspect, Naik's final view that Anand's novels repeat and reproduce social and socio-religious conflicts, would have been proved wrong.

Works cited

Novels

Anand, Mulk Raj, *Untouchable*, London: Lawrence & Wishart 1935 [London: Bodley Head 1970]

—, *The Coolie*, London: Lawrence & Wishart 1936 [*Coolie*, London: Penguin 1945]

—, *Two Leaves and a Bud*, London: Lawrence & Wishart 1937 [London: Liberty Press 1954]

—, *The Sword and the Sickle*, London: Jonathan Cape 1942

—, *Death of a Hero: Epitaph for Maqbool Sherwani*, Bombay: Kutub-Popular 1963 [New Delhi: Arnold-Heinemann 1988]

Silone, Ignazio, *Fontamara*, Zürich: Hebling & Oprecht 1933

Critical Studies

Derrett, M.E., *The Modern Indian Novel in English: A Comparative Approach*, Bruxelles: Edition de l'Institut de Sociologie, Université libre de Bruxelles 1966

Mukherjee, Meenakshi, *The Twice-Born Fiction: Themes and Techniques of the Indian Novel in English*, New Delhi, London: Arnold-Heinemann 1971

Naik, M.K., *Raja Rao*, New York: Twayne 1972

—, *Mulk Raj Anand*, London, New Delhi: Arnold-Heinemann 1973

Schorer, Mark, "Technique as Discovery", *The Hudson Review* (Spring 1948), 67–87

Human Labour and Alienation

Mulk Raj Anand's Novels

> *And as he thought of the conditions under which he had lived, of the intensity of the struggle and the futility of the waves of revolt falling upon the hard rock of privilege and possession, [...] he felt sad and bitter and defeated, like an old man.*
>
> *Coolie*[1]

THE FOLLOWING DISCUSSION OF LABOUR and alienation in Anand's novels is meant primarily as a contribution towards socio-literary investigations of literature and as an examination of the question as to how far the problem of labour — human labour as investigated into by the sciences of economics, sociology or political science — might be the object of literary criticism. The objection may be raised here that problems pertaining to human labour can hardly be of more than a purely thematic interest to the literary critic. To deal with this question adequately, then, will entail the task of touching briefly upon the methodological problems involved and to point out why, according to the definition of the concept of labour as it is understood here, we feel that analyzing the problem of human labour as depicted in literary works may offer an important insight into ideological aspects of such works and also into their artistic achievement.

First of all we shall deal with Marx's and Engels's concept of labour which then will take us to a short account of the forms of alienation of labour as historical phenomena caused by the development of factors of production and the ownership of the means of production. The concept of labour according to Marx, however, bears also on methodological questions,

1 Mulk Raj Anand, *Coolie*, ed. Atma Ram, *Mulk Raj Anand — A Reader*, New Delhi: Sahitya Akademi 2005, 157

problems of methodical approaches and the purpose of inquiries into the meaning and function of man's cultural products. This means that we shall have to refer to this aspect before our attention is turned to Anand's novels. There are good reasons why this writer has been chosen and we shall try to substantiate this choice in preference to that of any other Indo-English novelist by his unique ideological and artistic position in the field of Indo-English literature, as well as to the fundamental question of this paper.

Marx[2] defines labour as that specific activity of man which distinguishes him from even the most highly developed animals, the primates. In the working process man confronts nature in order to appropriate it in forms useful for his own life. Thus the working process is useful activity through which useful articles are produced. Through labour man learns to control nature and make her serve him. To help achieve this purpose in a more and more perfect manner man develops his means of production, which become more and more refined and complicated the further this process of appropriating nature advances. Labour is the eternal and natural condition of human life and thus independent from any specific form of life. Besides it is a free activity of man because its purposes are determined not by nature but by man himself. Thus labour means self-realization of man, an act of real freedom. Finally, as it is always performed in society, it is necessarily a social activity, though the forms of labour will differ according to the forms of society in which it is being performed. This means that labour is not an unchangeable activity which repeats itself through the same forms but it is a process leading to ever higher forms of activity because it is purposive activity.

Specific forms of labour which developed in the course of history differ in some respect from labour as such and as defined above. For instance, coinciding with the emergence of private ownership of the means of production which will now form the basis of society, classes emerge which participate in private ownership to a varying degree. As soon as man is separated from the means of production, as soon as they are no longer his property he is separated from the most important condition of labour and his work loses the quality of being a free and independent act, an act

2 All direct references to Marx and Engels are taken from: Karl Marx, *Texte zur Methode und Praxis II, Pariser Manuskripte*, Reinbeck: Rowohlt 1968
G. Klaus & M. Buhr, *Marxistisch-Leninistisches Wörterbuch der Philosophie*, 3 Bd., Reinbeck: Rowohlt 1972
Further references: S. Kaviraj, "Alienation and Literature", *Journal of the School of Languages* (Winter 1973-1974), 1-27

of self-realization. Man's labour has become estranged labour because not he but the owners of the means of production will determine what and how he has to work and to produce. Under conditions of a class-society work will appear as coercion to those who do not dispose of the means of production. Labour can be performed as physical or mental activity. This division develops hand in hand with the emergence of private ownership of the means of production. The two forms of labour become even opposed to each other in antagonistic class-societies where physical labour is reserved for the working-classes and mental labour for the owning classes.

Marx distinguishes several aspects of estranged labour which, however, all derive from its most important moment: man's alienation from the product of labour. After having 'lost' his means of production, including the power of disposing of his own labour, man is forced to work for the owners of the means of production who will determine which articles he will have to produce. The worker thus confronts the products of his own work as alien products; he does not realize himself through his work and in his products because he does not determine the purpose of his activity. His own products rule over him.

Alienation from the products of labour entails alienation in the act of production. Since the worker cannot decide which articles he has to produce the working process itself becomes something alienate to him. He will experience the act of production not as self-realization but as suffering, as a loss of his human nature.

Alienated labour causes man's alienation from the species. Man achieves self-realization as a human being, member of the species, by working upon the material world, nature, in order to appropriate it for his own purposes. The object of labour can thus be called realization of the life of the species. Alienated labour, however, takes man's object of production, nature, from him. Thus he loses the opportunity to develop his faculties and to employ them in a useful manner. Consequently, his essential nature cannot be realized, it appears as something alien to him, merely a means to secure his individual existence. Finally, alienation from the species means alienation of man from man. If man is alienated from his own nature he is also alienated from the human nature of his fellow-beings, a fact most obvious in the existence of antagonistic classes within a society.

Reflecting upon Marx's definition of human labour and his discussion of the various aspects of alienated labour under conditions of a class-society, we have to bear in mind that, in order to be able to assess the function of labour in Anand's novels, only one aspect of the problem has been referred to so far: Marx's ideas will help us select those passages in Anand's novels in which the problem of labour — in particular physical labour — is aesthetically presented in literary form, that is, through character and event. The question still to be answered is whether the concept of labour is of any relevance as a category in literary criticism. In other words, is there a logical correlation between the function of art — here, of literature — and the definition of man through labour?

In a passage on labour to be found in the so-called *Paris Manuscripts* Marx maintains that man as a member of the species behaves as a universal, free being. This means, as compared to animals, man produces on a universal scale; unlike animals he is not just subject to his immediate physical needs and thus is forced not only to reproduce himself through labour but he is able to reproduce nature. He can not only produce articles by imitating the process of work of any species but also produce according to the laws of beauty, that is, the laws inherent in objects. And it is through this activity that man achieves self-realization and forms the world freely and independently according to the laws of beauty.

If this assumption holds true, man's works of art are characterized by their specific form of 'appropriating' reality, i.e. according to the laws of beauty; but they are nevertheless products of human labour: "The evaluation and formation of objective reality (nature and society) according to aesthetic criteria form an integral element or the realization of man's essential faculties (through labour, it should be added, D.R.) and become manifest in all forms and fields of productive activity!"[3]

The subject of art is not an arbitrary one. In literature, we must admit, the most important subject has always been the totality of man's social activities and relations. If the artist 'appropriates' the world aesthetically by depicting man according to the laws of beauty he will do so by presenting man's essential nature, i.e. man as member of the species and that means: in his work.

Whether the term work is to be given a comprehensive and philosophical connotation is a question which would require further discussion. We shall be content to say that such a notion would subsume a definition of work in a restricted and concrete sense. This paper will be restricted to an analysis of those scenes in Anand's novels in which man is depicted performing physical labour. However, we can infer from what has been said above that as long as man's essential nature is not being presented aesthetically a writer's artistic achievement can obviously not be termed completely successful. Yet, this notion should not confuse the critic since he has to deal

3 Klaus/Buhr, vol. I, 120

with concrete literary works produced under specific historical conditions which themselves have to be taken into consideration when assessing the artistic achievement of works of art.

Though man at work is described more often by Anand than by any other contemporary Indo-English writer, the number of these depictions barely exceeds two dozen and there are several novels without any such scene. This is surprising because the subject matter of almost all novels is the life and fate of either an outcaste (*Untouchable*, *The Road*), lower-caste peasants (*The Old Woman and the Cow*, *The Village*), some of whom lost their land to the landlord or the money-lender (*Coolie*, *Two Leaves and a Bud*), industrial workers (*Coolie*), or craftsmen (*The Big Heart*). All the main characters in these works with the exception of Lalu (*The Village*) and Panchi (*The Old Woman and the Cow*) are forced to sell their labour in order to survive. In the case of Bakha (*Untouchable*) or Bikhu (*The Road*) their social status as outcastes does not permit them to rise in society and to perhaps secure the material means for themselves which might allow them to lead a more independent life. It is the caste system which forces them not only to sell their labour but also to do so under conditions laid down by the Hindu castes. Alienated labour is as much the fate of this social class as is their unalterable economic and social position. Alienation in the act of production as well as alienation from their fellow men is not the result of economic forces as under capitalistic conditions but of noneconomic forces, i.e. feudalism.

A second group of characters in these novels forced to sell their labour are Munoo, Hari (*Coolie*) and Gangu (*Two Leaves and a Bud*), former peasants who could not pay back their debts and high interest rates charged by landlord or money-lender and who were forced to sell their land and search for work elsewhere. While Munoo is made to experience a whole gamut of occupations — he works as a domestic servant in various households, as a market coolie offering his services to anyone, an unskilled worker in a small pickle-factory and a wage-earner in a cotton factory owned by English capitalists —, Hari earns his living in a factory and Gangu on a tea-plantation in Assam.

Anand makes use of these characters in order to illustrate the economic and social changes taking place in India under colonial rule during the period of developing capitalistic methods of production. He shows how a combination of economic and non-economic forces brings about a fundamental change of life to these members of Indian society. In *The Big Heart* yet another group is depicted: the thathiars or the coppersmith community of a large North-Indian town. Ananta, the protagonist of the novel, and Mehru, a minor character, represent two aspects of labour in this community of craftsmen. While Ananta is presented as a fairly independent worker whose income is based on piece work and who has his own small workshop, Mehru has already lost his independence as a craftsman and has started working as a labourer in a factory which has just started production of consumer goods. As in the two novels mentioned above, Anand presents the processes of change taking place under capitalistic conditions and affecting a traditional type of labour. Mehru and others of his craft indicate the fate of the whole community which even a highly skilled craftsman like Ananta will be unable to avoid eventually.

To sum up: by presenting a number of characters who for non-economic or economic reasons are forced to sell their labour in order to survive, Anand does not only show his interest in their individual fate but also illustrates the economic and social changes taking place in India under colonial rule and the gradual transformation of a feudal society into a capitalistic one. This preliminary insight into a characteristic feature of Anand's novels shows that he is well aware of the function of narrative writing which consists in revealing man's essential nature through the individual case. We shall now investigate the author's manner of portraying individual characters at work so that we may be able to assess the relationship of individual activity and its essential meaning. We have chosen a procedure which will deal with each novel by itself, because we are less interested in a systematic survey of scenes of labour than in a critical evaluation of the literary function of labour within the frame of a fictitious story. To begin with we will analyze two characters who can be considered the owners of their means of production: Lalu in *The Village* and Panchi in *The Old Woman and the Cow.*

At the beginning of the story, Lalu, a young peasant boy and the protagonist of *The Village*, is being shown at work in the fields. (26-31)[4] Here Anand illustrates Marx's definition of (disalienated) labour as an act of man's self-realization in a most convincing manner. Lalu's self-realization is not presented objectively but he is shown as being aware of his achievement. This also proves Anand's own awareness of the important meaning of this experience and his profound understanding of the character of human labour and its essential function for man. More than this, the author's artistic achievement lies not only in mediating his insight through this

4 The edition of Anand's novels used here is Kutub Popular, Bombay, *Coolie* (n.d.); *Untouchable* (n.d.); *Two Leaves and a Bud* (2nd ed. 1951); *The Village* (1954); *The Big Heart* (n.d.); *The Old Woman and the Cow* (1960); and *The Road* (1961)

highly individualized character but must also be seen in the fact that he makes him represent a certain historical stage in the development of man in India. This is how Anand proceeds.

Lalu is digging the ditch through which water from the irrigation system is to flow on to his family's fields. It is late in the afternoon towards the end of summer but the sun is still extremely hot in the Punjab at this time of the year. At the beginning the narrator only describes Lalu's actions which claim all his attention: "For a long moment his mind was a blank. He was only conscious of the mounds of moist earth yielding to his blade." (27) But then Anand turns towards Lalu's thoughts which result from his present activity: He contemplates the "peculiar knack" needed to hit straight and the fact that his skill has "not deteriorated through learning" (28) as the elders of the village always maintained. The awareness of the prejudicial nature of the view that physical and intellectual skills and qualities exclude each other — as the example of so many 'educated' city boys seem to prove — reveals that for Anand labour means essentially a combination of hand and brain while he repudiates a decision of labour reserving the manual part for one section of society and the intellectual one for another. Lalu continues: Learning and physical skills would enable him to "increase the productivity of the land, and set the house in order..." (28); "he would prove his worth to them." (29) Lalu's thoughts illustrate the idea that the abolition of the division of labour would enable man to fulfil his needs even more satisfactorily, and of controlling nature and make her yield more to man's will.

There is still another aspect of the relationship of man and nature as manifested in the act of work: man's control over nature is at once self-realization. The writer expresses this idea through a most simple image:

> As he began to dig deeper and hacked the earth again and again, till the water flowed through the shapely bed of the ditch, he felt an admiration for the energy that flowed with the laughter of the sun like tingling warmth in his body. (28)

The analysis of this scene has proven the almost philosophical meaning of man's relationship with nature. Characteristically, this does not suffice for Anand's purpose because he is not primarily interested in man as such but in Indian man living during a particular time: While at work Lalu's turban, meant to hold up his long hair which he, as a Sikh, is not allowed to cut, has opened. He reflects on the necessity of upholding traditions and beliefs under changed circumstances. Similarly, thinking about clothes which are not suitable for work makes him impatient with customs and conventions still in practice. Lalu's feelings and thoughts displayed do not only express his individuality but they reveal characteristics of the society which shaped him and illustrate the dialectical relationship between man and reality.

Anand depicting man at work does not only succeed in conveying a Marxian understanding of the relationship between man and nature and man and society as a dialectic relationship; he not only illustrates the central meaning of work for man but he also succeeds in presenting these ideas through the medium of literature in an aesthetically convincing manner by using the individual case to illustrate the essential nature of man.

There is another, rather similarly constructed scene depicting Lalu once more at work in the fields. (105-112) He is ploughing with the help of his bullocks and then starts reflecting on his work. Wondering about the obedience his bullocks show he ponders on the problem of obedience and submission generally and is reminded of an incident which had occurred only a few days before: after he had had his long hair cut, the whole village community, his family included, punished and humiliated him because of this sacrilegious act. Contemplating on breaking the bullocks' will thus helps Lalu to understand his relationship to traditional society: it is characterized by his complete dependence and society's claim to rule supreme over the individual.

At this point of the novel Anand introduces a new aspect of the character of labour. Lalu's shocking experience proves to be so strong that he is unable to overcome his frustration through work:

> He took the curve at the edge of the field and hurried Thiba and Rondu with a fierce push, inspired by the will to forget himself in his work. But his thoughts returned and he was torn and lacerated-full of a bitter hatred for the world. (109)

And later:

> He kicked the sod of the dark, moist furrows and looked round to see how much of the field he had ploughed. But his gaze turned inwards and strained to probe the depth of his dreams, in the dense gloom of his head. (111)

Labour can no longer be considered to bring about fulfilment and self-realization because, being always a social act but having lost its social function, it has become meaningless to the individual at war with his society, its values and norms. The alienation from man which Lalu experiences at the same time takes the form of alienation from the process of work.

Anand conveys this idea aesthetically and even makes Lalu understand part of the essential meaning of his experience:

> For what was life? [...] To be sure it was not all play, and one had to work. 'But I like work', he thought, 'if they will only love me more, and let me love them, I could soon work off their debts and relieve them of their troubles.' His soul swelled with adolescent exuberance and exultation, and he felt that his battles were half won. But what was the use? And if you couldn't do such a little thing as have your hair cut without being abused and beaten and insulted by the village, how could you do anything that went against their other superstitions? (111)

Precisely at this moment of his life Lalu realizes that he has to find his own way, and, indeed, looking at his further development as it is depicted in the second part of this novel and the following two parts of the trilogy, *Across the Black Water* and *The Sword and the Sickle*, we realize the author's idea of letting us watch Lalu's progress and his efforts to establish a new, more meaningful and more stable relationship between himself and other members of this society.

A final point is to be mentioned about this scene which indicates the change having taken place in Lalu's relationship to nature. While formerly it appeared to be one of harmony, alienation from man entailed alienation from nature — or, as Marx puts it, from the species. Nature appears to be distant, even unfriendly:

> And he went forward, dazed with the weight of his own perplexity, breathing evenly in the sunny stillness of the fields where the breeze was turning colder and colder with the damp odour of the newly turned earth, and where the transparent light of the sun shimmered through the elements and sighed among the blades of grass. (112)

We shall now look briefly at the second novel in which a major character is depicted as the owner of his means of production. Though Panchi, the antagonist in *The Old Woman and the Cow*, does not yet have to sell his labour but still owns his fields he is depicted as a completely alienated individual. The only scene which shows him at work in his fields (27-31) is a case in point. While ploughing with his bullocks, he is struggling continuously with them: this takes the form of either coaxing or brutalizing them. Work for Panchi is at once a necessity, a means to make ends meet, and an act of suffering. His thoughts of others, especial of his wife and relatives, reveal his alienation from man: unlike Lalu he is not concerned about their fate but only about his own. Panchi appears to be highly egoistic, full of self-pity and superstitious beliefs. He seems to have lost his humanity and is presented as a socially isolated person.

Panchi must be considered a unique creation among Anand's characters. Though there is no lack of totally alienated individuals in his novels they are almost without exception members of the owning classes. Since it is in their interest not to change economic or social conditions prevailing in an antagonistic class-society these characters appear to be static, 'one-sided', unchangeable, in short: types. Although they are alienated individuals they do not suffer from alienation as members of the working classes do. As Marx puts it:

> The owning classes and the proletarian class are both alienated. However, the owning classes are pleased with this condition and realize alienation as their own power; it appears to them as human existence. The proletariat experiences destruction through alienation.[5]

Panchi, on the other hand, does not belong to the owning classes but has internalized the values and norms of the ruling classes to such an extent that he identifies himself with them rather than with those of his own class. Thus his alienation from man takes the specific form of alienation from his own class.

In the scene depicting Panchi at work Anand succeeds in making transparent a degree of man's self-alienation which leaves no room for understanding oneself or others but will eventually lead to self-destruction, Panchi is the only example of a member of the dispossessed classes in whom Anand shows the full effects of alienation on man's mind, a depiction which reflects the author's insight into a development taking place under conditions of fully developed capitalism which did not yet prevail at the time when this writer composed his work. However, we have to keep in mind that Panchi plays the role of the antagonist in this novel whereas his wife Gauri, being the protagonist, embodies Anand's belief in the strength of man to create conditions under which self-realization will be possible again. Panchi, on the other hand, embodies Anand's fear of a potential development of man in India who will not learn to understand the reason for his suffering.

5 Marx & Engels, *Werke*, vol.2, 37 (my translation)

Alienation is the fate of those characters that have lost their own means of production and are forced to sell their labour. In our discussion of this group of individuals we shall restrict our analysis to that of Munoo, protagonist of one of Anand's earliest novels, *Coolie*. It is not surprising to find that this work contains by far the largest number of scenes showing man at work, if one keeps in mind that it was written in England in the early 1930s, a period well-known for many writers' commitment to the plight of the working-classes.

The first striking characteristic of the scenes depicting Munoo at work is the portrayal of the protagonist as a person for whom work is not an isolated act considered only as a means to secure his survival but as a social act: Munoo is always concerned either about the welfare of others (Prabha and his wife, Hari and his family) or about the way they react and behave towards him. He seems to realize more instinctively than consciously that it is through man's labour, understood as social activity, that the individual might prevent alienation from his fellow-men. In this context it is worthwhile to point out that Munoo meets people who accept him right from the beginning, like Sheila and her uncle Prem, Prabha and his wife, Hari and his wife, and their mutual friend Ratan, and even Mrs. Mainwaring, Munoo's last employer. On the other hand, there are those characters who try to teach him his place as a coolie like Bibiji and her husband; Ganpat, Prabha's business partner, or the manager of the cotton mill. The social context of Munoo's life as a worker sketched here is important because it is inseparable from the process of work itself: human attitudes and relationships are shaped and influenced by labour and must not be considered as completely independent of it. It will be one of the aims of the following discussion to point out how so-called moral — or less moral — attitudes of people towards Munoo are a reflection of their own notions of the function of labour. The scene describing Munoo at work in the household of Babu Natoo Ram, an employee of the local British-owned Imperial Bank, could be called a presentation of the initiation ceremony into alienated labour about which a young boy has not been taught the essential difference between play and — alienated — labour. He is still unaware of his economic and social position and reacts towards his new tasks in the only manner known to him through experience in his home village where "he remembered that he had often volunteered in a rush of sympathy to sweep the floor, to treat it with antiseptic cow dung and to run errands for [his aunt]." (31) Apart from being still too young to have disciplined his hands to the adequate performance of menial jobs" (31), as Anand puts it, he is faced with so many new impressions that he is unable to distinguish between his duties and those activities he likes to perform. Besides, he neither really cares to fulfil his duties 'properly', as his employers expect him to do, nor does he miss an opportunity to help or entertain others if he feels that he will make them happy.

Anand conveys Munoo's 'lack' of insight into the necessity of executing his duties in a manner expected from him by portraying his actions as having no effect on him, as being something indifferent to him. Two more literary devices contribute to the impression that Munoo is not affected by his work: the detailed description of Babu Nathoo Ram's household and the space devoted to Bibiji's curses and complaints about Munoo. By giving much importance to these aspects of Munoo's life Anand shows that work is of less importance than the conditions under which Munoo is working, in particular the relationship between employer and employee.

There is, for instance, Bibiji, his employer, who is presented as a completely alienated person. She constantly tries to teach Munoo his place as a servant, but she also complains about her own work: "'When will I get some rest! I slog, slog all day! I can't even get time to dress. Or to sit down with the neighbours for a chat. Or go to the shops." (14) Work to her is a burden which keeps her away from those activities which would give her fulfilment.

Munoo, the employee, on the other hand, has not yet experienced the alienating effects of work. It is only later that he begins to realize his social status in the family. Though the function of work dawns upon him at this moment, he is unable to fully understand its importance. Answering his own question as to why he is in this house he replies: "'Because my uncle brought me here to earn my living ...'" (36) The author adds: "It did not occur to him to ask himself what he was apart from being a servant, and why he was a servant." (36) Two scenes showing Munoo at work in a pickle factory (74-81; 88-90) add new touches to the aspect of labour discussed so far. Ganpat, one of the owners, does not hesitate to beat his workers if they are not quick enough. However, a more important aspect is Anand's description of the working place itself. Through its smallness, darkness and filthy condition, the stench caused by the ingredients used for the pickling process and the fumes of the fire, the depressing appearance of the workers themselves is intensified: they are either old and worn out by work or seem generally to be more inhuman than human and damned to spend their lives shut off from light and air. Munoo himself is shown as an outsider, an observer of the scene going on day in and day out. He neither interferes nor does he seem to have established any real contact with the labourers. He can only compare his present experiences with those in Bibiji's household, and this in turn increases his fatalistic approach to life: "It is sad that my good luck in finding work so easily should be spoilt by the presence of a cruel man." (75) Ganpat reminds him of Bibiji when he curses his labourers and accuses them of enjoying a holiday while he and Prabha were away to sell their products.

In the second scene taking place at the factory, Anand uses different narrative means to present men at work suffering under the conditions of labour. First he gives a short descriptive analysis of Ganpat's 'fate', his loss of income and his subsequent efforts in re-establishing his former economic and social status by over-emphasizing his role of employer. The writer confirms our impression of Ganpat's alienated nature.

Later, Anand uses the summary to indicate that "the only thing that relieved [Munoo's] fits of depression," — that is, "the comradeship which existed between him and the other coolies" (89), is of specific importance for Munoo's further development. Beyond this function, the experience of comradeship is given a deeper meaning because the labourers are shown as men realizing instinctively — though not consciously — the objective reason for their experience: the exploitation of their labour. Anand's coolies certainly do not know why "they would all fall to singing" (83), or does Munoo understand why, after singing with the others, he "regained the wild freedom of his childhood," or would want "to be a man, to flourish in the true dignity of manhood." (90) Yet the description of the labourers enjoying their freedom for a short while and the reference to Munoo's hopes and wishes must be considered an aesthetically convincing presentation of men's instinctive struggle against alienation. Anand does not stretch the authenticity of his characters, and makes Munoo react and feel according to his dispositions and the grade of his insight into his own status.

We are made to face yet another aspect of alienated labour in the scene where Munoo has to compete with "swarms of coolies" (122) at the vegetable market. The author is not primarily interested in competition as a characteristic feature of class-society but in its consequences for Munoo's psyche and his social relations. The only chance to find a job is outwitting his competitors, because he is physically too weak to impress a potential employer as a good labourer. Munoo employs his wit and proves to possess profound insight into the psyche of people: he either spreads the rumour that the market will be closed on the following day or uses an especially cultivated pronunciation of the word 'mother' when addressing elderly ladies in asking them for a job. However, his idea of preferring to work for elderly ladies proves to be a failure because in them he meets his equals, a rather tough-bargaining, miserly group of employers. The touch of humour presented in these encounters cannot hide the ugly fact that work under these conditions is not only humiliating but alienates Munoo even more from man and himself.

Having reached Bombay where he meets Hari and his family, a disowned peasant looking for work at a factory, Munoo is made to experience industrial labour under capitalistic conditions. Here alienated labour rules their lives absolutely. When Hari and his wife Lakshmi hear the factory whistle in the morning, their nerves are set on edge and the fear of being late and losing their jobs makes them behave like automatons and not like members of a family. (175-176) Working conditions are much the same as those which Munoo experienced in the pickle factory, if not worse: Chimta Sahib, the English manager, curses and beats the coolies freely, the deafening noise of the machines, the stench of cotton and oil and the unbearable heat of a summer's day in Bombay are even worse than anything Munoo has experienced until now. Besides, while the work he performed so far still seemed to be a challenge to his skills, the mechanical and repetitive action he is now made to perform increases his suffering. The incident of his cotton shirt being snatched by a machine and torn into shreds appears to be symbolic of Munoo under control of those who force him to sell his labour.

Capitalistic conditions do not only bring about the alienation of man in the process of work, they also prevail during the period of reproduction of his labour: there is just one water pump for hundreds of coolies, "not a canteen, nor a cookshop, nor even a confectioner's shop" (181), and, of course, there is no doctor at hand in case of accidents.

Conditions of labour at this cotton factory in Bombay are also the cause of man's alienation from man. When Hari informs Munoo that his little son was injured by a machine, "Munoo felt hard and could not sympathize. He just looked blankly into Hari's face and remained dumb, as if now his heart strings had contracted." (181) However, what follows is perhaps more important for a critical judgement of Anand's achievement than the almost naturalistic dimension of his description of the coolies' exploitation. Munoo's lack of feeling for Hari proves to be of a temporary nature only: "[his] heart went out of him. He felt he must go and bear the child to the hospital." (182) Still, his reaction is, rather, an instinctive one, because he is unable to see the real reason for his indifference for Hari's suffering. Rather, a more specific form of alienation is revealed in his self-accusation that he, being an orphan, must have been the cause of Hari's bad luck. The hold of Hindu superstitions, or, to put it more properly, the influence of Hindu ideology — that is, of the owning classes and their ideologists — on a coolie's mind is so strong that he is unable to recognize the real cause of man's suffering and man's alienation from man. Capitalistic labour conditions and an ideology derived from feudalism are responsible for Munoo's false notions about himself and his social relations. He seems to be bound to a vicious circle:

> the tiny skiff of his soul tossed to and fro on the soft, sun-speckled edge of this foam, as if it were a small point struggling in vain to cross the river, and as if it were threatened with extinction by an unforeseen storm. (82)

While the aesthetic presentation of Munoo's alienation and his suffering has been convincing until now, the conclusion of the scene cannot be described as artistically successful. While Munoo is portrayed as the victim of capitalism and feudalistic ideology, at one moment he is suddenly made to remember his wishes and hopes for a better life. (183) It is less Anand the Marxian thinker who was perhaps urged to add such a 'positive' outlook to this scene than Anand the humanist whose humanism, as M.K. Naik concludes in his critical appraisal of the author, is eclectic and tries to combine ideas stemming from very different ideologies.[6]

This conclusion is confirmed if we look at the only scene in Anand's novels in which the relationship between capital and labour is presented not as one embodied in the relations between single individuals but masses of workers and their leaders on the one hand and the management of a capitalistic enterprise on the other. (219-226) After short-work has been announced, workers and trade union leaders meet to discuss how to react to this provocation. Several positions are presented; first of all there is the attitude of the majority of the coolies who by all means want to work, regardless of the terms of labour offered by the employers because lack of work means starvation or, even worse, death by hunger. Then there is Ratan and a group of trade-union leaders who are able to analyse the relationship of capital and labour in general and also the particular situation at hand. They appeal to the emotions of the masses, the day-to-day sufferings experienced by them as exploited labourers, and they are well on their way to winning back the support of the majority after the president of the trade union had gained points when he suggested that his organization, the AITUC, would try to work out a compromise between the workers and the management. Anand seems as much set against this line of approach as the masses of the workers, who unite in a chorus and shout the charter of their demands from the management. Before any decision can be taken,

6 M.K. Naik, *Mulk Raj Anand*, New Delhi: Arnold-Heinemann 1973, 16

the rumour spreads that Muslims have kidnapped Hindu children, and the gathering of workers splits up into two religious communities fighting against each other instead of uniting their efforts against those who exploit them materially and ideologically.

Anand probably chose this solution because he wanted to point out how strong the hold of religion on Indians was at the time when the events are supposed to have taken place; besides, the historical development in India has certainly proved that he was right in that a portrayal of Indian workers acting consciously as a class rather than members of religious communities or castes would have revealed a dogmatic attitude on the part of the author. Still, choosing this solution appears somewhat defeatist because it suggests that alienation of man from man having taken the form of religious fanaticism and communal enmity is not only inevitable but that a fact like proletarian experience and the creation of a proletarian public seems generally impossible. It is logical then that Munoo, affected by the course of events, is separated from his friends and colleagues and is forced once more to face the hardships of life by himself. More than that, he begins to identify himself more and more with the norms and values of those who employ and rule him, though at times he still realizes instinctively that this does not mean self-fulfilment.

It is no easy task to state in a few sentences how far Anand succeeds in *Coolie* in conveying not only the various forms of man's alienation but, more important, a perspective of overcoming alienation caused by capitalism. Though, as we have said above, the historical conditions referred to and, we should add, the selection of a character like Munoo as the protagonist of the novel, inherently restrict a 'positive' perspective, we must admit that Anand succeeds less in advancing a philosophically and aesthetically convincing 'solution' than in presenting the essential function of labour and the various forms of alienation in this novel and elsewhere.

India, with its different methods of production which exist side by side, is depicted from a different angle again in *The Big Heart*. Expressed in terms of human labour, it is the transformation of the period of manufacture to that of industrial capitalism on which Anand focuses his attention. Ananta, the coppersmith, who owns a little workshop and lives on piece-work, is still engaged with manual production, which is gradually being replaced by industrial labour. Here, Mehru, a skilled worker and former coppersmith, has found work in a factory recently established by the head of the guild of thathiars or coppersmiths and the head of the "utensil sellers community."

Strange though it may appear at first, Anand is not interested in describing the extent of alienation in the work process as it is experienced by Ananta on the one hand and Mehru on the other. It is rather the degree of alienation of man which characterizes those scenes in which the complexity of labour is depicted; and, paradoxically, alienation seems to have affected Ananta and his employer more deeply than Mehru and his 'superiors.' While Lal Chand, who gave Ananta the order to make a large copper cauldron, is only interested in lowering the coppersmith's wages and in increasing his own profit, Ananta is dumbfounded that the head of his own community has taken to acting as capitalist rather than a brother-thathiar. He is unable to establish communication with him, and in the end Ananta says bitterly: "I had better go home and change my profession." (101) Through these words, though hardly grasped by Ananta himself, the author shows us that a change in the relationship of man and working process has already taken place. The idea that a craftsman achieves a realization in the product of his labour has long been false.

This conclusion is confirmed when we look at the very first scene of *The Big Heart*: Ananta is working upon a large cauldron "imprinting evenly spaced rows of bright moonstrokes" on it. (11) However, he does not concentrate on his work; it is rather a mechanical action which he performs deftly and quickly while his thoughts have turned towards the nightmare he had had the previous night. An explanation for Anand's procedure may be found when we look at the central conflict in the novel: it is caused by the opening of the factory and the consequent loss of work for many coppersmiths. The depicting of Ananta at work and selling his cauldron reveals that Anand does not look back nostalgically to a period when man achieved fulfilment in the production of articles. On the contrary, the author tries to convey the positive meaning the introduction of industrial labour may have. And this may explain why Mehru, working at the factory now, is less affected by the alienation than we should expect. It is true that he is discontented with his work: the machines frighten him, his work as a sweeper and, soon afterwards, as a labourer performing the most simple and boring actions serving a machine, make him recall the more satisfying work in his own shop. However, his thoughts turn to his time off and he imagines what complicated and useful articles he could produce then so that he would really find satisfaction in his work. Besides, the mechanical work done at the factory gives him time to turn his attention to his relationship with others. Although there is the fear of losing one's job and also envy and the attempt to exploit each other, we feel that Anand realizes the historical necessity of replacing outmoded methods of production by more modern ones. At the same time, he sees a chance for man to use these methods of production to his own human advantage by, for example, trying to overcome alienation from man and from the work process. Anand's historical views, then, prove to be of a dynamic character but, again, potential 'solutions' of man's alienation are made a task of the individual's goodwill rather than of man's efforts to understand the essential relationship between capital and labour in a capitalistic society.

Bakha (*Untouchable*) and Bikhu (*The Road*) represent the group of labourers mentioned first, the outcastes. It is Bakha's duty to clean the primitive public latrines situated close to the outcaste colony of a small North Indian town. He does his work in a manner so efficient that to the onlooker he appears almost too intelligent, too superior for this sort of activity. (7-11) Labour as described here, is at once part of a man's life and something separate from it, an activity which remains alien to him. Anand compares Bakha's working with the movement of a wave: "he seemed as easy as a wave sailing away on a deep river" (7); and, expressed once more in a less metaphoric manner: "though his job was dirty he remained comparatively clean. He didn't even soil his sleeves." (7) But this is only part of Bakha's reality. His labour is intrinsically connected with his social station. One of the officers Bakha serves, a high-caste Hindu, presents him with a hockey-stick, and this evokes the habitual, almost inborn "trait of servility in Bakha." (8) Social status and labour define his relationship to caste Hindus and serve him to identify himself. Though Bakha seems to be in harmony with his work, "he slowly slipped into a song [...] and he went forward with eager step, from job to job, a marvel of movement, dancing through his work" (8), Anand takes pains not to mislead us about Bakha's attitude towards his work. He does not want to tell us that there is dignity even in the meanest labour: "A soft smile lingered on his lips, the smile of a slave overjoyed at the condescension of his master, more akin to pride than to happiness." (8) Bakha is not really anxious to do more than is expected and would like to have a different job: "he preferred to imagine himself sweeping the streets in the place of his father. That is easy work, he said to himself." (10) And it turns out in the end that the impression of efficiency and concentration Bakha creates is nothing else but the outward manifestation of his efforts to suppress the thought of his work; as Anand puts it at the end of the scene:

> he worked unconsciously. This forgetfulness or emptiness persisted in him over long periods. It was a sort of insensitivity created in him by the kind of work he had to do, a tough skin which would be a shield against all the most awful sensations. (11)

It is Anand's purpose to show that even a person belonging to the lowest social class is essentially a human being who suffers from having to perform alienated labour forced upon him by caste society. The seemingly 'unconscious' attitude to alienated labour expressed by Bakha, either through suppressing any thought of it or through performing it in a most mechanical manner, is the author's literary means of conveying his purposes.

The theme of solidarity and self-realization through labour — though hinted at already in *Coolie* — is taken up once more in *The Road* and is developed here in a more convincing manner. Untouchability was abolished by law after India had become independent. Bikhu, a young outcaste boy is thus given better chances than Bakha to overcome the exploitation by the higher castes. Besides, the government tries to improve the lot of the outcastes by offering them work in government schemes: they help break the stones needed for the construction of a road which will connect their village with the city of Delhi. This in itself is to be understood as a symbolic act opening the Indian village to the world and asking caste and outcaste inhabitants of the village to share alike in the work. Bikhu realizes that because of the opposition of caste Hindus their work might not be finished and the chance of starting construction of the road may be foiled. (86-88) However, the outcaste women offer their help which is gladly accepted by the supervisor and the men and now all hope to finish their work in time.

Labour as described here is given the function of — literally as well as symbolically — liberating man from his bondage, from being forced to live an alienated life. To take part in this work is a free decision of those who accept the offer, the work process itself a realization of man, because through it he will produce something which is useful to him; labour, indeed, has won back its essential function of being useful activity in the sense Marx defined it. But labour here also means realization of man as member of the species: all alienated relationships can be overcome, those between different social groups as well as those between the generations or sexes. The strength solidarity created is even noticed by caste Hindus. (88) In Bikhu, this feeling of victory is made manifest when he is described as having become one with his work and the lives others. (107) Neither his mother's prejudices nor, in the end, those of a Hindu boy of his age can take away this experience of self-fulfilment. (108)

It is in this short novel that Anand, more than in any other work, has found a more profound insight into 'possible solutions', of overcoming alienation. That this does not mean that he is an idealistic dreamer becomes clear when we look at the conclusion of *The Road*: Bikhu is depressed that the prejudices of caste Hindus still exist and will continue to make human beings like him suffer. What is important, however, is the fact that Anand here does not sacrifice a philosophically tenable 'solution' for a naturalistic depiction of his story as he did in *Coolie*. On the other hand his dream has the power of potential realization. Although the novel as such has not been considered artistically successful by most critics, we must admit that Anand, philosophically speaking, has achieved more in those passages depicting man at work than in many others which are integral parts of more successful literary works.

Concluding, we can say that the author shows throughout a profound understanding of the character of human labour and the various forms of alienation which are caused by specific historical conditions and determine the relationship between man and his work. Altogether, he succeeds in presenting this theme in a manner that is aesthetically convincing. It is only in one of his more recent novels that a more comprehensive treatment of this theme can be noticed, and, although its artistic execution may not be altogether successful, the meaning labour is given in *The Road* indicates that Anand has achieved an even deeper insight into its complexity.

Works cited

Novels

ANAND, Mulk Raj, *Coolie*, Bombay: Kutub Popular, n.d.

—, *Untouchable*, Bombay: Kutub Popular, n.d.

—, *Two Leaves and a Bud*, Bombay: Kutub Popular, 2nd ed. 1951

—, *The Village*, Bombay: Kutub Popular 1954

—, *The Old Woman and the Cow*, Bombay: Kutub Popular 1960

—, *The Road*, Bombay: Kutub Popular 1961

Critical Studies

KAVURAJ, S., "Alienation and Literature", *Journal of the School of Languages* (Winter 1973-74), 1-27

KLAUS, G. & M. Buhr, *Texte zur Methode und Praxis II, Pariser Manuskripte*, Reinbeck: Rowohlt 1968

—, *Marxistisch-Leninistisches Wörterbuch der Philosophie*, 3 Bd., Reinbeck: Rowohlt 1972

NAIK, M.K., *Mulk Raj Anand*, New Delhi: Arnold-Heinemann 1973

The *New Poets' Manifesto*

P. Lal and Contemporary Indian English Poetry

Our English host was gracious
We were soon at ease:
Or almost:
The Servants
were watching. (Gieve Patel, "Evening")[1]

BEFORE DISCUSSING SOME OF THE TRENDS in modern Indo-English poetry, I'd like to refer to the principle issues of the debate about the meaning and function of English poetry written by Indians, a debate which has been raging ever since P. Lal published his controversial article in 1951 in the Bombay *The Sunday Standard*, subsequently republished as "Introduction" to *Modern Indo-Anglian Poetry*, edited by Lal and K.R. Rao in 1959.[2] Lal's credo which, according to him, "became the New Poets' 'Manifesto'",[3] is not only to be understood as a piece of critical writing in its own right and as an essential contribution towards the definition of Indo-English poetry but, I believe, has also stood the test of being an accurate prediction of the major development of Indian poetry in English during the last twenty years.

In his attempt to break with the tradition of Romanticism symbolized by such outstanding figures as Sri Aurobindo and Sarojini Naidu, Lal rejected

1 Gieve Patel, "Evening", ed. P. Lal, *Modern Indian Poetry in English: An Anthology and a Credo*, Calcutta: Writers Workshop 1969, 395

2 Cf. P. Lal, ed., *op.cit.*, iv

3 All quotations from the New Poets' Manifesto in: *Modern Indian Poetry in English*, iv–xiii

the idea of "reading poetry for spiritual propaganda or propaganda of any sort" and asked for poetry that "must satisfy me as poetry"; hence, his postulate that poetry "must deal in concrete terms with concrete experience" and "be free from propaganda." Whether the language used by Indians was King's, Queen's or Indian English was of much less importance than the fact that it was a vital language which was made to serve the poets' purpose. Insisting on concrete experience as an essential element of poetry it was logical that "all forms of imitation" were to be condemned while experiments were commendable as long as they did not lead "to excessive obscurity." This means that a poet's liberty to express his most subjective experiences would fail to serve the poem if it impeded or even destroyed communication with the reader. Poetry, above all, had to reflect the age in which it was written. The problem of communication is taken up in Lal's final argument. In the present age of "mass approval and hysteria" there is "the need for the private voice", which ought to make use of the lyric form as the one best suited because of its direct "appeal to that personality of man which is distinct, curious, unique and idealistic." Though this demand on poetry seems to indicate elitist thinking it also means that poetry as an act of communication is a socially responsible act.

It is interesting to compare what Lal had to say almost twenty years later when reviewing what had happened to Indo-English poetry since. In his summary of the demands on the writer to write good writing phrases such as "realistic poetry" and "private voice" do not occur again. Instead, "originality and experiment [...] intensity and strength of feeling [...] clarity in thought structure [...] and vitality" emphasize the relationship between poet and poem but seem to give hardly a thought to the one between the author and reader or author and reality. It would need a critic's investigation to analyze whether the shift of emphasis of the critical argument reflects the development of Indo-English poetry.

Here, it will be less my task to discuss the premises and implications of Lal's concept of poetry than to assess the character and extent of its accuracy by examining a number of poems written by four of the — to my mind — leading contemporary Indian poets: Nissim Ezekiel, Kamala Das, Mary Erulkar and P. Lal. Though my approach and selection is subjective, I am certain that the inclusion of other poets and poems would basically corroborate my findings.

Many of Ezekiel's early poems, it seems, convincingly illustrate Lal's demand for "concrete experience in concrete terms." The reader acquainted with Toru Dutt, Sri Aurobindo, Manmohan Ghose or Sarojini Naidu and their "poetry [...] dedicated to an expression of spiritual vision"[4] is struck by the familiarity of themes and feelings dealt with, by the frequent use of colloquialisms and by the simplicity of structure in poems such as Ezekiel's "Case Study", "Love Sonnet"[5] or "Night of the Scorpion."[6] He often uses topographical settings against which he projects his themes ("Urban", "A Morning Walk"[7] or "In India")[8]:

> The city like a passion burns.
> He dreams of morning walks, alone,
> And floating on a wave of sand.
> But still his mind its traffic turns
> Away from beach and tree and stone
> To kindered clamour close at hand. ("Urban")

Here as elsewhere, Lal's "the din and hubbub, the confusion and indecision, the flashes of beauty and goodness of our age"[9] form an essential part of Ezekiel's poems:

> Barbaric city sick with slums,
> Deprived of seasons, blessed with rains,
> Its hawkers, beggars, iron-lunged,
> Processions led by frantic drums,
> A million purgatorial lanes,
> And child-like masses, many tongued,
> Whose wages are in words and crumbs. ("A Morning Walk")

Whatever location or incidents (e.g., lovers' union in "Marriage", a pilgrimage in "Enterprise"[10]) are intended to serve the poet as a solid and reliable point of reference, they almost invariably prove less so and many of Ezekiel's poems end on a note of doubt or self-doubt, uncertainty or resignation. It is this gradual, almost imperceptible transformation of certitude to a doubtful or questioning attitude which helps the reader gain insight into a new truth. Ezekiel's technique of first arresting the reader's attention by making him remember a well-known experience, by gradually causing him to feel doubtful and by finally summing up for him how wrong he was, can be observed in "Enterprise":

4 V.K. Gokak, *Studies in Indo-Anglian Poetry*, Bombay 1972, 145
5 Nissim Ezekiel, *The Unfinished Man*, Calcutta: Writers Workshop 1960
6 Lal, *op. cit.*, 175–176
7 Ezekiel, *op.cit.*
8 Lal, *op.cit.*, 177–179
9 Ibid., xiii
10 Ezekiel, *op.cit.*

It started as a pilgrimage,
Exalting minds and making all
The burdens light. The second stage
Explored but did not test the call.
The sun beat down to match our rage.

But when the differences arose
On how to cross a desert patch
We lost a friend whose stylish prose
Was quite the best of all our batch.
A shadow falls on us — and grows.

When, finally, we reached the place,
We hardly knew why we were there.
The trip had darkened every face,
Our deeds were neither great nor rare.
Home is where we have to gather grace.

Ezekiel's poems certainly cannot be accused of containing propaganda of any kind; rather, they end more often than not on a banal note (e.g. "Love Sonnet", "Commitment"[11]), and we are not always sure about the intensity and strength of Ezekiel's feelings.

The use of a visible background like the town ("Summer in Calcutta"[12]), the sea ("The Suicide", "Composition"), and airport ("Palam"), the burning ghats ("The Joss-Sticks at Cadell Road"), or a certain season ("Jaisurya"[13]) also characterize many of Kamala Das's poems. Similarly, the frequent use of simple colloquial English, the absence of hard words and the rare occurrence of complicated syntactical structures make her poems comparable with Ezekiel's:

When I die
Do not throw the meat and bones away
But pile them up
And
Let them tell
By their smell
What life was worth
On this earth
What love was worth
In the end. ("A Request"[14])

11 Ibid.

12 Lal, *op.cit.*, 107

13 Kamala Das, *The Descendants*, Calcutta: Writers Workshop 1967, 1–4, 29-35, 10, 23, 27–28

14 Ibid., 5

However, the function, the metaphorical and symbolical content of images such as town or sea, airport or burning ghat differ distinctly from those in Ezekiel's poems. Reality does not prove to be questionable but hides its essential meaning. The search of the self is directed at the truth of life and death ("The Suicide"), of constancy ("Substitutes", "Contacts") and love ("The Invitation", "The Conflagration"[15]):

Bereft of soul
My body shall be bare
Bereft of body
My soul shall be bare

Which would you rather have
O kind sea?
Which is the more dead
Of the two?

Yet I never can forget
The only man who hurts.
The only one who seems to know
The only way to hurt.

Holding you is easy
Clutching at moving water,
I tell you, sea,
This is easy.
But to hold him for half a day
Was a difficult task

But, when he did love,
Believe me,
All I could do was sob like a fool. ("The Suicide")

The intense urge to know is complemented by a strong rejection of temporary, man-made solutions trying to answer the question of who the self is:

I don't know politics but I know the names
of those in power, and can repeat them like
Days of week, or names of months, beginning with
Nehru …
Don't write in English, they said,
English is not your mother-tongue …

15 Ibid., 6–7, 19, 14–15, 20

Dress in saris, be girl,
Be wife, they said. Be embroidered, be cook,
Be a quarreller with servants. Fit in. Oh, . . .
Who are you, I ask each and everyone,
The answer is, it is I . . .
I too call myself I. ("An Introduction"[16])

In what is one of the most well-known contemporary Indo-English poems Das endows each seemingly simple reflection and question with the intense feeling of being personally affected by the concrete world around — politicians, language, skin colour, marriage — and the world inside — loneliness, joy and love, shame and pain. In a much less sophisticated manner than in Ezekiel's poems Das expresses poetically what Lal claims theoretically: the need for the private voice so that that personality of wo/man, which is distinct and unique, can be reached. Das's almost total lack of emotional inhibition, an attitude so alien to the Indian psyche, her obsession to possess and make her own what she can name, make her an exception on the Indian poetry scene. It is this obsession with the truth which enables her to create original poems even when at times the sentiments expressed appear trite ("My love is an empty gift, a gilded empty container, good for show, nothing else ...": "Captive"), or the images used are clichés ("There was a time when our lusts were like multicoloured flags of no particular country ...": "Convicts"[17]).

In Ezekiel's and Das's poems India, more often than not, is the *locus in quo* which inspired the poet; she serves him as setting and background and generally becomes the "objective correlative" of his and her feelings and thoughts. Though it may be tempting to substitute Lal's "concrete" by "Indian", I believe that this was certainly not his idea when he spoke of poetry. This view is substantiated when we look at Mary Erulkar's poems. A few of them are included in *Modern Indian Poetry in English* while her first collection, *Mandala 25*, was published by the Writers Workshop, an institution established in 1958. It set itself the task to focus "on English creative and transcreative work by Indians, or such work by foreigners as deals with, or is inspired by, Indian life and culture."[18]

A few poems contain overt references to or images taken from India:

16 Lal, *op. cit.*, 104–105

17 Das, *op. cit.*, 17, 26

18 P. Lal, *The Man of Dharma and the Rasa of Silence*, Calcutta: Writers Workshop 1974, Appendix, 14

Let me kneel like a root of lotus.
Lotus in the praying waters, let me fold
my hands to the mystic bud,
firm as the hand of god
god's hand in flickering maya
maya of man's illusory world.
Let lotus of god, lotus of man,
god and man, flesh at last to light. ("The Still Violence"[19])

The poem "Whale"[20] concludes

I come budded, full blooded,
with edens dead in my apple-red arms,
India,
my whale,
my whaler.

Still, these are exceptions rather than the rule. In rendering recurring themes poetically, Erulkar takes recourse more often to images which seem to be uppermost in her mind. She appears to depend on her surroundings, the stimuli she receives and the observations she makes. The distinctive feature of her poetry is not the presence of India but the immediate transformation and symbolization of observations, stimuli and visible pictures into poetic language. Rarely in an Indian poet do we meet with such diverse imagery ranging from unusual poetic topoi like science ("Moon Gate", "The Architecture of Lilacs", "The Infinite Distances of Atoms"), to more conventional ones like religion ("After Estrangement", "The Still Violence", "A Pardon for Judas", "Embarked NOW"[21]); nature ("A Leavetaking", "Evening"[22], "Flying a Kite", "The Gulf Stream"); or womanhood ("Baldela Rose", "Mujer, Mujer", "For a Childbirth", "The Second Wife Speaks"[23]). In her longer poems, however, she succeeds in blending the at times most diverse images into a structured totality:

Where Europe and America build their arches
the pale women lean like fountains in the wind
between the stone images: and there
the iridescent children like bubbles float
in the laburnum-lighted squares.

---

19 Mary Erulkar, *Mandala 25*, Calcutta: Writers Workshop 1972, 13

20 Ibid., 42

21 Ibid., 15-16, 17, 34, 18, 13, 37, 43

22 Lal, ed., *op; cit.*, 163, 165

23 Erulkar, *op. cit.*, 21, 22-23, 27, 30–31,44

And in the long snow-candled nights
the women move in moonlight ephemerally,
phosphorescent in jewels and the rare
northern lights of their ice-bound hair,
before the sun comes with gulls and whitewinged air.
("The Third Continent"[24])

Many of her poems are among the most experimental in the contemporary literary scene and excel with their fusion of images, boldness of metaphor, use of rhetorical means and syntactical structures:

Dream. Yes,
in my kindled dream,
in a light black as cornflowers,
and the sun
half a lifetime away,
the lions come hooped in their blazing hair.
Iphigenia,
the hour
of fading lilacs may come too soon;
Annapurna, the bread may lie
unbroken for ever in a beggar's bowl.
The lions await me in their terrible noon.
("The Lonely Departure for Cythera")[25]

It seems, the poet has taken Lal at his word when she insists on her most personal need for the private voice, though at times it is not easy to grasp the full meaning of a poem like the one quoted above, or "Dying, Alcestis Dreams of Him",[26] "The Third Continent" and "Mujer, Mujer". She often appears on the verge of losing control over the abundance of images in face of intensely felt experiences, such as time lost, the immutability of the law of change, the cycle of life and death, and suffering caused by the elusiveness of life. However, Erulkar's poetic sensibility and her creative use of the language make her one of the outstanding and convincing voices of "the confusion and indecision, the flashes of beauty and goodness of our age."

To conclude, it is only fair to ask in how far Lal's reflections on modern Indian poetry in English have been of any bearing on his own work. What,

24 Ibid., 36
25 Ibid., 26
26 Ibid., 48

essentially, makes his poems incomparable with those discussed already is their poise stemming from a certitude, an inner conviction which not only enables the poet to observe in a controlled manner the transience of life, of human passions and thoughts but also to symbolize his belief in a quality of life, the truth of which eludes final comprehension and can at best be grasped poetically as beauty. It is the controlled balance between the mind's understanding of visible reality and a belief in the essential harmony and beauty of life which creates the poems' unique appeal in Lal's collections *Love's The First,*[27] *The Parrot's Death & Other Poems*[28] and *'Change!' They Said.*[29] The following poem may stand for many, excepting perhaps some of a highly personal nature collected in *The Parrot's Death* which are not easily accessible:

> In you something knows,
> After refusal, crying;
> But regret was not in the rose,
> Though beautiful and denying.
> If our hearts learn cruelty
> To lead only to regret,
> Were it not better frailty
> Possessed us yet?
> –As the warm rose, loved by each wind,
> Insensibly gives laughter,
> But does not argue in the mind
> If good or evil after. ("Rose"[30])

In his usually short poems Lal does not often refer overtly to India ("Images at Dawn", "Boat on the Hooghly", "The Refugees at Sealdah Station", "'Change!' They Said", "Jawaharlal Nehru"[31]) but deal with common human experiences like love ("The White Rose", "Nocturne", "I Cannot Say My Love, My Dear",[32] "The Simplest Love", "The Bee's Love"); beauty, including the beauty of nature ("A Song for Beauty",[33] "The Crickets"[34]); the plea for an understanding of life ("For My Daughter", "For My Son Ananda"[35]); and the transience of life ("On Transience", "The

27 Lal, *Love's The First*, Calcutta: Writers Workshop 1963
28 Lal, *The Parrot's Death & Other Poems*, Calcutta: Writers Workshop 1960
29 Lal, *"Change!" They Said*, Calcutta: Writers Workshop 1966
30 Lal, *Love's The First*
31 Lal, *"Change!" They Said*
32 Lal, *Love's The First*
33 Lal, *The Parrot's Death & Other Poems*
34 Lal, *"Change!" They Said*
35 Lal, *Love's The First*

Bronze Girl", "The Old Man"[36]). Similarly, he chooses the simple word or phrase as in "The Bee's Love":

This bee is sensible,
Loving fragrance, not flower;
Saint-like and stone-like,
Limiting desire.

But lovers are wiser
Than saints or stones,
Loving rings round dark eyes
And brittle bones.

Love like a flower
Has roots that reach
Beyond fragrance, beyond power
Of loving speech.

As a structural device he uses juxtaposition, often of man and nature. Whether the effect achieved is the recognition of analogies or of essential dissimilarity of, to take the examples at hand, lovers and rose or a bee's and man's love is of secondary importance compared to the recognition of their true character. This means that the sequence and structuring of phrases constitutes the meaning of these poems.

When rains fall
Is all astir
My green soul,
My prisoner.

November,
Middle age
Struggles, needing
More than a cage.

Soul is to cage
As love to foe.
My loved one, my bird,
Take heart and go. ("The Parrot's Death & Other Poems")

Though Lal's poems certainly cannot be called obscure, his succinct style and economic use of the language as well as the, at times, structural

36 Lal, *The Parrot's Death & Other Poems*

complexity of his works characterize them as very personal expressions of common human experiences.

Like Ezekiel, Das and Erulkar, Lal has developed his own distinct style and has proved that modern Indian poets, far from being propagandistic or imitative, not only make creative use of the English language but also succeed in satisfying their wish to communicate their experiences and thoughts poetically as they appeal to the reader's need to gain insight into the different facets of "India's cultural ethos" which Lal spoke of,[37] an ethos shaping the sensibility of the contemporary Indian poet who while being a realistic observer of life around him strives, in the best Indian tradition, to transcend its ephemerality in his quest for truth.

Works cited

Poetry Collections

DAS, Kamala, *The Descendants*, Calcutta: Writers Workshop 1967

ERULKAR, Mary, *Mandala 25*, Calcutta: Writers Workshop 1972

EZEKIEL, Nissim, *The Unfinished Man*, Calcutta: Writers Workshop 1960

LAL, P., *The Parrot's Death and Other Poems*, **Calcutta: Writers Workshop 1960**

—, *Love's the First*, Calcutta: Writers Workshop 1963

—, " *'Change!' They Said*", **Calcutta: Writers Workshop 1966**

—, ed., *Modern Indian Poetry in English. An Anthology and a Credo*, Calcutta: Writers Workshop 1969

—, *The Man of Dharma and the Rasa of Silence*, Calcutta: Writers Workshop 1974

Critical Studies

GOKAK, V.K., *Studies in Indo-Anglian Poetry*, Bombay 1972

37 Lal, *The Man of Dharma and the Rasa of Silence*, Appendix, 14

History and the Individual

Salman Rushdie's *Midnight's Children* and Anita Desai's *Clear Light of Day*

To understand just one life,
you have to swallow the world.

Salman Rushdie: *Midnight's Children*

'Nothing's over', she agreed.
'Ever', she accepted.

Anita Desai: *Clear Light of Day*

SALMAN RUSHDIE'S NOVEL *Midnight's Children* and Anita Desai's *Clear Light of Day* are essentially concerned with man's quest for his identity, and both authors relate the quest of their individual hero or heroine to the past of their lives. However, Rushdie and Desai proceed very differently as a glance at their understanding of the terms 'history' and 'the past' shows. The former makes his narrator, Saleem Sinai, move in time and space: Covering the years from 1915 to 1978, Saleem narrates the fate of his family over three generations. Along with his grandparents he takes us from Kashmir via Amritsar to Agra where their five children are born. His parents settle temporarily in Delhi, move to Bombay where Saleem is born exactly on the stroke of midnight of India's independence, and finally migrate to Rawalpindi in Pakistan where they perish in the 1965 India-Pakistan war. Saleem subsequently lives in the border area of Pakistan, is sent to Bangladesh just before East Pakistan declares its independence in 1971, returns to Delhi, is taken to Benares by force and finally settles in Bombay to write his book because, as he says, he wants to preserve memory and save it "from the corruption of the clocks."[1]

1 Salman Rushdie, *Midnight's Children*, London: Pan Books 1982, 38. All further references (MC) are

Anita Desai, as in most of her earlier novels, restricts the little action there is in *Clear Light of Day* to one place, Delhi, and here, more specifically, to the house and the garden of the Das family and its immediate neighbourhood. The times dealt with are the late 1930s, 1947 to 1948, and a few days in the 1970s. Like *Midnight's Children*, the immediate action of the novel is the present: Rushdie makes Saleem tell the story of his family in 1977 with the narrator interrupting himself every so often in order to comment on his present situation, on the act of writing, on history and a number of related issues. The omniscient narrator in *Clear Light of Day* recounts the story during a few days in the hot season in the early 1970s using the reunion of the two sisters to take them back into their childhood and adolescence with Tara giving way to her reminiscences and compelling Bim to follow her. While to Saleem the past constituting the present is full of changes in the life of the nation as well as in that of his family and is conceived of as a continuous and at times fast moving process, to Tara and Bim, on the other hand, past and present in Delhi appear at times almost unchanged and without movement except, perhaps, a slow movement towards decay and, at other times, as two different worlds with a past to which they by no means want to return. Tara's words, "I'm so glad it is over and we can never be young again", are confirmed by Bim who adds, "I never wish it back. I would never be young for anything."[2] And yet, subconsciously they know that the present cannot be understood and be made an integral part of their selves as long as they look at the past from a preconceived and prejudiced point of view. The author shows, in the course of her novel, how both women in the end accept their childhood because "It's never over. Nothing's over even" (CLD, 174), thereby gaining that insight into the continuance of the historical process with which Saleem sets out to tell his story.

Both writers do not confine themselves to a retelling of history through the portrayal of individual characters; rather, by interrelating character and event they reveal their deep interest in the central epistemological category of recollection, the category which constitutes on the one hand the aesthetic genres of the autobiography and the biography, and on the other hand the academic discipline of history. Recollection is not being made use of as a dream but as a mirror in which man tries to recognize the aspirations and strivings of mankind to recognize the totality of his own self as well as that of his species.

to this edition and are included in the text

2 Anita Desai, *Clear Light of Day*, New Delhi: Allied Publishers 1980, 43. All further references (CLD) are to this edition and are included in the text

Again, both writers differ in the way they deal with recollection. While Anita Desai works through her characters' interaction, especially through dialogue and reminiscence, thus building up a concept of history in an indirect and implicit manner, Rushdie's narrator Saleem is a very self-conscious person who uses different means: he conceptualizes and verbalizes, for instance, the term recollection in phrases such as there "is no escape from past acquaintance. What you were is forever who you are" (MC, 368); or, towards the end of the novel, when he sums up his insight: "Who what am I? My answer: I am the sum total of everything that went before me, of all I have been seen done, of everything done-to-me." (MC, 383)

Another difference in narrative procedure is the intricate relationship between historical events and personal experiences in the Sinai family which enables Rushdie to build up a myth of history which is as provocative as it is questionable. In *Clear Light of Day* there are parallels between the historical process and individual experiences, especially in the second part of the book where the times are marked by departure and death, not only in the Das family but also in the life of the Indian nation. The years 1947-48 with the partition of the subcontinent, the enforced exodus of millions from their homes, violence, death and, finally, Gandhi's assassination, are of profound meaning for the Das children, but still, it appears that history and individuals are linked by coincidence rather than by the same intrinsic logic we encounter in *Midnight's Children*.

Let us ask now how Saleem, Tara and Bim, the main actors in these two novels, conceive of the past and thus, through their memories, reflect their authors' notions as to how to deal with history. Saleem, the chronicler of events, moves through time and space in order to grasp the totality of the Indian subcontinent. History to him is a closely knit, complex and intricately interrelated sequence of events not ruled, as it seems, by any logic exterior to it; rather, it creates its own logic. He returns again and again to a central passage of his story, i.e. Nehru's letter to his parents on the occasion of his birth on 15 August 1947, the day India became independent. "We shall be watching over your life", it said, "with the closest attention; it will be, in a sense, the mirror of our own." (MC, 122) This letter gives us the clue as to why it is that when Saleem retells the history of his family he, at the same time, writes the history of the subcontinent. His motivation — and that of Rushdie, we should add — appears moralistic in that it attempts to answer the question he asks the Midnight Children, all those born on the day of independence. It deals with the notions of purpose and meaning: "'We must think'", I said, "'what we are for.'" (MC, 228)

On the surface Saleem's hope to save memory from "the corruption of the clocks" (MC, 38) indicates a Western concept of history and reality which takes both for granted, for tangible truth. On the other hand Saleem's method of combining the individually subjective with the supra individually objective, i.e. the family history with that of the subcontinent, is prompted by the disposition of the Indian mind to see correspondences in seemingly unrelated events:

> As a people we are obsessed with correspondences. Similarities between this and that, between apparently unconnected things make us clap our hands delightedly when we find them out. It is a sort of national longing for form — or perhaps simply an expression of our deep belief that forms lie hidden within reality; that meaning reveals itself only in flashes. Hence our vulnerability to omens. (MC, 300)

Logically, then, to Saleem there is no fundamental doubt in the perhaps unreliable nature of his story. As he argues, the only reality for man is the one derived from his recollection, from his memory:

> 'I told you [Padma] the truth [...], Memory's truth, because memory has its own special kind. It selects, eliminates, exaggerates, minimizes, glorifies, and vilifies, also; but in the end it creates its own reality, its heterogeneous but usually coherent version of events; and no sane human being ever trusts someone else's version more than his own.' (MC, 21)

Towards the end of his account Saleem reveals his ulterior motive, the reason why he wants to preserve the past, using the comparison of pickling fruit to preserve it:

> To pickle is to give immortality [...] The art is to change the flavour in degree, but not in kind; and above all [...] to give it shape and form — that is to say meaning.
>
> One day, perhaps, the world may taste the pickles of history I [...] hope [...] they possess the authentic taste of truth [...] that they are, despite everything, acts of love. (MC, 461)

Recapturing the past, then, is to be understood not only as man's attempt to give meaning to life, whatever the extent of his own imperfect vision, but, more importantly, as an act of love. Bim and Tara, by contrast, conceive of the past as a period essentially lacking in positive meaning. However, sharing a number of memories makes them reflect and comment upon them: the rose-walk in the garden, Raja's illness, meeting the neighbours, playing by the river, Hyder Ali on his horse, Aunt Mira's arrival, and the fires burning on the horizon in that fateful summer of 1947. Seemingly disconnected events establish a logical sequence of their own and evoke strong emotional and psychological responses in both of them. This gives scope to the author to probe into her characters' interior landscapes which are embedded in the same historical background of the 1930s and the 1940s and which share the same very few exciting events in otherwise altogether quite unexciting lives.

They agreed, we said, never to return to the past, their childhood, "all that dullness, boredom, waiting" (CLD, 4), where life seemed to have by-passed them. Still, there is Tara's need to return home at regular intervals in order, as she says, "not to lose touch [...] to find out and make sure again." (CLD, 6) Bim, on the other hand, obviously had never seriously thought of leaving the house, that symbol of the past both try to feel indifferent to. Imperceptibly, however, the past creeps back into their thoughts and words; Tara and Bim realize how much they have been shaped by it — and to what an extent it has distorted their views of each other and of the family altogether. As Tara admits reflecting on her sister's mental make-up:

> She had always thought Bim so competent, so capable. Everyone had thought that [...] But Bim seemed to stampede through the house like a dishevelled storm [...] Tara saw how little she had really observed — either as a child or as a grown woman. She had seen Bim through the lenses of her own self, as she had wanted to see her. And now, when she tried to be objective [...] she found she could not — her vision was strewn, obscured and screened by too much of the past. (CLD, 148)

And the past had meant, over the years, to be excluded from Raja's and Bim's world of make-believe, to be dependent on Bim's exuberance, to feel terrified and looked down upon at school where Bim excelled, to be forced to take part in activities she abhorred and got sick over, to be despondent at the way the days never seemed to pass, the future never to begin. The past also meant feeling guilty for having left Bim behind to look after Baba, and for having run away from Bim once who had been attacked by a swarm of bees in an old tomb in the Lodi Gardens. Tara had escaped all these memories as soon as an opportunity offered itself: marriage and a life far away from home. Now she feels that her guilt has to be redeemed, that Bim has to forgive her so that she can live with the past. But, as she realizes, her sister has not only attached little attention to the incident in the Lodi

Gardens but also says that Tara had done the right thing in going away. What else should she have done? Thus her sister, willingly or unwillingly, forces Tara to accept the past as it was, by looking straight at it, by living with it instead of being absolved from it.

Bim, too, reflecting on their childhood, gradually realizes how distorted her own vision of the past is. Her decision, years ago, not to leave the house but to look after Raja and Aunt Mira, thus, to become an independent woman and to earn her own living, had not really been founded on a realistic assessment of her own personality because she had always tried to behave the way others expected her to. She had known this instinctively for a long time, certainly since Dr Biswas, their young family doctor, had told her he understood why Bim chose to stay at home and look after Baba and Aunt Mira: they needed her support and it would be selfish to marry him. Yet ever since she had tried to suppress her memories of this incident because she had acted in a way she had not really felt like. Now, under the pressure of Tara's reminiscences and guilt feelings, she is unable to hold out any longer herself: she abuses Baba, storms at him and sees in her mentally retarded brother the reason for all her failures. However, soon after her emotional outburst Bim is honest enough to admit that it is her distorted view of the past and of herself which made her attack innocent and helpless Baba who, in any case, had never even encroached on Bim's support and patience. She admits that "I myself haven't been able to manage on my own." (CLD, 155)

For Tara and Bim, to turn to the past means to take courage and face the truth in order to live with it. If people succeed in doing so, they will realize that life means love, love for others, not self-love which needs the applause of others. As Bim sees it at the end:

> Although it was shadowy and dark, Bim could see as well as by the clear light of day that she felt only love and yearning for them all, and if there were hurts [...] then it was only because her love was imperfect and did not encompass them thoroughly enough [...] All these would have to be mended, these rents and tears, she would have to mend and make her net whole so that it would suffice her in her passage through the ocean. (CLD, 165)

Let me now try to assess the artistic realization of the relationship between history and the individual by looking at the interaction and interdependence of character and event in both novels. In Rushdie's book there is virtually no event which is not given an individual as well as an historical meaning. To cite only a few: Saleem's grandparents on their way from Kashmir to Agra stop over in Amritsar where Aziz experiences the Jallianwallah Bagh massacre in 1919. It is the day when he realizes how different his wife is from what he imagined her to be: orthodox, family-centred and strong-willed. Saleem's parents marry the day in 1945 when the first atom bomb ever is being exploded to destroy thousands and to usher in the nuclear age; they depart for Bombay on 4 June 1947, the day partition and the date of independence are announced by Nehru and Mountbatten; they acquire their own house on 15 August 1947, the day Saleem is born, from the Englishman Mr Methwold who claims that his ancestors were instrumental in establishing British rule in India; Saleem's grandfather returns to Kashmir on the same day in December 1963 when the prophet Mohammed's hair is stolen from the shrine in the Hazrat Bal mosque in Srinagar; on 23 September 1965 India's air force strafes Rawalpindi and Saleem's family is killed, his parents, his grandmother and an aunt; Shiva, the narrator's powerful adversary, moves in with Parvati-the-witch on the day in May 1974 when India explodes its first nuclear test bomb in Rajasthan and enters the nuclear age; their son Adam is born on 25 June 1975, the day the Emergency is declared for the first time in the country. More examples could be cited to demonstrate Saleem's belief that

> I was linked to history both literally and metaphorically, both actively and passively, in what our [...] scientists might term 'modes of connection composed of dualistically combined configurations' of the two pairs of opposed adverbs given above. This is why hyphens are necessary: actively-literally, passively-metaphorically, actively-metaphorically and passively-literally, I was inextricably entwined in my world. (MC, 238)

Since there can be no doubt about the close interconnection of character and event the question arises what pattern of history emerges. What is Saleem's and his family's fate, and does the first truly mirror that of the subcontinent? The story proper begins when Saleem becomes aware of his gift to read the minds of other people and of the existence of the Midnight Children who are also uncommonly gifted. Three of them prove to be outstanding: "Shiva, born like Saleem 'on the stroke of midnight' had been 'given the gifts of war'; Saleem, 'the greatest talent of all', had been endowed with 'the ability to look into the hearts and minds of men'". (MC, 200) Having been expelled from a children's gang he decides to set up his own: "a gang which was spread over the length and breadth of the country, and whose headquarters were behind my eyebrows, called "Midnight Children's Conference, my very own M.C.C." (MC, 207) And then there is Parvati-the-witch, the most powerful of the female Midnight's Children and only next to Saleem and Shiva because she was "born a mere seven seconds after midnight on August 15th, [and] had been given the powers of the adept, the illuminatus, the genuine gifts of conjuration and sorcery." (MC, 200)

These three children are closely linked to each other. Saleem's power to communicate with all the Midnight Children is being used with the intention to turn his mind "into a kind of forum in which they could talk to one another through me." (MC, 227) Only Shiva can close "off from me any part of his thoughts he chose to keep to himself." (MC, 226) Against his objection but with Parvati's assistance Saleem becomes their leader, their chief who soon proceeds to find out from the children about "the notions which plagued me all this time, the notions of purpose, and meaning. 'We must think', I said, 'what we are for.'" (MC, 228) After all, there must have been an agency which endowed all of them with supernatural, or rather, superhuman gifts. Saleem's unspoken assumption of the existence of an historical 'first cause' is soon questioned because many different, often mutually exclusive answers are being offered to his query: collectivism and individualism, filial duty and infant revolution, or science and religion. Full of premonition he concludes that "not a single one of us suggested that the purpose of Midnight's Children might be annihilation; that we would have no meaning until we were destroyed." (MC, 229)

Worse is to follow: the children symbolizing India's potentiality to build her future for each of its citizens, to build "the noble mansion of free India, where all her children may dwell", as Nehru had declared once (MC, 118), do not only differ ideologically, but strife, envy, selfishness, narrow-mindedness, regionalism and communalism gradually lead to the "disintegration of the Midnight Children's Conference — which finally fell apart on the day the Chinese armies came down over the Himalayas to humiliate the Indian fauj" (MC, 254), that is, in 1962. Besides, and perhaps more importantly, there is Shiva, Saleem's adversary, who had scoffed at the idea of the M.C.C., "that club-shub stuff [...] for you rich boy." (MC, 228) Intimately linked to Saleem both children were exchanged soon after their birth without the knowledge of their parents so that Shiva is actually the son of Amina and Ahmed Sinai while Saleem's parents are Vanita, a poor musician's wife, and Methwold, former English landlord and owner of the Sinai house in Bombay. Shiva is condemned to a life of poverty and crime; he rejects Saleem's search for the purpose and meaning of their lives because poverty leaves no room for idealistic philosophizing: "'Rich kid', Shiva yelled, 'you don't know one damned thing! What purpose, man!

What thing in the whole sister-sleeping world got reason, yara? Where's the reason in starving, man?'" (MC, 220) And after the disintegration of the Midnight Children's Conference Shiva presses home his point that

> 'there is no third principle; there is only money-and-poverty and have-and-lack [...] there is only me-against-the-world [...] and the world is no place for dreamers [...] look at Birla and Tata, and all the powerful: they make things. For things, the country is run. Not for people.' (MC, 255)

Saleem, unable to retort to Shiva's cynical analysis of the world, takes refuge in the idea that "if there is a third principle, its name is childhood. But it dies; or rather, it is murdered." (MC, 256) This is little consolation for never finding an answer to his search for meaning.

Perceived not so much as realistic human beings but, rather, as metaphorical and symbolical representatives Saleem and Shiva embody the principles of preservation and destruction, of idealism and materialism, of good and evil, of selfless search and selfish "struggle of oneself-against-the-crowd." (MC, 282) The historical process is based on the dualism of opposing forces with the principle of Shiva, destruction, increasingly determining present and future. Accordingly, Shiva's rise in the nation to become "India's most decorated war hero" (MC, 407) after the two wars against Pakistan in 1965 and 1971 is juxtaposed with Saleem's decline. Not only does the latter lose his control over the Midnight Children (who had lost faith in him after India's defeat by the Chinese and had fled from him), but his family is also destroyed and his sister disappears. Saleem, degraded to sniffing out the Indian enemy — a faculty which had replaced his telepathic powers — succeeds in surviving the war in Bangladesh and, with the support of Parvati-the-witch, returns to Delhi where he lives among magicians and conjurers in a slum. After a short while he is again forced to leave, is arrested and questioned about the Midnight Children whom he betrays to the new political power, the widow and her son. His own downfall and that of the children is brought about in Benares, symbolically one of the most holy places of Shiva worship in India, where all of them are castrated and thus, ironically, freed from their linkage with the country's history. Saleem and all the others end as "broken promises, made to be broken." (MC, 440) Regretting that he had ever thought and dreamt of a purpose in life; he comes to the conclusion "that privacy, the small individual lives of men, are preferable to all his inflated macrocosmic activities." (MC, 435)

In the light of Saleem's downfall and withdrawal into his private shell and Shiva's rise — who, incidentally, creates a new race of children, bastards and products of his illegitimate and clandestine relations with numerous 'society ladies' — the question arises as to what extent Rushdie's-Saleem's story expresses a pessimistic view of history in that man is unable to stem the process of decay and destruction which, in turn, reveals that history by its own intrinsic logic moves towards its own annihilation. For Saleem there is no question: "I will soon be thirty-one years old. Perhaps. If my crumbling, over-used body permits. But I have no hope of saving my life" (MC, 9) But then, introducing his long story on such a resigned note he implicitly questions his statement by underlining his view that there is, after all, some meaning, and this lies in employing one's recollection in order to give history immortality. This suggests that man's purpose in life as well as in history is to preserve it, hand its meaning down to others for them to listen to and, perhaps, to learn from. Saleem, so it appears, has learnt his moral lesson. Yet underneath we detect another more embracing dimension to Saleem's account, a philosophical quest. Rushdie, apart from telling a moral story, is basically concerned with the crucial question of Indian philosophy and the Indian mind, i.e., the perception of reality and illusion as a precondition of man's liberation, moksha. A look at a few explications given by Saleem as well as at some symbols in the story will verify this assumption.

We have already referred to memory's truth, to memory "[which] creates its own reality" (MC, 211), an assertion that reality can be defined only as a subjective entity; it cannot claim to be truth as such. Even more so, our perception of what we call reality, the working of our senses which provide the data for our recollection, our memory, is restricted by its very nature. Saleem illustrates this in differing ways:

> Reality is a question of perspective, the further you get from the past, the more concrete and plausible it seems — but as you approach the present, it inevitably seems more and more incredible. Suppose yourself in a large cinema, sitting at first in the back row, and gradually moving up, row by row, until your nose is almost pressed against the screen. Gradually the stars' faces dissolve into dancing grain; tiny details assume grotesque proportions; the illusion dissolves — or rather, it becomes clear that the illusion itself is reality. (MC, 165-66)

Related to this statement is Saleem's reflection on the concept of history as perceived in Hindu cosmology. "History", he says, "in my version [entering] a new phase on August 15th, 1947" (MC, 194), is inextricably bound to the age of Darkness, Kali-Yuga, and thus is, by cosmological law, a period of decay resulting in the perversion of all values and virtues. The moral issue turns into a philosophical one because in the face of Hindu cosmology a few years in the history of man or a nation are but the most fleeting and meaningless fractions of moments in Brahma's life: Kali- Yuga comprising 432,000 years is only a tenth of the Maha-Yuga cycle which in turn is the one thousandth part of "just one Day of Brahma" (MC, 194), whose life spans a hundred years. Reality is, indeed, illusion within the context of Brahma's life, irrespective of whether we take Hindu cosmology literally in a religious-philosophical sense or understand it as a myth created to grasp the relationship between reality and illusion. Saleem's despondency with his times is, perhaps, to be understood as expressing his resigned insight into man's non-knowledge, avidya, his failure to ever grasp the meaning of history the way historians and historiographers trust their ability to acquire it. Does not Rushdie's absurd story linking, even fusing the history of a nation with that of a family chosen at random expose, in its absurdity, the extent of the historian's and historiographer's hubris to explain to us what really happened in the past?

Next to reflection, episodes in the story illustrate the same predicament. Saleem cuts out newspaper items, for instance, words, syllables and letters, to piece them together to form a message to Commander Sabarmati that his wife betrays him. (MC, 259-60) Seemingly important political newspaper items are cut up at random to constitute a new message on reality when rearranged in a new way. Saleem's act reveals the absurdity of the historian's claim to render history objectively; rather, history can be bent to serve subjective and individual purposes.

Finally, Rushdie-Saleem employ symbols which at times grow into myths as in the case of the perforated bedsheet kept as a family treasure like a few other items, e.g. the silver spittoon, the green metal box, or Saleem's umbilical cord. Initially, the bedsheet with a hole at its centre served as a screen to hide a woman's body from the prying eyes of a male doctor permitting him only to inspect that part of the body which required treatment. Aziz, the young doctor, is often called to treat Naseem, a landowner's daughter, who is obviously a hypochondriac. He becomes haunted by the "phantasm of a partitioned woman" (MC, 25) whom he glues together in his imagination. Finally he falls in love with his image of Naseem "because through [the perforated sheet] he had seen the things which had filled up the hole inside himself." (MC, 27) After their marriage is agreed upon and Aziz comes to know his wife in her 'unpartitioned' nature, he realizes how little reality tallies with his imagination. Through the symbol of the perforated sheet we are again made aware of man's imperfect perceptive and — in the case of Aziz also his imperfect mental powers.

With the passage of time the sheet becomes moth-eaten. Aziz discovers on 14 August 1947 "that the hole had grown that there were other, smaller holes in the surrounding fabric." (MC, 111) They permit us, in the sense of the symbol's meaning, to recognize more of reality (illusion) by curtailing man's imaginative powers, by making them more and more superfluous — in much the same way as when we retreat from the screen in the cinema. The passage of thirty-two years, from 1915 to 1947, has taught Aziz much about the woman behind the sheet whom he had once fallen in love with.

A final reference to this symbol corroborates our analysis of its meaning. Saleem's family and along with it the past and its history are destroyed in the India-Pakistan war of 1965. They have ceased to exist as tangible objects and will survive only in Saleem's memory: "Sheets of flame rose from a Rawalpindi bungalow, perforated sheets at whose centre hung a mysterious dark hole [...] and one by one the war eliminated my drained, hopeless family from the earth." (MC, 342)

Compared with this novel, *Clear Light of Day* appears to be not only much less ambitious in its philosophical scope but also more traditional in its narrative technique. Anita Desai, in the main, employs traditional narrative modes such as flashback, perspectivism, stream-of-consciousness, point of view and, related to this, associative thought processes that centre on a limited number of memories which are gradually transformed into meaningful symbols. The first and the last chapter deal with the present, and the narrator switches her focus repeatedly from one sister to the other. Both are given equal room for reminiscence, for expressing their thoughts and exchanging their views. Very often, especially in the first chapter, visual impressions form the starting point of reminiscences: the rose walk in the garden, the veranda of the house, or one of its rooms, the pond at the back of the garden where the cow had drowned, the road to the river Jumna where the children used to play and see their neighbour on his horse, the path across to the Misras, their other neighbours. Again and again visual impressions associate events, incidents, experiences related to tangible reality. Since Bim and Tara are hardly shown outside their house, their garden or their immediate surroundings, the past remembered appears simple and transparent. Bim, accordingly, sums up her concept of life at the end of the first chapter, the first day after Tara's arrival:

> Isn't it strange how life won't flow, like a river, but moves in jumps, as if it were held back by locks that are opened now and

> then to let it jump forward in a kind of flood? There are these long still stretches — nothing happens — [...] and then suddenly there is a crash — mighty deeds take place [...] That summer was certainly one of them — the summer of '47'. (CLD, 43)

Bim's words serve the narrator as a cue to probe into their truth by turning back to 1947 and 1948, those eventful years in India's and the Das family's history, as we have said already. The flashback offers the opportunity to modify the narrator's point of view by alternately relating his story to one or the other of the Das children as well as to Aunt Mira. Tara's and Bim's notions of the past and each other are thus being scrutinized, verified, modified or proved wrong or distorted. Characters appear more complex and gain greater depth, especially Aunt Mira whom the children had always referred to as "the tree that grew in the centre of their lives." (CLD, 110) Paradoxically, we see her now in all her frailty, her mental insecurity and physical weakness. We are made aware of the total extent of her dependence on others as a widow to which she had been condemned according to Hindu custom after the early death of her husband when she herself was only twelve years old. The horrors of Aunt Mira's childhood, adolescence and mature life are juxtaposed with Tara's and Bim's — partly imagined — abhorrence of their own childhood experiences, thus putting their feelings and their psychological reactions into perspective since their own childhood had never really impinged on their freedom or their mental and psychological stability to the extent it had affected Aunt Mira's psyche, which finally succumbs to the strains experienced in the past and breaks.

A further flashback, presumably to the late 1930s, in the following chapter of the novel extends our understanding of the Das family even further because it deals with childhood proper when a person's personality is being formed. The events narrated here make us understand why Raja, Tara and Bim reacted towards their family life in 1947 and 1948 the way the preceding chapter had told us: Raja leaving his home to join the Hyder Ali family in Hyderabad; Tara marrying a young diplomat, and Bim rejecting the advances of Dr Biswas and his mother to marry him. To Raja, romantic and poet, departing had meant the realization of his childhood dreams "of coming alive to ideas, to images picked up in the books he read." (CLD, 120) To Tara, the over-sensitive and lonely child, breaking away from her home had meant escaping from a world where she had experienced again and again "the spider fear that lurked at the centre of the web-world." (CLD, 135) Finally, to Bim, her decision to stay on had been caused by Dr Biswas's words that she, Bim, obviously wanted to dedicate her life to her aunt and her brother. (CLD, 97) All of them, as we learn now, acted out of mistaken or misconceived notions of themselves: Raja did not lose his dependence on Hyder Ali and his family, nor Tara her anxieties and fears, or Bim her lack of organising life for others. Thus, by directing her explorative beam of light deeper and deeper into their lives, the past of her adult characters, Desai reveals more and more of their true selves to us and to them. Tara and Bim eventually realize who they really are so that they can live on more truthfully to themselves and each other. Bim becomes reconciled to her life in the house which initially only appeared to satisfy her expectations from life; Tara accepts living with her past failings, as we have seen, without blaming others or seeking their forgiveness. The past, re-experienced in its fullness, needs no further explanation: "Everything had been said at last, cleared out of the way finally. There was nothing left in the way of a barrier or a shadow, only the clear light pouring down from the sun." (CLD, 177)

Comparing the approach of the two writers to what is essentially the same question, man's quest for meaning, we can draw the conclusion that while Rushdie/Saleem come to understand the individual by grasping the meaning or meaninglessness of history, Tara and Bim discover it by rediscovering their own and true selves. What both writers suggest and where they agree philosophically is the necessity of an awareness that the power of love does not only help in finding the answer to one's quest — different though an answer may be — but that love and acts of love are the means available to man to prevent his destruction and, along with that, the destruction of history. Paradoxically, Salman Rushdie, having lived for a long time outside India, appears to be closer to it than Anita Desai, to whom India is her home. Rushdie, rendering the action of his novel through the narrator's discourse and comments, through structuring motives, images and symbols, shows how close he is to the Indian philosophical tradition: by fusing moral and philosophical issues as well as different modes of perception of the world, by rejecting the belief in man's ability to write and think objectively about history, he demonstrates that reality can only be grasped through myth — or literature. Anita Desai, on the other hand, is much closer to Western philosophical and humanistic concerns; her concept of reality is that of a tangible though perhaps distorted entity. It is one which it is man's and woman's task to find for himself or herself.

Works cited

Desai, Anita, *Clear Light of Day*, New Delhi: Allied Publishers 1980
Rushdie, Salman, *Midnight's Children*, London: Pan Books 1982

Indian Women Writing in English

A Brief Look at Short Stories of the 1970s and Early 1980s

"We are looking for a girl, simple yet sophisticated", his mother had said. "My son is working in a foreign company. His wife must be able to entertain and mix with the foreigners." She had made the word 'foreigners' sound like Martians. Simple and sophisticated, I had wondered. Was I that? It had seemed that I was, for my mother joyfully told me that they had agreed to our proposal. No one had asked me if I had agreed. It had been taken for granted. I had taken it for granted myself, when, suddenly a few days before the wedding, I had gone to my father, stricken by doubts. "Why?" he had asked me again and again. And "what will you do then?" In a panic I had asked myself, 'What will I do?' and I had thought of a thousand answers, but none to the question, 'What's wrong with him?' I had nothing to say either when my father said quietly, "I have two more daughters to be married."

There was no talk, no word between us. Just this relentless pounding. His movements had the same rhythm, the same violence as the movements of the sea; but, I thought, I could have borne the battering of the sea better. For that would hurt, but not humiliate like this. And at last, mercifully, it was over, my body having helped him by some strange instinct beyond and outside me. And the cry I gave was not for physical pain, but for the intrusion into my privacy, for the violation of my right to myself. I drew the sheets over myself and lay quietly, afraid to move, thinking of nothing, my mind an absolute blank.[1]

---

1 Shashi Deshpande, *The Legacy and Other Stories*, Calcutta: Writers Workshop 1978

THESE TWO SHORT PARAGRAPHS which were not chosen at random illustrate tellingly what the modern Indian English short story written by women is all about: it deals with young single or married women, housewives and mothers, or the relationship of husband and wife. The narrative action is concerned with a woman's psychological, emotional or intellectual needs, problems and conflicts as they arise out of her status and role in a comparatively conservative society. The experiences of the main character or characters in these short stories draw our attention to the modern Indian woman's predicament with regard to her establishing herself as an individual in her own right vis-à-vis a society which, by tradition, has reserved and continues to prescribe certain functions and roles to its women. The narrator's point of view chosen by the female author is almost always that of the protagonist, and there are numerous examples of stories told by the main character herself. Their language reflects the tensions between a well-established sociolect — or rather, sexolect — and the attempts of women to break linguistic barriers and create for themselves an idiom which is meaningful and conveys to others experiences of an awareness of self which cannot always be grasped cognitively. Let me illustrate these points by looking more closely at the two passages quoted.

The first one shows us a narrator who, initially, functions as an onlooker or commentator rather than the central character on the stage. The young woman who is being discussed here reports the comments passed upon her and only gradually includes herself in the deliberations of those who are deciding her fate. The sexolect of this passage and the narrator's attempt to break through the barriers it has constructed around her illustrates the shift of the narrator's point of view on the linguistic level. The person talked about and referred to is not "a woman" but "a girl"; she is to combine an appealing facade with passivity and obedience — "sophistication with simplicity" — and is expected to react chameleon-like to the needs of either her future social group or her tradition-oriented husband. "Mother", "they" and "father" are the institutions on whom the burden and the responsibility rests to see to it that "daughters [are] to be married", or that an unwritten social law is being executed. The momentous decision on the future life of an individual is reduced to an act of barter, a proposal. When the young woman steps into the action herself her words indicate the newness of the experience she is undergoing. At first she can only put her reactions into questions. "Was I simple and sophisticated?"; "What will I do?" Later on she becomes just speechless being unable to answer her own and her father's questions.

This short scene which, in the context of the story, is relived in the narrator's memory on the evening of her wedding night which she and her husband are going to spend in a lonely house by the sea, presents us with a young woman who is in the process of trying to grasp what is happening to her and what her relationship to her husband and herself really means. The point I want to make here is not to maintain that women writing from India till now had not been concerned with the individual woman's plight and her efforts to assert her dignity as a person but that, in the modern short story written by women — and, I should add, in the novel, too — a shift of emphasis has taken place. Woman now insists on her right to reject a life which is prescribed by a male-dominated, anti-individual society. What is more: She now has the courage to say so clearly.

This becomes quite obvious when we look at the second passage which we find at the end of "The Intrusion". To start with, the rather detailed description of the sexual act especially when composed by a woman and seen by her means breaking a very important taboo Indian society has imposed on its members, a taboo imposed, moreover, by a society which is well known for its sexual hypocrisy and prudishness. But to go even further and expose one's most intimate emotional and psychological experiences and reactions is almost an act of self-immolation, of wilfully relinquishing one's right to be accepted as a normal member of society. Shashi Deshpande's description of her narrator's sense of victimisation and isolation, of a dichotomy of body and soul, the outside world and her inner self, of the humiliation she feels at being treated like an object of gratification, and, finally, of her experience of emptiness, uselessness and fear takes us into realms of the female psyche which no writer of the previous generation had dared put into words as candidly. What at the beginning of the story appeared to be yet another cliché-ridden exposure of the oppression of women in India turns into an act of self-assertion, an assertion, however, which is still not in a position to go beyond rejecting traditional role conceptions and replace them by new ones. Shashi Deshpande's story ends on a note of almost deliberate detachment which does not indicate in the least how her young woman will develop in future:

> When sensation and feeling came back with a surge, my first thought was that I could not hear even the sea now. And I wondered why till I realized that there was another sound drowning it. I looked at him. He was lying on his back, his legs flung apart, snoring loudly and steadily. (48)

The language, too, underlines the dichotomy experienced by the woman: The pounding of the sea is distinguished from that of her husband's bodily movements, her own sensations, temporarily numbed, come back in a surge — nature re-establishing itself — and her husband's snoring drowns the sound of the sea.

Much the same can be said about other women writers and their short stories with regard to theme, narrative episode, character constellation and message. Among the nine collections I have gone through which include about a hundred and fifty stories there are of course examples which do not offer any new insight, which repeat cliché situations and conflicts in a cliché manner. This is due mainly, I believe, to the fact that Indian magazines, weeklies or monthlies, and the big English newspapers have offered their pages to women's stories. A new middle-class readership has established itself for which all these journalistic publications are catering, and many of the readers are middle-class women whom the editors hope to reach. Nevertheless, many of the stories written by young women who are by now quite well-known through their contributions to Indo-English literature deserve the critic's attention, and it is these stories which share their essential characteristics with "The Intrusion". The man–woman relationship, the experiences of a young girl or a young woman, the assertion of the older woman, her loneliness and isolation and the ostracism woman is forced to accept in a caste- and class-ridden society, are the main themes to which Padma Hejmadi, Sunita Jain, Raji Narasimhan, Jai Nimbkar, Malathi Rao, Vasantha Ravindran, Vera Sharma or Indu Suryanarayan return again and again.

In Raji Narasimhan's "The Last Embrace"[2] the narrator's wife has decided to leave him, to "retire from Life", as she told him. Similarly, their daughter has begun to live on her own, having turned her attention away from home towards a young man with whom she has fallen in love. Joshi, the narrator, feels his male supremacy being questioned which makes him ponder as to how he can once again reaffirm it by "a last embrace". Little is said about his wife's motives, just that he has lost his importance for her which, perhaps, he never had really possessed during their married life. In Narasimhan's "A Village Story"[3] a woman leaves her husband and starts teaching in a village. When he visits her to take her back she coolly sends him off. Sunita Jain's "The Landing"[4] describes a woman and her

2 Raji Narasimhan, "The Last Embrace", *The Marriage of Bela*, 63–71

3 Ibid., 89–98

4 Sunita Jain, "The Landing", *A Woman is Dead*, 16–23

children's return to India from the United States leaving her husband and their father behind because they want to live a a more meaningful life without him. And finally, in Shashi Despande's "Rain"[5] a young doctor is shocked by his woman friend's apparent callousness. She is obviously not upset at all when the telephone rings in the midst of their love-making and the hospital informs her that her husband has just died. Having earlier closed a previous chapter in her life, she will not allow its past to intrude and upset her.

Stories such as these exemplify that their authors are neither concerned with an analysis of their heroines' past tribulations nor are they anxious to justify their decisions to be free by, for example, paying attention to possibly rewarding prospects of their new lives. Rather, they confine themselves to portraying a woman's deliberate step to liberate herself from the shackles of traditional roles. It is the act itself of a woman's decision to leave her husband or partner in order to start a new life that is the point the writers want to make. Besides, little attention is being paid to questions of motivation and consequence, or of morality and ethos; an astounding fact considering Indian social practice and the high regard placed on respectability.

Against stories setting out to define new and anti-traditional images of women and posing a challenge to their readers' conceptions or misconceptions of their roles, a second type of narration depicts women who have already established their own independence and consequently have to cope with a world around them that is not really amenable to their new roles. Narasimhan's "End of Probation" and "Their Woman Colleague"[6] depict professionally successful women whose careers rankle their male colleagues' minds. Yet again, this kind of 'new' woman confronting male role playing is not actually probed into. Does the author purposely shun it or perhaps prefer the open ending of her story — as modern writers are apt to do — in order to invite her readers' responses? A reason for her strategy may also be found in Indian society's notoriety for punishing women for their alleged 'failure' or their choice of the 'wrong path'. Their punishment would take the form of feeling isolated, frustrated, self-questioning and resigned, as in Malathi Rao's story "The Metaphor of Stone."[7] On her birthday fifty year old Anita remembers her past, her lost hopes, her loneliness and the meaninglessness of being a woman. In Indu

5 Shashi Deshpande, "Rain", *The Legacy*, 58-66

6 Raji Narasimhan, "End of Probation", "Their Woman Colleague", *The Marriage of Bela*, 21–28, 29–33

7 Malathi Rao, "The Metaphor of Stone", *Come for Coffee, Please*, 18–26

Suryanarayan's "The Journey"[8] an elderly woman also reminisces on the past, when on a train journey she suddenly realizes that the man opposite her had ruined her father and thrown the burden of responsibility onto her; a weight that had affected her whole life, had in fact allowed her to live on her own, yet at the expense of permanently feeling the "stabbing pain" of a bad conscience. The victimization of the "failed" or "fallen" woman may make her face her self-negation because economic necessity forces her to end her rebellion and play those roles society has reserved for her, that of the mistress or the beggar. Vera Sharma's "The Unrepentant"[9] tells of a young widow and her illegitimate child who is eventually unable to bear the charity and righteousness of a Christian hostel and who escapes into the safety of a petty businessman's secure arms as his mistress. Indu Suryanarayan's "Drying Tears in the Sun"[10], on the other hand, traces the fate of an orphan girl who after having been seduced and born a child sinks to the lowest level in society, becoming a beggar woman who depends on charity. Finally, the same predicament is faced by women whose rebellion is quickly smothered and whose future lives are made to conform to society's expectations, for instance in Malathi Rao's "The Blue Muffler"[11] and in several Deshpande stories like "A Liberated Woman", "An Antidote to Boredom", "The Dim Corridor", or "The Eternal Theme".[12]

The thematic and ideological preoccupations of the modern Indian short story by women, and even more so the way these stories are being told and given linguistic and formal contour, reflect upon present-day efforts of the women in India to redefine themselves in the context of the tremendous economic, social, and cultural changes that have occurred over the last twenty or so years. These changes have brought about the emergence of new social classes such as the petit bourgeoisie and the 'new' middle class. Almost without exception, the younger generation of Indian women writers introduced here belongs to the middle class, a social formation that has adapted to western education, anglicised views, has set their minds on job-security, on an occupation in the administrative, the professional, educational and managerial branches of either the public or the private sector. This generation, born between the late 1930s and the 1940s, has

8 Indu Suryanarayan, "The Journey", *Drying Tears in the Sun*, 96–100

9 Vera Sharma, "The Unrepentant", *The Unrepentant*, 9–14

10 Indu Suryanarayan, "Drying Tears in the Sun", *Drying Tears in the Sun*, 45–57

11 Malathi Rao, "The Blue Muffler", *Passion Fruit*, 41–52

12 Shashi Deshpande, "A Liberated Woman"; "An Antidote to Boredom"; "The Dim Corridor"; "The Eternal Theme"; *The Legacy*, 21–29, 67–76, 77–85, 96–103

not personally experienced the struggle for independence but has grown up in a country where erstwhile important literary themes like dealing with colonialism and the nationalist struggle against it, the cultural clash between East and West, or the confrontation of tradition and modernity have more or less lost relevance. The wide-spread national struggles of the pre-war and war periods have been replaced by economic and social tensions and contradictions amongst the social classes and castes of India. Middle class writers have turned to questions and problems besetting their own social and economic conditions and paying attention to the private sphere. The Indian women short story of the 1970s and early 1980s is to be placed in this very context, and the increasing number of women writers is directly related to the thematic shift in emphasis and, of course, to the specific effects the changes referred to have had on their status and new perceptions of their own roles.

Women writers' noticeable preference for the short literary genre is also related to improved conditions of literary production, the expansion of the publishing industry, the spread of magazines and journals and a corresponding growth of readership. Prospective women writers used these opportunities and were supported by for example a modern publisher like P. Lal and his Writers Workshop in Calcutta who introduced many new voices to the reading public, which, incidentally, explains the large number of titles referred to in this essay. Comparatively secure economic conditions of many well-educated middle-class women began to form a solid basis for those among them who wanted to turn to writing, usually in their spare time but also because of the particular appeal this literary genre may have had for the female Indian sensibility which has earlier found expression mainly through poetry. Yet the poem, the private voice, left little scope to represent the social dimension of life in India while the novel characterized by the realistic mode of narration often enough sacrificed the subjective and personal to the general. As a literary form which would achieve both, to depict the inner and outer world, woman's personal affectedness by social and cultural realities and their composition, the short story appears to have appeared especially suitable to combine the epic art of extension with the "poetic art of ellipsis,"[13] to achieve conveying their situation and their world. The story forms chosen corroborate this reading. Stories are told straightforwardly and realistically with little attention paid to experiment. It is the message that matters and not how it is presented.

13 Thomas A. Gullason, "The Short Story: An Underrated Art", *Studies in Short Fiction* 2 (1964), 28

Works cited

Short Story Collections
HEJMADI, Padma, *Coigns of Vantage*, Calcutta: Writers Workshop 1972
DESHPANDE, Shashi, *The Legacy and Other Stories*, Calcutta: Writers Workshop 1978
JAIN, Sunita, *A Woman is Dead*, Calcutta: Writers Workshop 1980
NARASIMHAN, Raji, *The Marriage of Bela*, Calcutta: Writers Workshop 1978
NIMBKAR, Jay, *The Lotus Leaves and Other Stories*, Calcutta: Writers Workshop 1971
RAO, Malathi, *Passion Fruit*, Calcutta: Writers Workshop 1980
—, *Come for Coffee, Please*, Calcutta: Writers Workshop 1982
RAVINDRAN, Vasantha, *The Old House and Other Stories*, Calcutta: Writers Workshop 1982
SHARMA, Vera, *The Unrepentant and Other Stories*, Calcutta: Writers Workshop 1982
SURYANARAYAN, Indu, *Drying Tears in the Sun*, Calcutta: Writers Workshop 1982

Critical Studies
GULLASON, Thomas A., "The Short Story: An Underrated Art", *Studies in Short Fiction* 2 (1964), 13-31

Marginalizing the Centre — Centring the Periphery

The Critical Debate on 'Indian' Literature in English

THE DEBATE ON THE ROLE and the status of literary texts in English written outside Great Britain and the United States has, in the course of the latter half of this century, found its rightful place in the academy. And among the various literatures in English, writings by Indians do not only, and justifiably so, claim the longest history dating back to the early years of the last century, but have also been exposed to the perhaps most vigorous and controversial critical debate both inside and outside the country. To attempt thus a general critical survey of the reception of Indian literature in English would entail extensive research and necessarily result in a detailed and comprehensive presentation, a task that can only be hinted at here. What this paper then will set out to do is to present a provisional report on work in progress by sketching the historical background to the discourse of the reception and a few of its characteristic features. Accordingly, attention will be called to the last three decades, and, more specifically, to the discussion during this period on Indo-English writing in general.

The critical realization of a remarkable tradition of Indian creative writing in English could only be a question of time but did not, initially and in spite of Iyengar's work,[1] occur in places of higher learning but outside the English departments of the country's colleges and universities. Thus, on the occasion of the Second All-India Writers' Conference in Benares in October and November 1947, the All-India Centre of the P.E.N. led the way, and the writers assembled here discussed Indian literature, including

1 K.R. Srinivasa Iyengar, *Indian Writing in English*, Bombay: Asia Publishing House 1962, 2

its Indo-English brand.[2] Iyengar defined the critic's task as not merely that of analysing the text but also of contextualizing his reading and modified Taine's 'race', 'milieu' by emphasizing that the critic "should also learn to locate each work of literature in its unique context in terms of place, time and circumstance and judge it in relevance to them."[3] Once again, this literature is to be approached in cross-cultural terms:

> As regards Anglo-Indian literature, the 'race' is the mixed Indian race, a resultant of invasions, conquests, and occupations extending over a period of 4 or 5 thousand years; the 'milieu', the variegated Indian subcontinent, comprising extremes of every kind, heir to a geography and cultural heritage all its own; and the 'moment', the meeting of the West and India.[4] (22)

Almost forty years later Feroza F. Jussawalla's *Family Quarrels: Towards a Criticism of Indian Writing in English*[5] links up to Iyengar's view by arguing a combined textual-analytical and contextual-culture study approach with regard to the evaluation of the Indian writer's use of English and his or her execution of literary themes. Grounding her methodological considerations on J.R. Firth's definition of 'context of situation' as "the series of contexts of both verbal and non-verbal that make up a text..." (89), and on Braj B. Kachru's application of this concept to the (creative) use of English in India (98), Jussawalla rejects the, in her eyes, dominant approach hitherto practised by Indian critics who ignore the "context of situation, the language- and culture-contact situation in India." (137) Although she does not suggest the adoption, let alone the imitation, of Western critical theories, her expatriate status and her obvious distance to the Indian critical scene explain perhaps why she advocates Stanley Fish's concept

2 K.R. Srinivasa Iyengar, "Literary Criticism", ed. The P.E.N. All-India Centre, *Writers in Free India: Proceedings of the Second All-India Writers Conference*, Bombay: The P.E.N. All-India-Centre 1955. K.R. Srinivasa Iyengar sums up his remarks on "Indo-English Literature" (181–189), on the hopeful note that "... the career of Indo-English literature is not ended, and ... the best is yet to be", at the same time requesting his listeners to "look upon Indo-English literature as an Indian literature among other great Indian literatures..." (188) Cf. also K.R. Srinivasa Iyengar (ed.), *Indian Writers in Council: Proceedings of the First All-India Writers Conference*, Bombay: The International Book House 1947, and Sir Bomanji Wadia's contribution to the Jaipur conference in 1945 on "The Indispensability of English to Indian Culture." (243–246)

3 K.R. Srinivasa Iyengar, "Literary Criticism", *Writers in Free India*, Bombay: International Book House 1950, 99

4 Iyengar, *Indian Writing in English*, Bombay: Asia Publishing House, 2nd enlarged ed. 1973, 22 [Lectures, University of Leeds 1962]

5 Feroza F. Jussawalla, *Family Quarrels. Towards a Criticism of Indian Writing in English*, New York: Peter Lang 1985, 43

of the 'interpretive community' that, being itself contextualized, "could draw both on the important native Indian traditions in criticism and on contemporary linguistic analyses." (X) Mention should also be made here

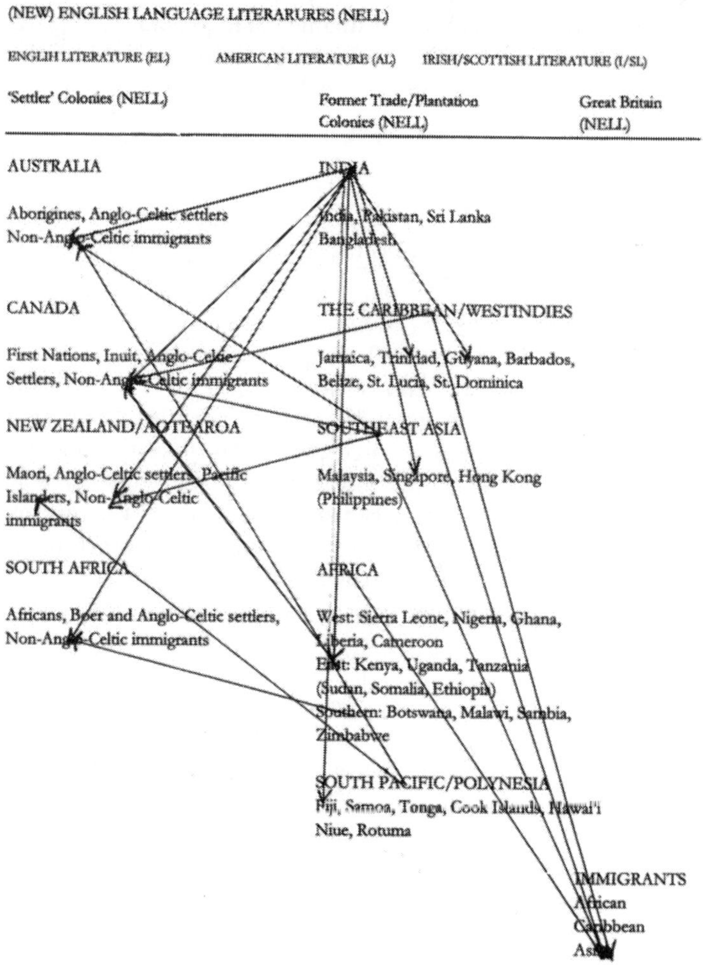

of the fact that Jussawalla's critical survey of the development of Indian criticism is not any longer nationalist and thus concerned with questions like: "'Should we use English?' or 'How can we Indianize English?', but rather 'How best can we use the English language to reflect our society and culture?'" (17)

Having necessarily digressed into linking up important methodological tenets of the post-war period and the beginning of Indo-English criticism in the early 1960s with a critical position of the mid-1980s grounded on socio-linguistics and culture studies, I must return to a second non-university institution which was instrumental in promoting Indo-English literature and criticism, viz. *The Writers Workshop* founded in Calcutta in 1958 by P. Lal and

> a group of writers who agree in principle that English has proved its ability, as a language, to play a creative role in Indian literature, through original writing and transcreation. Its task is that of defining and substantiating the role by discussion and diffusion of creative writing and transcreation from India and other countries.[6]

The position of *The Writers Workshop* on the role of English voiced rather adamantly here and substantiated unequivocally in a number of critical analyses of Indo-English writing, especially of poetry, in its main outlet *miscellany*, must be held responsible perhaps not for setting up but for bringing to the fore the two opposed critical camps of the defenders and the opponents of creative Indian writing in English: the 'localists' and the 'internationalists'. The controversy itself ranges across the diametrically opposed camps of those who defend or deny the creative use of an acquired language. Ferozewalla's conclusion about the Indian critical scene and her view on the 'localist' camp neatly sums up the situation:

> ... questions regarding the use of English and the identification of the Indianness of the subject matter have been the main concerns of the critics. Nationalistic rejection of English was coupled with an acceptance of the Whorfian hypothesis that a consciousness conditioned by an Indian language could not be conveyed through English. Indian critics seemed to accept Whorf's hypothesis about language determining the 'house' of one's consciousness all too readily.[7]

Lal's position, shared by many Indian writers in English,[8] was first taken

6 P. Lal, *The Concept of an Indian Literature: Six Essays*, Calcutta: Writers Workshop 1968, VI

7 Feroza F. Jussawalla, *Family Quarrels*, 33. See also the chapter "Family Quarrels", *ibid.*, 1–37, for a succinct though not uncontroversial presentation of the Indian critical scene

8 Cf. P. Lal (ed.), *Modern Indian Poetry in English*, Calcutta: Writers Workshop 1969; a comprehensive anthology complemented by poets responding to a questionnaire Lal had sent out to them. Cf. also statements made by Anand, Narayan and Rao on the creative use of English: Mulk Raj Anand, "Pigeon-Indian: Some Notes on Indian-English Writing"; and R.K Narayan, "English in India: The Process of Transmutation", ed. M.K. Naik, *Aspects of Indian Writing in English*, Delhi: The Macmillan Company of India 1979, 24–44 and 19–23 respectively. Raja Rao, "Foreword",

to task in the journal *Quest* in 1959; it was subsequently defended in several of his essays and also discussed in a *Writers Workshop* symposium held in 1960 as well as in the Indian press in 1961/62.[9] His emphatic insistence at the time on "the private voice" and the appeal of creative writing "to that personality in man which is distinct, curious, unique and idealistic",[10] clearly went against the grain of views held by more traditionally-oriented critics because it openly professed affinities to European Romanticism. Incidentally, it also rejected such tenets of Sanskrit aesthetics which were later to be suggested as forming part and parcel of the "Indian critic's equipment and training" in a 1984 Seminar on "A Common Poetic for Indian Literatures" organized at Dhvanyaloka in Mysore[11] by C.D. Narasimaiah, one of the most eloquent advocates of Indian writing in English. As was argued there, "the expression of personal emotion in art, *except as transmuted into artistic terms, when it becomes impersonal,* [my emphasis] has not been of any interest to the Indian critic...", while "the way a work affects the reader" occurs in the following manner:

> The reader enters into a dialogue, *hrdayasamvada*, with the work of art before him, and as the engagement with the work advances by stages variously described as *ahlada*, *rasollasa*, *cittavistra*, it matures into an absorption, *tallinatha* in it: for the duration of this condition, the reader has achieved his detachment or release from his egocentric predicament.[12]

Yet while Narasimhaiah pleads for

> taking you back to Bharata and his followers [...] not only because they are Indian and help to recover our *svadharma* but because they provide us with a poetic which could stand up to the menace of realism which has circumscribed Western thought...[13]

Kanthapura, London: George Allen and Unwin 1938

9 P.Lal, "Indian Writing in English. A Reply to Mr. Jyotirmoy Datta", [orig. 1959], P. Lal, *The Alien Insiders*, Calcutta: Writers Workshop 1987, 9–19; "Workshop Symposium", *Writers Workshop — a miscellany of creative writing*, 2 (October 1960), 13–22; *Indian Writing in English — a Symposium*, Calcutta: Writers Workshop n.d. [1962]; P. Lal, "Indian Writing in English", P. Lal, *The Concept of an Indian Literature*, Calcutta: Writers Workshop 1968, 41–49

10 P. Lal, "Indian Writing in English", 19

11 Dhvanyaloka, a research centre founded by Narasimhaiah, became in the 1970s the heart and hub of Indo-Anglian and Indian criticism in the country

12 "Appendix: Towards the Formulation of a Common Poetic for Indian Literatures Today", eds. C.D. Narasimhaiah and C.N. Srinath, *A Common Poetic for Indian Literatures*, Mysore: Dhvanyaloka 1984, 167

13 Narasimhaiah, "Introductory", *op.cit.*, 8

the critical movement towards the re-appropriation of traditional Indian aesthetics, as given voice here,[14] in spite of a differing critical methodology, seems to share with Lal and *The Writers Workshop* the belief in Indo-English literature as an Indian literature. And still, Narasimhaiah's opening remark in this context "that the mainstream of Indian thought is Hindu and the *mainstream* of literary sensibility is Sanskrit as the back-bone of the country's cultural unity"[15] appears to contradict this view unless, as I would suggest here, Indo-English literature is now being marginalized and assigned a place at the periphery of Indian culture.

Interestingly, while Narasimhaiah's critical preoccupation with defining the 'Indianness' of Indo-English writing and the 'Indian sensibility' of its authors, pursued by him from the beginning of his career,[16] appears to have led him towards an unequivocal centre-margin relationship of Indian and Indo-English writing. As opposed to him, Lal seems to have moved from his earlier romantic perception to, on the one hand, a contextualizing approach placing those Indian writers who have stayed on in the country and their "self-search, quest for tradition and myth knowing..."[17] more closely to their own cultural background. On the other hand and more importantly, Lal now implicitly subscribes to the multicultural composition of this literature when he calls attention to the motley crowd of writers in English and their vastly differing ethnic, linguistic, educational, religious and geographic background.[18]

---

14 See also R.B. Patankar's summons: "Let us look for our roots where they are most likely to be found — in India as it was just before the British advent. It is only if we start from there, that we shall discover/create a common poetic for modern Indian literatures." R.B. Patankar, "The Three Alternatives", *A Common Poetic for Indian Literatures*, 63

15 C.D. Narasimhaiah, "Introductory", *op.cit.*, 2. P. Lal has already taken up this point in 1974 in his essay "What is Indian in Indian Literature?" by arguing that there "has never been an 'Indian' literature for the simple reason that there never has been a very clearly defined sense of Indian nationhood." P. Lal, *The Lemon Tree of Modern Sex and Other Essays*, Calcutta: Writers Workshop 1974, 24

16 Cf. his statement in: "Raja Rao: The Metaphysical Novel (*The Serpent and the Rope*) and its Significance for our Age", C.D. Narasimhaiah, *The Swan and the Eagle. Essays on Indian English Literature*, Delhi: 2nd ed. 1987: "... I had during those years [i.e. the early 1960s] a special interest in Indian fiction, had been looking for a great Indian novel, and reading *The Serpent and the Rope* I remember I felt a sudden thrill that here at last was the finest and fullest possible expression of an essentially Indian sensibility." (159)

17 P. Lal, "The Alien Insiders", P. Lal, *The Alien Insiders*, 33

18 "The only pan-Indian language, English attracts the most diverse types. *They are all Indians* [my emphasis]: a Chinese-Sikkimese Catholic schooled in Darjeeling now working in a Bombay advertising firm; an Indian Jew who lives in Bombay...; a young woman novelist with a German mother and a Bengali father married to a Gujarati; a Mohammedan woman novelist from Lucknow; ... a young Bengali poet from a traditionally anglicised family; an Anglo-Burmese novelist...; a Kannada novelist who speaks and writes in French as fluently as he does in English; ... a Tamil-

While I will have to return to the Dhvanyaloka project of "constructing a critical framework" based on the assumption that the "*Rasa-Dhvani* theory is more widely known in Indian literatures than any other critical system and its concepts are in vogue in our arts and literatures", which makes it "more capable than any other existing theory of serving as the basis of a common poetic for Indian literatures",[19] *The Writers Workshop* activities in the early 1960s need some further elaboration by calling attention to the involvement, incidentally, for the first time, of foreign critics in the debate on the binary of English and Indianness. In contrast to several, mainly British critics who had responded favourably to the early Anand and Narayan novels and their linguistic and literary achievement,[20] the historian Michael Edwardes, author of a *History of India*, the writer John Waine and David McCutchion, Reader at Jadavpur University near Calcutta in the 1960s, took a rather critical stance, with Edwardes praising only Rudyard Kipling (!) and R.K. Narayan as having

> given me a genuine feeling about the country, [whereas] Indians writing in English are merely Indians writing in a foreign language. I do not think that they are Indian novelists at all [...] Indians writing in English are writing specifically for a foreign market. They are, therefore, more inclined to supply what they feel the market requires rather than writing something from their experience or out of their heart.[21]

While Edwardes obviously holds the view "that a consciousness conditioned by an Indian language could not be conveyed through English", David McCutchion, as sceptical of Indians making creative use of English as of the vagueness of the term 'Indianness', believes that the use of English quite generally and "inevitably brings with it the association of English literature and an English context." Thus while "Indian imagery and Indian tradition is experienced by most Indians only through the regional

speaking Indian Christian woman novelist married to a Telugu-speaking Hindu now teaching in an American university..." P. Lal, "The Alien Insiders", *op.cit.*, 33–34

19 "Appendix", *A Common Poetic for Indian Literatures*, 164, 169

20 For early European responses to Mulk Raj Anand, cf. Saros Cowasjee, *So Many Freedoms*, Delhi: OUP 1977, esp. 41–82, where he discusses Anand's *Untouchable* and *Coolie*; see also his "Select Bibliography", 196–198. Critical response to R.K. Narayan's early novels can be found in Hilda Pontes, *R.K. Narayan*, New Delhi: Concept 1983, 37–39

21 "Baldoon Dhingra interviews Michael Edwardes", *Indian Writing in English — a Symposium*, Calcutta: Writers Workshop, n.d. [1962], n.p. [2, 3]. See also C.D. Narasimhaiah's critique of John Waine's statement that "the Indian's use of English has been at the level of a *lingua franca* and lacks the fineness of nuance that makes literature possible." C.D. Narasimhaiah, *The Swan and the Eagle. Essays on Indian English Literature*, Delhi, 2nd ed. 1987 [1968], 2

languages [...] English will create a scholarly remove — the language of universities and museums."[22]

While this is a rather static view of language which erases the dynamism inherent in language-contact situations, such as 'English in India', 'Indianness' and its defenders come in for the type of dynamic criticism lacking in McCutchion's reflection on language. Who, he ironically asks, "is to say in what 'Indianness' consists, or where it is to be found: in the sutras or on Howrah Station, in Kalidasa or with the Swatantra Party, in a village mela or at the Lokh Sabha?" [23]

His final suggestion, somewhat surprising though, points in the direction of Lal's conjecture of the multicultural character of 'Indianness', present in Indo-English writing when there is a reflection of "the conflicts and reconciliations of European and Indian traditions [... which is] the most outstanding feature of contemporary Indian culture."[24]

Although McCutchion repeatedly returns to the bone of contention of Indo-English criticism,[25] and confirms his conviction that "there seems to be no *a priori* reason why great literature should not be written in English by Indians",[26] he noticeably begins to shift his attention to aesthetic considerations, as to whether, for example, "Indian literature in English [is] going to set itself standards or not."[27] The question of literary value remains important because neither "critical standards at home and patronizing approval from abroad" nor "Iyengar's loving survey"[28] will shake his conviction "that so much Indian writing in English is second-rate",[29] and that the "language is characterized by a mixture of pretentiousness and vulgarity, generally bathetic, and complete insensitivity to metaphorical undertones."[30] "The problem of literary value, our aesthetic response, still remains."[31]

In the 1960s then, the stage for the critical reception of Indo-English literature was set with opposed though mixed factions of Indian and European critics who had institutionalized a discourse on the binary

22 "Workshop Symposium", *miscellany* 2 (October 1960), 18

23 Ibid., 22

24 Ibid., 23

25 David McCutchion, *Indian Writing in English*, Calcutta: Writers Workshop 1969

26 *op.cit.*, 34

27 David McCutchion, "The Indianness of Indian Criticism", *op.cit.*, 75

28 "Indian Writing in English", 28, 29

29 Ibid., 10

30 Ibid., 19

31 Ibid., 17

opposition of language and sensibility, English and Indianness, and who claimed that the validity of their arguments and judgements were rooted in uncontroversial aesthetic assumptions readily at the disposal of practicing critics.[32] The general debate has continued into the 1990s and, perforce setting aside contributions of the late 1960s and the 1970s, I want to turn to methodological considerations proposed during the last ten to fifteen years.[33]

The discourse has finally shifted from non-academic to academic institutions, the beginnings of which were noticeable with Narasimhaiah's, Lal's and McCutchion's affiliations with university departments in the late 1960s; new centres of Indo-English literary studies sprang up at the universities of Mysore, Dharwar, Pune, Hyderabad, Gulbarga and New Delhi and at Indian Institutes of Technology in Madras, Bombay and New Delhi. Besides, university journals made their appearance, among them *The Literary Criterion* and the *Literary Half-Yearly*, *The Journal of Indian Writing in English* and *LittCrit*, or *The Osmania Journal of English Studies*. Finally, we notice the world-wide dissemination of studies in the new or post-colonial literatures in English and their gradual integration into university study programmes; the founding of research associations and the occasional collaboration between Indian and Western researchers. Concomitant with the entry of Indo-English studies into the university, there has been a shift in discursive practice in that for one, the problems of the creative writer has receded into the background and cleared the way for methodological considerations directed at devising an aesthetic theory of the relational integration of language, sensibility and artistic value.[34]

32 It should be added here that Bruce King, in his exhaustive study *Modern Indian Poetry in English*, Delhi: OUP 1987, relativizes the importance of the methodological reflections pursued by *The Writers Workshop* by arguing the influence of the 'Bombay poets', viz. Nissim Ezekiel and a whole group "marginal to traditional Hindu society not only by being alienated by their English-language education but also, more significantly, by coming from such communities as the Parsi, Jews, Christians, or by being rebels from Hinduism and Islam, or by living abroad." 3–4

33 Vasant A. Shahane in a brief survey praises the efflorescence of Indo–Anglian criticism and argues that "the genesis of criticism of Indian writing in English has been 'academic.'" He omits, though, the contributions of the *Indian P.E.N.* and *Writers Workshop*. Useful is his reference to a number of hitherto virtually unknown Ph.D. theses and critical texts of the 1920s and 1930s, while his comment on the achievement of non-Indian critics remains ambivalent. On the one hand he praises the ease with which they lay their hands "on what is 'Indian' in our sensibility", on the other he calls them "liable to be misleading due to their *innate incapacity* [my emphasis] to realize the 'Indianness' of Indian literatures [sic!] in English." Vasant A. Shahane, "Criticism of Indo-English Writing: Achievements and Failures" *Littcrit* 8, 1 (1982), 13-19; here 14

34 Cf. "Towards an Aesthetic of Indian English Literature", M.K. Naik, *Studies in Indian English Literature*, Delhi: Sterling 1987

For another, by opening up to the global Indian criticism has begun to relativize its often close affinity to the T.S. Eliot / F.R. Leavis 'school' and has returned to its own philosophical and aesthetic tradition.

In this context, the 'angle of attack' naturally differs with regard to epistemological categories like 'Indianness' or 'text' of variegated central concern. Iyengar, for instance, in a short note, felt called upon to define 'Indian sensibility' as "the 'rasa', the quality of our confrontation of Reality", which he perceives as a sufficiently flexible and 'open' concept to be concretized by specific Indian attitudes. But although he does not regard these as monolithic and rejects their equation with Hinduism, he seems to posit an unhistorically pure and static *rasa* which in its 'historical manifestations', though, and especially nowadays, might suffer fraction and fragmentation from the "challenges of an emerging planetary civilization" and thus will make it "more than Indian."[35]

Indian critics in a seminar on "Identity of Text: Problems and Reliability of Reader Response", again organised at Dhvanyaloka in 1986, attempted to relate Indian aesthetic concepts of the poet-reader relationship to Western reader-response theory, by giving attention to the 'text'. S. Laxmana Murthy, for instance, argued, and he did so in contradistinction to the deconstructionists' 'infinite referral' of meaning or signification, that in traditional Indian aesthetics

> [i]t appears that the Intentional and the Affective are accommodated in recovering the poetic statement in full [,] exercising caution not to let these dwindle into fallacies. [Accordingly] 'a stable identifiable literary text' [is posited] squarely between *kavi* [poet] and *sahridaya* [reader]

He further held that the establishment of this 'rapport' between the two depends on the shared knowledge of "the norms of linguistic community".[36] Obviously then, one of the logical conclusions of this tenet for the reception of Indo-English literature would lie in the difficulty, if not incapacity of English to achieve such a rapport, since it is to be doubted that *kavi* and *sahridaya* share throughout "the norms of linguistic community." Such a posited textual identity thus relativizes the status of Indian writing in English.

35 K.R. Srinivasa Iyengar, "Towards an Indian Sensibility in Indo-English Fiction" *Littcrit* 8, 1 (1982), 42–46; here 42, 44

36 S. Laxmana Murthy, "Reader's Response: An Indian View", *The Literary Criterion* XXI, 4 (1986), 10–16; here 15. Cf. also Swapan Majumdar, "Is there a Reader in the Class?", *op.cit.*, 58–62, who briefly alludes to Hans Robert Jauss, Wolfgang Iser and the "Konstanz School" and suggests that "classical Indian literary criticism has a lot to contribute to the consolidations of the premises of the Response theory" (61), without, however, substantiating his assertion

In response to Murthy's advocation of the *rasadhvani* concept, C.N. Ramachandran pointed out that this school would, like the 'Vakrokti' School of Kuntaka,

> flounder unless [both] fall back upon the 'given' of highly trained and initiated reader[s], [who, however, hardly exist], especially [not] in the modern world with its spread of literacy to all sections of the society and its clearing off the linguistic, cultural, and geographical bounds of readers.[37]

Yet in spite of his reservations, Ramachandran does not follow deconstructionism in its critique of Saussure and its denial of "the 'essence' of a text" and "a distinctive status to [sic] literary works",[38] but maintains that "a text has no identity of its own except the one given it by the reader." This, of course, is a far cry from considering the reader's realization of a text as "release from his egocentric predicament"[39], as maintained in the "Common Poetic"-seminar in 1984. Though objections were raised against Ramachandran and Murthy,[40] the conclusion to be drawn from this seminar is that against the epistemological problem of a suppositious constant, viz. 'Indian sensibility' — which, of course, relates to the central Hindu philosophical concept of *Brahman/atman* and *maya* — 'text' in its 'historical manifestation(s)' has been more strongly foregrounded in the more recent methodological debate. An impression confirmed, incidentally, by Kapil and Ranga Kapoor's note on "Third World Poetics. The Indian Case", and their "proposal to revive Indian poetics" in "terms of revival of Sanskrit poetics." This is being translated as revitalizing those 'schools' which based their aesthetics on "the scientific study of language", resp. "the special use of language as medium of art."[41] Circumventing the issue of poet-reader-relationship, 'text' with these critics is given the status of an autotelic entity to be submitted to descriptive linguistic and rhetorical analysis. This is an unexpected relapse, it appears, into the pre- reader-response era of New Criticism, although paradoxically, the Kapoors castigate Indian critics for not having used "frameworks" such as "hermeneutics, structuralism, post-structuralism [and] deconstruction."[42]

---

37 C.N. Ramachandran, "In Search of the Text: A Comparative Study of Western and Eastern Concepts", *The Literary Criterion* XXI, 4 (1986), 69–79; here 77, 78

38 Ibid., 73

39 Cf. note 12

40 *The Literary Criterion* XXI, 4 (1986), 101–106

41 Kapil Kapoor and Ranga Kapoor, "Third World Poetics. The Indian Case", *ACLALS Bulletin*, 7th series, No. 5 (1986), 48–57; here 52

42 Ibid, 48

While lack of space prevents further comments on the recent general Indian critical discourse,[43] a few remarks on the non-Indian contribution[44] must suffice.

Klaus Börner's essay "The Reception of Indian Literature in English in the West",[45] refers in its main argument distinctly to the Indian aesthetics discourse of the 1980s. Attempting to explore the question whether "the new literature (in English) call[s] for a new criticism" (307), he spells out a series of reception situations, among them one in which "the reader is German, author and reality are Indian, [and] the text is Indo-English." (312) Setting aside here the problematic situation of the German reader, Börner's discussion on the possibility of mediating such texts cross-culturally concentrates on the by now familiar discourse of the use of English — which, as he indicates, must be tackled socio-linguistically — and of 'Indianness'. Here he seems to corroborate implicitly "the nationalists or regionalists who think that English only superficially affects a deep rooted Indian identity" (314), and to follow Narasimhaiah's and other traditionalist Indian critics' validation and valorisation of Sanskrit aesthetic theory as constituting a tenable modern Indian poetics. His argument is that "the utterly non-western synthesis of religion, philosophy and aesthetics that constitutes the eastern modes of perception" has remained dominant, because "in the eastern reception of art the fatal secularization or dissociation of sensibilities has not taken place." (318) Börner thus posits the continuance of a distinct Indian sensibility, when reflected philosophically, has obviously found its 'objective correlative' in Sanskrit aesthetics, especially as regards the poet-reader-relationship articulated in *rasadhvani*.

In contrast to Börner, a rather different methodological approach of non-Indian critics has set great store on relating Indian writing in English to, as Syd Harrex and Guy Amirthanayagam have put it, "the complex process of cultural hybridization" with its historical roots of imperialism and "multi-ethnic creativity in spoken and written English."[46] Accordingly,

---

43 Cf. also Vasant A. Shahane, "Indo-English Literature: Its Major Concerns and Its Academic Rationale", ed. A.K. Srivastava, *Alien Voice. Perspectives on Commonwealth Literature*, Lucknow: Print House India 1981, 9–30

44 Cf. Kirpal Singh, ed., *Through Western Eyes: Foreign Responses to Indian Writing in English*, Calcutta 1984, which is based on a "Special Double Issue" of *The Journal of Indian Writing in English* 8 (1980)

45 Klaus Börner, "The Reception of Indian Literature in English in the West", *German Studies in India* 9, 4 (1985), 177–190; repr. in: ed. Abhai Maurya , *India and World Literature*, New Delhi 1990, 305–321

46 S.C. Harrex & Guy Amirthanayagam, "Introduction: Notes towards a Comparative Cross-Cultural

the catalyst for many writers here "is the *cross-cultural* [my emphasis] character of their situations and identities." (3) Nonetheless, both critics are careful in pointing out that, although Indian writers share in this process, they are yet "heir to a number of major cultural traditions" (17) that continue to shape them.

While a methodological exploration, for example, of the linguistic processes giving expression of the experience of cultural hybridisation, is not being attempted here, it is given some scope in John Oliver Perry's "Is Indian English an 'Alien Tongue'?"[47] He pursues some of those linguistic aspects of the multi-functional nature of Indian English Börner may have had in mind. Discussing socially, culturally and historically differing Indian English varieties, Perry admits that

> it cannot reasonably be claimed that the full panoply of India's multicultural traditions can be captured in Indian English, [but adds that this] limitation [...] also applies to all the geographically identified regional languages; none can incorporate all the rest. (49)

On the other hand he claims — probably much to the chagrin of the 'localist' defenders of one and only one Indian 'reality' — that

> Indian English can and does embody many different distinctly Indian realities; it is a more multi-cultural language medium in its many effective uses, poetic and practical, than probably any other language used in India. (40)

In this context even Bill Ashcroft, Gareth Griffith and Helen Tiffin's study of the new, or as they prefer to say, post-colonial literatures, *The Empire Writes Back*,[48] represents a fundamental theoretical non-Indian intervention into the Indo-English critical discourse. Viewing the Sanskrit aesthetics debate of the 1980s as "in part at least [...] a debate about decolonization" (117), the three Australian critics bracket it with the world-wide post-colonial process of abrogating Western cultural hegemony and appropriating one's own cultural identity, but warn us at the same time, that its outcome in India is "difficult to predict." (121) Referring to the

Criticism", eds. Guy Amirthanayagam and S.C. Harrex, *Only Connect. Literary Perspectives East and West*, Adelaide/Honolulu: CRNLE and East-West Center 1981, 1–27; here 1

47 John Oliver Perry, "Is Indian English an 'Alien Tongue'?", *The Literary Criterion* XXV, 3 (1990), 38–55

48 Bill Ashcroft, Gareth Griffith, and Helen Tiffin, *The Empire Writes Back. Theory and Practice in Post-colonial Literatures*, London: Routledge 1989

practice and theory of Indo-English writing, they confine themselves to affirming Meenakshi Mukherjee's generalizing evaluative statement made in the mid-1970s, that the Indian writers' choice of English "is in no sense a bar to this work being profoundly Indian in concern and potentially as rich a means of reproducing Indian society and thought." (123)[49]

The discourse of post-colonialism has, with a very few exceptions, hardly drawn in Indo-English critics. Among them, Arun P. Mukherjee's intervention, "The Exclusion of Postcolonial Theory and Mulk Raj Anand's 'Untouchable': A Case Study",[50] deserves attention, as it represents a basic critique of the theoretical assumptions of this discourse. Questioning the validity of post-colonial constructs, such as "the binary oppositions of colonizer/colonized, domination/resistance" (30), the positing of a "unitary subject" (34) and "a unitary 'colonised consciousness'" (44), Mukherjee generally accuses the post-colonial theoreticians (including Diana Brydon, Abdul R. JanMohamed, Leslie Monkman, Benita Parry or Stephen Slemon) of re-introducing a "'universalist' aesthetics, albeit from the left this time" (29) by suggesting a

> 'postcolonial' essence [...] that is supposedly shared by geographically dispersed and historically, culturally, linguistically, politically, and racially different societies and the texts produced by their members. (29)

Mukherjee rests her counter-arguments on at least two premises; first, that there exists in post-colonial societies the

> Bakhtian 'heteroglossia' [...] of social discourses [...] that arises from conflicts of race, class, gender, language, religion, ethnicity, and political affiliation and forms, in Jameson's terms 'the social ground of a text' (34),

and secondly and concomitant with this heteroglossia that

> our cultural productions are also created in response to *our own* [my emphasis] cultural needs and desires to interrogate 'our class structures, our familial ideologies, our management of bodies and sexualities, our ideologies, our silences'. (33)

Deconstructing Mulk Raj Anand's *Untouchable* (1935), "one of the canonical texts of Indo-English literature", (35) Mukherjee then proceeds to illustrate

49 Quoted from Meenakshi Mukherjee, *Considerations*, New Delhi: Allied 1977, n.p.

50 Arun P. Mukherjee, "The Exclusions of Postcolonial Theory and Mulk Raj Anand's 'Untouchable': A Case Study", *ARIEL* 22, 3 (July 1991), 27–48

that, far from being a post-colonial novel, "the textual discourse can be called patronizing" (38) in that it represses and denies the "actions and discourses of the untouchables themselves."(38) Historically speaking, they were very well in a position to act at the time Anand wrote this novel, which Mukherjee calls an "embourgeoisified version of [the untouchables'] story" (36) and aligning itself with the "version of nationalist historiography." (39) "The 'heteroglossia' of the novel is, ultimately, constituted of middle class voices alone." (40) Rejecting a "homogeneous postcolonial consciousness" (33), Mukherjee emphatically implores post-colonial critics to realize the "pluralistic and heterogeneous nature of the 'socio-ideological' discourses of postcolonial cultures." (45)

To conclude: The more audible voices in the concert of Indo-English literature and its critical reception, however, will most probably be found among a younger generation who, setting aside their continued response to the work of the founding fathers of the Indo-English novel, will increasingly be concerned with the after-effects of the paradigmatic change in the Indian literary scene brought about by Rushdie's *Midnight's Children*. A collection of essays edited by Viney Kirpal, *The New Indian Novel in English: A Study of the 1980s*, and Feroza Jussawalla and Reed Way Dasenbrock's "Introduction" to their *Interviews with Writers of the Post-Colonial World* are just two instances of a fresh response to Indo-English works which differ from their predecessors in more than merely their non-realistic narrative mode.[51]

Commenting upon the newness of quite a few works of the 1980s, Kirpal notices their openness to new forms and themes, their "vast emotional, political, cultural, geographical and historical sweep", and "protagonists [who] are insecure, anxious, tense, sceptical people sitting on the edge of the world." (xvii) Affirming the post-colonial outlook on the Indo-English novel, the critic does not only relate the 1980s novel to the "mixed Indian tradition" (xxi), including the presence of minority communities, but implicitly also advocates a shift in the theoretical discourse to correspond to the shift in literary practice.[52] Still, readings of Rushdie's works for example, illustrate that the new critical task is not as easy to accomplish as a programmatic outline may suggest. Neither Makarand R. Paranjpe's sweeping generalizations about the novel of the 1960s and 1970s, or his cursory pro-

51 Ed. Viney Kirpal, *The New Indian Novel in English: A Study of the 1980s*, New Delhi: Allied Publishers 1990; eds. Feroza Jussawalla and Reed Way Dasenbrock, *Interviews with Writers of the Post-Colonial World*, Jackson & London: University Press of Mississippi 1992

52 Cf. also Novy Kapadia, "Narrative Techniques in the New Indian Novel", Kirpal, *op.cit.*, 239–250

nouncements on Rushdie as a hoax and *Midnight's Children* as phoney and "one great, big, confused bluff",[53] nor Jussawalla's diatribe against *The Satanic Verses* because of the author's alleged 'Orientalism' and, interestingly, the novel's lack of "a good story, a moral vision, and a narrative technique that keeps the reader engrossed,"[54] quite fulfil the high expectations raised in Viney Kirpal's "Introduction".

Looking back at the long tradition of Indo-English writing, it is surprising to note that its reception both in practical and theoretical terms has, on the whole, mainly been an affair of a comparatively small group of Indian and an even smaller number of non-Indian critics. Besides, it has been restricted almost exclusively to 'high' literature, thereby denying popular or mass literature the attention it certainly deserves, especially since its reading may offer access to elusive aspects of literary practice in India. Finally, linguistic studies, in spite of the work done by Braj B. Kachru and a few others, are almost non-existent. The field of Indo-English literature needs further cultivation, and since it continues to grow it will, hopefully, invite many more critical readers.

Works cited

ANAND, Mulk Raj, "Pigeon-English: Some Notes on Indian- English Writing", ed. M.K. Naik, *Aspects of Indian Writing in English*, Delhi: The Macmillan Company of India 1979, 24–44

ASHCROFT, Bill, Gareth Griffith, and Helen Tiffin, *The Empire Writes Back. Theory and Practice in Post-Colonial Literatures*, London: Routledge 1989

BÖRNER, Klaus, "The Reception of Indian Literature in English in the West", *German Studies in India* 9, 4 (1985), 177–190

COWASJEE, Saros, *So Man Freedoms: A Study of the Major Fiction of Mulk Raj Anand*, Delhi: OUP 1977

DHINGRA, Baldoon, "Baldoon Dhingra interviews Michael Edwardes", *Indian Writing in English — A Symposium*, Calcutta: Writers Workshop n.d. [1962]

HARREX, S.C. and Guy Amirthanayagam, "Introduction: Notes towards a Comparative Cross-Cultural Criticism", eds. Guy Amarthanayagam & S.C. Harrex, *Only Connect. Literary Perspectives East and West*, Adelaide/Honolulu: CRNLE and East-West Center 1981, 1–27

IYENGAR, K.R. Srinivasa, *Indian Writing in English*, Bombay: Asia Publishing House 1962

—, ed., *Indian Writers in Council: Proceedings of the First All-India Writers Conference*, Bombay: The International Book House 1947

—, "Towards an Indian Sensibility in Indo-English Fiction", *LittCrit* 8, 1 (1982), 42–46

JUSSAWALLA, Feroza F., *Family Quarrels. Towards a Criticism of Indian Writing in English*, New York: Peter Lang 1985

—, "Post-Joycean / Sub-Joycean: The Reverses of Mr. Rushdie's Tricks in *The Satanic Verses*", ed. Viney Kirpal, *op.cit.*, 227–337 [sic!]

---

53 Makarand R. Paranjpe, "Inside and Outside the Whale: Politics and the New Indian English Novel", Kirpal *op.cit.*, 213–226; here 220 and 221

54 Feroza Jussawalla, "Post-Joycean/Sub-Joycean: The Reverses of Mr. Rushdie's Tricks in *The Satanic Verses*", Kirpal, *op.cit*, 227–337 (sic!); here 232 and 236

—, and Reed Way Daysenbrock, *Interviews with Writers of the Post-Colonial World*, Jackson and London: University Press of Mississippi 1992

KAPADIA, Novy, "Narrative Techniques in the New Indian Novel", ed. Viney Kirpal, *op.cit.*, 239–250

KAPOOR, Kapil and Ranga Kapoor, "Third World Poetics. The Indian Case", *ACLALS Bulletin*, 7th series, No.5 (1986), 48–57

KING, Bruce, *Modern Indian Poetry in English*, Delhi: OUP 1987

KIRPAL, Viney, ed., *The New Indian Novel in English: A Study of the 1980s*, New Delhi: Allied Publishers 1990

LAL, P., "Indian Writing in English. A Reply to Mr. Jyotimoy Datta", P. Lal, *The Alien Insiders*, Calcutta Writers Workshop 1989 [orig. 1959], 9–19

—, "Workshop Symposium", *Writers Workshop — a miscellany of creative writing* 2 (October 1960), 13–22

—, *Indian Writing in English — A Symposium*, Calcutta: Writers Workshop n.d. [1962]

—, *The Concept of an Indian Literature. Six Essays*, Calcutta: Writers Workshop 1968

—, ed., *Modern Indian Poetry in English*, Calcutta: Writers Workshop 1969

—, *The Lemon Tree of Modern Sex and Other Essays*, Calcutta: Writers Workshop 1974

MAJUMDAR, Swapan, "Is there a Reader in the Class?" *The Literary Criterion* XXI, 4 (1986), 58–62

MCCUTCHION, David, *Indian Writing in English*, Calcutta: Writers Workshop 1969

MUKHERJEE, Arun P., "The Exclusions of Postcolonial Theory and Mulk Raj Anand's *Untouchable*: A Case-Study", *ARIEL* 22, 3 (July 1991), 27–48

MUKHERJEE, Meenakshi, *Considerations*, New Delhi: Allied 1977

MURTHY, S. Laxmana, "Reader's Response: An Indian View", *The Literary Criterion* XXI, 4 (1986), 10–16

NAIK, M.K., *Studies in Indian English Literature*, Delhi: Sterling 1987

NARAYAN, R.K., "English in India. The Process of Transmutation", ed. M.K. Naik, *op.cit.*, 19–23

NARASIMHAIAH, C.D., *The Swan and the Eagle. Essays on Indian English Literature*, Simla: Indian Institute of Advanced Study 1969 [Delhi, 2nd ed., 1987]

—, "Appendix: Towards the Formulation of a Common Poetic for Indian Literature Today", eds. Narasimhaiah and Srinath, *A Common Poetic for Indian Literatures*, Mysore: Dhvanyaloka 1984

PARANJPE, Makarand R., "Inside and Outside the Whale: Politics and the New Indian English Novel", ed. Viney Kirpal, *op.cit.*, 213–226

PATANKAR, R.B., "The Three Alternatives", eds. C.D. Narasimhaiah and C.N. Srinath, *op.cit.*

THE P.E.N. ALL-INDIA CENTRE, *Writers in Free India*, Bombay 1950

PERRY, John Oliver, "Is Indian English an 'Alien' Tongue?" *The Literary Criterion* XXV, 3 (1990), 38–55

PONTES, Hilda, *R.K. Narayan*, New Delhi: Concept 1983

RAMACHANDRAN, C.N., "In Search of the Text: A Comparative Study of Western and European Concepts", *The Literary Criterion* XXI, 4 (1986), 69–79

RAO, Raja, "Foreword", *Kanthapura*, London: George Allen and Unwin 1938

SHAHANE, Vasant A, "Criticism of Indo-English Writing. Achievements and Failures", *LittCrit* 8, 1 (1982), 13–19

—, "Indo-English Literature: Its Major Concerns and Its Academic Rationale", ed. A.K. Srivastava, *Alien Voice. Perspectives on Commonwealth Literature*, Lucknow: Print House India 1981, 9–30

SINGH, Kirpal, *Through Western Eyes: Foreign Responses to Indian Writing in English*, Calcutta 1984

‘In the Days When the Love Laws Were Made’

Arundhati Roy’s *The God of Small Things*

AFTER HAVING READ ARUNDHATI ROY’S story *The God of Small Things*, these words raise a number of questions in my mind; questions of the meaning of history, tradition and modernity, of law and of love, of society and the individual human being — in a country that I think I have come to know a little over a period of more than thirty years. I am well aware that to know a country even ‘a little’ is a highly pretentious statement, not the least because the India that is meant here is a mental construct, an intellectual abstraction that has to be translated into a myriad of concrete space-time shapes to give it meaning. Into that of Kerala in the 1960s and 1990s, for example; or more precisely, into a small Kerala village community. A community like Ayemenem, near Kottayam, where the story’s fateful events take place during a fortnight at the end of 1969; events that would forever affect the lives of a Syrian-Christian family.

I also ask myself, whether having visited several parts of Kerala in the past will help me towards answering my questions. Or perhaps, my having read other stories from and about Kerala. For example, Meena Alexander’s autobiography *Fault Lines*, which introduced me to a particular social segment of the Syrian-Christian community. Or the first part of Salman Rushdie’s *The Moore’s Last Sigh* with its portrayal of a coastal, urban, pluralistic religious society and its twentieth century economic and cultural history. Or Thakazhi’s *Chemmeen*, the famous fisherman story of many years ago, which was turned into a film and is mentioned in Roy’s novel. (218) Or finally, Kamala Das’s stories and poems which have certainly opened windows for me, especially her "An Introduction" and "My Grandmother's House".

Taking my cue from Das's texts as well as from several of her love poems and relating them to *The God of Small Things*[1], it does not seem far-fetched then to suggest that independent-minded women writers from Kerala like Kamala Das, Meena Alexander or Arundhati Roy have been concerned with the fate especially of the young woman, and her relationship to society — or to return to Roy's phrase, to the 'love laws' decreed in the past but still valid and ruthlessly put into effect even today, as the novel's story illustrates.

At the end of the introductory chapter, "Paradise Pickles & Preserves", the narrator reflects upon the time frame of her story (which we do not yet know in all its details). Distinguishing between the actual story to be told "for practical purposes, in a hopelessly practical world ..." (34) that does not cover more than two weeks, and its historically representative meaning she suggests:

> to say that it all began when Sophie Mol came to Ayemenem is only one way of looking at it.
> Equally, it could be argued that it actually began thousands of years ago [...] before Marxism came [...] the British [...] the Dutch [...] It could be argued that it began long before Christianity arrived in a boat and seeped into Kerala like tea from a teabag.
> That it really began in the days when the Love Laws were made.
> The laws that lay down who should be loved, and how.
> And how much. (33)

The historical perspective invoked here touches upon two interesting aspects, a socio-cultural dimension and a political-aesthetic one, to which I shall turn later. Its socio-cultural reference suggests a fissure between the history of Christianity in South India and 'Love'. Christ's dictum, "love thy neighbour as thyself", we are meant to understand, has perhaps never really taken root in the Syrian-Christian community's socio-religious make-up. On the contrary. *The God of Small Things,* I think, 'argues' that Christian love in its several forms — God's love and human conjugal, parental, brotherly and sisterly, neighbourly and sexual love — have come to be regulated and subjugated by the 'love laws'; by such rules, to be more precise, that govern interpersonal relations and were instituted and sanctioned during the pre-Christian era

1 Arundhati, Roy, *The God of Small Things*, London: Flamingo/Harper Collins 1998. All further references are to this edition.

in Kerala; in sum, by a remarkably resilient conception and practice of love insisted-upon and applied ever since, which would denounce, reject and, if the need arose, simply annihilate any alternative idea and practice of love in any religious community, including that of the Syrian-Christians.

In an interesting excursion into the history of the relationship of Christianity and casteism (which is, after all, the 'love laws' site), the narrator supplies evidence of their supreme power. The conversion of untouchables to Christianity did not remove their social stigma and make them 'brothers in Christ'. On the contrary: "They were made to have separate churches, with separate services, and separate priests. As a special favour they were even given their own separate Pariah Bishop." (74)

The God of Small Things demonstrates the virtually unbroken tradition and almost unquestioned rule of these 'love laws' in the configuration of a conflict between their defenders and their challengers. As for the constellation of its adverse parties, the logic of this conflict obviously demands typifying those who unquestioningly defend the immutability of tradition. Their opponents, on the other hand, would have to be more individualized, as they are modern, questioning, even doubting human beings, who suffer from contradictory pulls — desires, emotions and views — in their search for a personal identity beyond the constriction of the 'love laws'. Thus on one side of the dividing line we meet Baby Kochamma, a spinster of almost sixty years of age, who is the perhaps outstanding, although not the only advocate of the 'love laws'. I would go even further and maintain that the narrator foregrounds Baby Kochamma's physical appearance, her views, reflections, feelings and generally scheming nature to such an extent that she at times turns out as a caricature of herself. On the opposite side we find her niece Ammu, twenty-seven years old, divorced and the mother of the twins Esthappen Yako and Rahel. She is the central antagonist in the struggle against the 'love laws' and the most individualized of all the characters.

As far as stereotyping is concerned, I note, of course, the narrator's (and implied author-narrator's) obvious rejection of — and suffering from! — pre-Christian, that is to say, Hindu-based and caste-grounded perception of interpersonal relationships. A perception which I similarly reject because I believe that it is an ideological construct that serves, first and foremost, the maintenance of power by those who wield it: the upper over the lower castes; caste members over untouchables; man over woman and children; the wealthy over the poor. But I am also aware of the danger of being too easily manipulated by the narrator's tendency to stereotype her figures; and aware, similarly, of the danger of too quickly identifying with her critical stance towards, for example, Baby Kochamma who, after all, is not a demon but a *human being.* There is then the need on the reader's part of perceiving of her as a *literary construct* that serves the narrator's purpose of examining the roots of the 'love laws' and of exposing their anti-human nature. Which, incidentally, reminds me of the narrator's likewise sceptical investigation into that brand of Marxism that is professed by Comrade Pillai when Velutha approaches him for help:

> '... Comrade [he said], you should know that Party was not constituted to support workers' indiscipline in their private life.'
> Velutha watched Comrade Pillai's body fade from the door. His disembodied, piping voice stayed on and sent out slogans. Pennants fluttering in an empty doorway.
>
> *It is not in the Party's interest to take up such matters.*
> *Individuals' interest is subordinate to the organization's interest.*
> *Violating Party Discipline means violating Party Unity.*
>
> The voice went on. Sentences disaggregated into phrases. Words.
>
> [...]
>
> And there it was again. Another religion turned against itself. Another edifice constructed by the human mind, decimated by human nature. (287)

As this passage illustrates, Baby Kochamma is not the only typified figure in the narrative. Others, too, are ostensibly meant to serve the same function of exposing 'the religion' of the 'love laws'. Comrade K.N.M. Pillai shuts the door on Velutha because the young man's 'indiscipline' in his private life neither serves his own political ambitions nor his business interests. As the master of his house he addresses his wife with 'edi' (or 'hey, you', as the narrator helpfully explains to the non-Malayalam speaker and reader). He makes his niece Latha and son Lenin obediently rattle off English literary texts to impress the visitor, memorized words which they neither understand nor pronounce intelligibly. And he orders 'edi' around to serve the men, stay in the background and hold her tongue. Similarly typified characters are Inspector Thomas Mathew; or a "posse of Touchable Policemen [...] A cartoonplatoon" (304) of six men who catch sleeping Velutha and kick him to death; or Velutha's father Vellya Paapen who has totally internalised the 'love laws', gives his son's illicit relationship with Ammu away to Mammachi and even waits for Velutha to kill him, because he had dared to humiliate the very family who had given "his father, Kelan, title to the land on which their hut now stood." (255)

Various Ipe-family members are drawn as types filling out traditional social and gender roles. Benaan John Ipe or Pappachi, Ammu's father, rules his household like a tyrant, and neither his educational background nor his respectable professional position prevent him from beating up his wife and daughter — though not his son — regularly and ruthlessly. Mammachi, suffering wife, is the doting Indian mother of a son for whom she has a special entrance built to the house to facilitate the visit of his women who, after all, minister to "a Man's needs." (168) Yet after she has heard of her daughter's affair with an untouchable, which triggers off a vividly detailed fantasized picture of their love act, she

> nearly vomited. *Like a dog with a bitch on heat.* Her tolerance of 'Men's Needs' as far as her son was concerned, became the fuel for her unmanageable fury at her daughter. She had defiled generations of breeding [...] and brought the family to its knees. [...]
>
> Mammachi lost control. (258)

Finally, her son Chacko, who long ago had just managed to pass his exam at Balliol College in Oxford, but had thereafter failed in almost every other respect, including in his marriage to Sophie Mol's English mother Margaret, and now in running the family pickle factory. Though he can discuss history, hates to admit that they "were a *family* of Anglophiles" (52), and teaches the twins to understand difficult English words, he has turned — or returned — into the stereotypical Indian family man. In charge of the Ipe-household he asserts his position whenever he can. Thus he cynically puts his sister down by telling her, "'What's yours is mine and what's mine is also mine'", since "as a daughter [she] had no claim to property." (57)

Set against this range of stereotyped figures there is, as I have said, Ammu, portrayed as an individual character. I would also include the three children Estha, Rahel and Sophie Mol and, to some degree, Velutha. Ammu's individuality rests in her double role as the searching and lonely antagonist and the acting protagonist of the final part of the narrative. She antagonizes her family by marginalizing herself socially: escapes from her parents' home as a young woman; marries a man of her own choice and separates from him after only a few years. Once in Ayemenem, she widens the rift by constantly challenging her elder brother's views and attitudes and by keeping distant from her mother and her aunt. When she suddenly realizes her love for Velutha and does not hesitate to enter into a tabooed relationship with him, a Paravan employed by her mother, it is this single act of Ammu's breaking society's 'love laws' that causes their defenders to react and that pushes the narrative to its climax. She herself may not always be free of stereotypical views, for example in her critique of others as social conformists or of men as male chauvinists. Yet such accusations protect her and hide her loneliness, her homelessness. She does indeed never find and never have a home. Like other family members who for a time had lived elsewhere — Pappachi, Baby Kochamma and Chacko — Ammu's move to Ayemenem initially appears as her homecoming, although being a divorced woman with children does not make her really welcome. Ironically, she finally finds her home in 'The History House': the deserted and dilapidating house of the "Black Sahib. The Englishman who had 'gone native'" (52); which later becomes the refuge of the children and finally the place where Velutha is murdered.

The three children are not yet old enough to have become aware of the question of individual identity, but it is Roy's gift of credibly portraying their childlike nature which endows them with individuality. As grown-up people, twenty-three years after Ammu's and Velutha's love was destroyed, I still recognize Estah and Rahel as individual personalities, albeit as totally changed ever since the children were forced by Baby Kochamma to 'admit' Velutha's alleged crime of having abducted and then murdered Sophie Mol. Estha's mental disturbance, I feel, sets in when the "Inspector asked his question. Estha's mouth said Yes. Childhood tiptoed out. Silence slid in like a bolt." (320) Taking leave from Ammu and Rahel and being 'Returned' to his father on Chacko's orders, Estha "left his voice behind" (326) at the Cochin Harbour Terminus, never to see his mother again and never to speak a word after his 're-Return' to Aymenem twenty-three years later, sometime in 1993. Rahel, just back from America at Baby Kochamma's request to look after her brother, had at the time of departure "doubled over and screamed and screamed" on the station platform. (326) Her life has since been empty without her twin brother, without Ammu who had died a few years later, and with her own aimless drifting from place to place. But being now together again, sisterly and brotherly love re-asserts itself against the 'love laws' — which would, of course, forbid their lying together :

> she sat up and put her arms around him. Drew him down beside her.
> They lay like that for a long time. Awake in the dark. Quietness and Emptiness.
> Not old. Not young.
> But a viable, die-able age.
>
> [...]

> But what was there to say?
> Only that there were tears. Only that Quietness and Emptiness fitted together like stacked spoons. [...] Only that what they shared that night was not happiness, but hideous grief.
> Only that once again they broke the Love Laws. That lay down who should be loved. And how. And how much. (327-8)

I mentioned that I read Velutha as a partly individualized figure, and I think this is due to the several points of view employed. There is, first of all, the narrator's own voice drily describing Velutha's childhood and his return to Ayemenem after four years of absence. Or on the fateful day of Ammu's and Velutha's mutual recognition as man and woman, it is his physical appearance that invites the narrator's attention. (174) Further, he is seen through the eyes and the mind of other characters. His father, for example, recognizes an assuredness in Velutha which he himself does not possess and which worries him. Estha and Rahel who quickly befriend the young man are impressed by his craftsman's skilled hands. And there is, of course, Ammu who, as it were, takes over the narrator's angle by concentrating on Velutha's physique: his body, cheekbones and smile. Later again and dreaming about him, Ammu is mainly taken up by his physical appearance — which incidentally also takes centre stage in her mind as in the narrator's in their love-making. Velutha, it appears, is constructed as a type of the *noble untouchable*. Ammu in her dream even raises him to the level of 'The God of Loss', 'The God of Small Things': a symbolic heightening of this character which assumes central importance in the narrator's story.

Still, there is a third point of view: Velutha's own thoughts and feelings as presented directly to the reader, and it is here where he gains individuality: through *his* realization of a 'new world' of wonder and fear:

> In that brief moment, Velutha looked up and saw things that he hadn't seen before. Things that had been out of bounds so far, obscured by history's blinkers.
> Simple things.
> For instance, he saw that Rahel's mother was a woman.
> That she had dimples when she smiled. [...] He saw too that he was not necessarily the only giver of gifts. That *she* had gifts to give him too.
> This knowing slid into him cleanly, like the sharp edge of a knife.
> Cold and hot at once. It only took a moment. (176-7)

Similarly, in their first night together it is Velutha himself who conveys the turmoil of his emotions, his joy, love, apprehension, self-accusation and hope. And again, shortly before his life is ended, his happiness and hope:

> He was suddenly happy. *Things will get worse,* he thought to himself. *Then better.* He was walking swiftly now, towards the Heart of Darkness.
> As lonely as a wolf.
> The God of Loss.
> The God of Small Things.
> Naked but for his nail varnish. (290)

However, at this point I would like to put forward an essential observation on the novel as a whole. A very careful reading of these sentences — which should and could easily be complemented by many more examples — reveals a characteristic narrative strategy, a specific employment of point of view which, I believe, sets the tone and mood not only of passages quoted here but of the whole story of *The God of Small Things*: The *persona* of the narrator is never very far from the scene narrated. "The knowing slid into him cleanly, like the sharp edge of a knife", or the final four lines of my last quotation, are *her* words, not Velutha's. To add just one final example. When he swims towards Ammu who is sitting on the stone steps leading to the water,

> [h]e watched her. He took his time.
> Had he known that he was about to enter a tunnel whose only egress was his own annihilation, would he have turned away?
> Perhaps.
> Perhaps not.
> Who can tell? (333)

The narrator's presence makes itself felt here; she foregrounds herself not only here but throughout her narrative; which is to say, underneath the realistic story Roy has created a subtext, the mimetic mode is counterpoised by the fabulist; or to use the narrator's own words:

> Perhaps it's true that things can change in a day. That a few dozen hours can affect the outcome of whole lifetimes. And that when they do, those few dozen hours [...] must be resurrected from the ruins and *examined.* Preserved. Accounted for.
> Little events, ordinary things, smashed and *reconstituted. Imbued with new meaning.* Suddenly they become the bleached bones of a story. [my emphasis] (32–3)

"Imbued with new meaning" — the "little events", the *small things*. In the manner Ammu and Velutha,

> on the thirteen nights that followed this one, instinctively [...] stuck to the Small Things. [Because the] Big Things ever lurked inside. They knew that there was nowhere for them to go. They had nothing. No future. So they stuck to the small things. (338)

The fabulist mode then, by constantly transcending the mimetic, reveals the 'Big Things' through the 'Small Things', gives those who challenge the 'love laws' tragic stature in their failure. This is achieved through a number of rhetorical and structuring narrative devices of which only a few should be mentioned here. Obviously most noticeable is the narrator's repetition of words and of often elliptic sentences as well as her use of innumerable similes and comparisons. Their frequent employment gradually endows them with symbolic power which in turn contributes towards an intricate pattern of the meaning of events and actions and of the personality of the actors. To quote, out of context and at random, some significant examples: The God of Small Things; Pappachi's moth; Touchables; a chink in History; hole in the Universe; when the Love Laws were made; a cold moth lifted a cold leg; infinnate [sic!] joy; viable die-able age; later — Lay Ter; no Locusts Stand I; things can change in a day; the time was ten to two; mosquito on a leash; like old roses on a breeze; click and click; tomorrow; he left no footprints in sand, no ripples in water, no image in mirrors — and so on.

Structurally, *The God of Small Things* is the creation of a highly reflective and intellectual artistic mind that breaks up the linear time sequence of the story and mingles and combines present, past and future, memories, dreams and allusive foresight as effortlessly as it shifts from one point of view to another — and I have not referred to all of them. The pattern that emerges resembles a carpet with its basic structure woven in the first chapter and its details then added, returned to and reworked one by one. Here, a particular and unique design in its overall pattern should not be overlooked because it reveals itself as a combination of the two historical dimensions of the novel mentioned earlier, the socio-cultural and the political-aesthetic. I am referring to the chapters "God's Own Country" and "Kochu Thomban". Both present us with Ayemenem or Kerala in the 1990s as experienced by Rahel after her return, and precisely because of their differing time level, they raise the question of the political-aesthetic site of *The God of Small Things*.

"God's Own Country", the name given to a tourist resort near the river with the old but now renovated 'History House' as its centre, ironically negates its very meaning because it is a purely man-made business venture set up at the expense of nature and people; of the river, its fishermen and the villagers of Ayemenem. The river greets Rahel "with a ghastly skull's smile, with holes where teeth had been, and a limp hand raised from a hospital bed." (124) The imagery of sickness and disease is further complemented by images of the filth and stench of the "shanty hutments" on the river bank, where people have been screened off from the resort. "God's Own Country" is fake history and fake culture. The ancestral Kerala homes with their furniture and knick-knacks bought from old families and the "trunkated kathakali performances" in the evenings are "toy histories for rich tourists to play in." (126) Similarly, Ayemenem has not only "swelled to the size of a little town" but also turned into a potentially violent community because of its "press of people". (128) Only Comrade K.N.M. Pillai has remained unchanged: smug, economically well-off and socially true to stereotype in appearance and his own peculiar brand of English. Indeed, true to his conviction: "Change is one thing. Acceptance is another." (279)

Juxtaposing "Kochu Thomban" with "God's Own Country" means moving from one make-believe world into another; yet from a tone of sarcasm and irony to one of praise, and from a mood of suppressed anger and sadness to one of rapture, peace and acceptance. The narrator's description of Rahel's visit to the temple to offer a coconut to the elephant turns into a rhetorically impressive praise song of oral quality about Kathakali Man and his performance, followed by a similarly dense description of his enactment of kathakali, or the retelling of the main story of the Mahabharata. It is an exceptional piece of writing, quite unique within the novel, in which the narrator appears to totally identify with her narrative and to merge with its content. She obvioully underwrites Ayemenem men's need

> to ask pardon of their gods. To apologize for corrupting their stories. For encashing their identities. Misappropriating their lives; [for] turning to tourism to stave off starvation. (229)

But does she also identify with the story the way the dancers do? With the story's meaning and the function it has for these men? That is, to identify with their religion, their culture and cultural history? And with Kunti who "invoked the Love Laws"? (233)

The narrator's emphatic soliloquy bears echoes for me of Raja Rao's old woman narrator in *Kanthapura*. Yet eventually she steps back after the dancing has come to an end and the make-belief world of the dancers is laid to rest. Now we are made to look into the minds of Rahel and Estha (who had joined her in the temple):

> There was madness there that morning. Under the rose bowl. It was no performance. Esthappen and Rahel recognized it. They had seen its work before. Another morning. Another stage. Another kind of frenzy [...] The brutal extravagance of this matched by the savage economy of that.
> They sat there, Quietness and Emptiness [...] Trapped in the bog of a story that was and wasn't theirs. (235-6)

Here we are again, at the textual level, of being told of 'Small things' containing 'Big things'. Violence, destruction and death as the story of a culture, of its history, reaching back to the times when the 'love laws' were made.

I return to my questions raised at the beginning, of the meaning of history, tradition and modernity, of the individual and society. What do I call the political-aesthetic site of *The God of Small Things*? Does it appeal to tradition in the sense of upholding the 'love laws', of merging with the kathakali meaning, as the dancers do, or of feeling helplessly lost in the face of the dehumanizing effects and the ecological damage capitalism has brought to the countryside? Or does it appeal to modernity in the sense that the 'love laws' must be abolished since they destroy women and men who strive for their self-realization as individuals? There is no question that *The God of Small Things* rejects modernity in the cloak of "God's Own Country", as much as it does tradition as the rule of the 'love laws'. The answer then must obviously be searched elsewhere. In the fate of Estha and Rahel? Or in that of the kathakali dancer? In 'Quietness and Emptiness', or in the dancer who has turned into

> Regional Flavour [... who] checks his rage and dances [...] collects his fees [...] stops by the Ayemenem temple, he and the others with him, and they dance to ask pardon of the gods. (231)

Or must the novel not be placed in today's post-colonial world? As a representation of the pull between tradition and modernity where neither the one nor the other offers ready-made formulas as to how to live in it? And where, perhaps, Chacko is the 'true' representative of its heterogeneity, its hybridity. He who in spite of the stereotypical role he is cast in, is never really able to strip himself off his colonized mind: the ex-Balliol student with his rowing oar from Oxford, his European suit and his knowledge of English, his idea of modernizing the pickle factory by buying the latest in machinery, and his final, though similarly unsuccessful migration to Canada as an antiques dealer.

> Happy, however, are the K.N.M. Pillais.
> Perhaps.
> But who wants to be a Pillai?

Works cited

ALEXANDER, Meena, *Fault Lines: A Memoir*, New Delhi: Penguin Books 1993

DAS, Kamala, "An Introduction"; "My Grandmother's House", *Summer in Calcutta*, Calcutta: writers workshop 1965

ROY, Arundhati, *The God of Small Things*, London: Flamingo/ Harper Collins 1998

RUSHDIE, Salman, *The Moor's Last Sigh*, London: Jonathan Cape 1995

THAKAZHI, *Chemmeen*, Kottayam: National Book Stall, D.C. Books 1956

R. K. NARAYAN
Centenary - 2006
The Guide

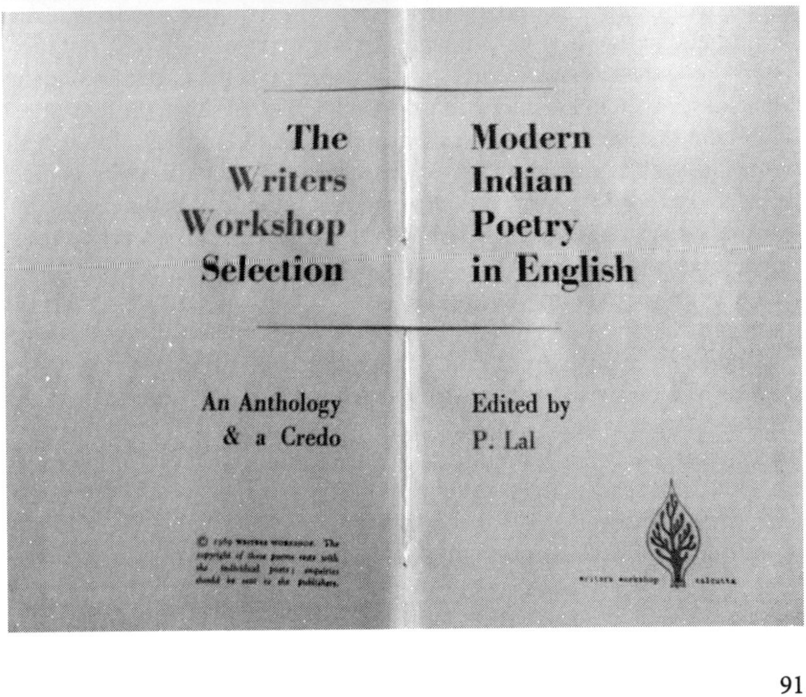
The Writers Workshop Selection

Modern Indian Poetry in English

An Anthology & a Credo

Edited by P. Lal

Global Fantasy — Glocal Imagination

The New Literatures in English and their Fantastic ImagiNations

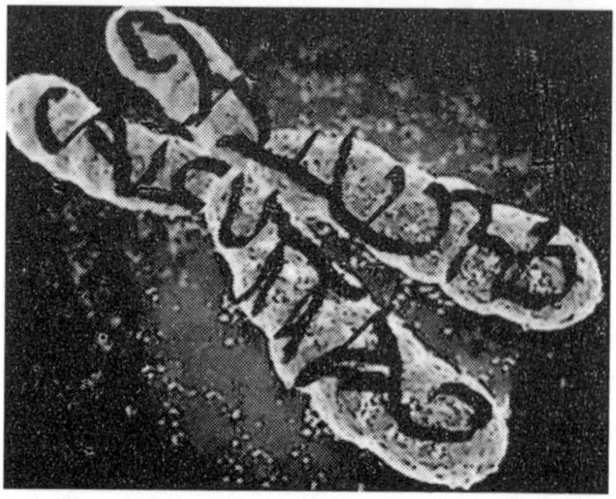

As my cue I take the word 'imagination' and aim to explore its power to transcend borders: borders drawn on maps separating one nation state from another; the border that writers and readers deal with in their task (or need) to distinguish between the world 'out there' and the border that finds expression and is represented through the artist's creative use of the word, but also as it is realized in the act of reading; the border within that imagined world that separates what we refer to as 'realist' or mimetic in the sense of its imaginary mirroring of the world 'out there' from the fantasized world that finds little or perhaps no correspondence whatsoever even to the mirrored world 'out there'. In short, the fantastic. It is a realm that invites comparison with the world of dreams, although the fantastic and the dream differ structurally. While the former is as much subjected to our basic perceptions of the 'real' grounded in time, space and causality, the latter is just as bereft of them: to understand it requires access through dream analysis.

Of course, different though the world of fantasy may be from our perceptions of the 'real' world, we cannot ultimately devise a world populated by beings and brought alive by their action and interaction beyond the border of our sensual perceptions, of our experience of the world 'out there'. Fantastic stories may be as far removed from our reality as we can imagine, yet they are still based on and controlled by overt violation of what is generally accepted as possibility. In other words, they invert elements of this world.[1] Distinctions, however, can be made depending on the distance created between the 'here' and the 'there', and this becomes

1 Rosemary Jackson, *Fantasy: The Literature of Subversion*, London & New York: Methuen 1981, 8

obvious when we think of examples of fantastic writing. The world of *The Lord of the Rings* is populated by strange creatures but also by beings who share many features with human beings in our world; so does its moral value system, its location and topography and the causality of its dramatic actions. Much further removed is Amos Tutuola's world of *The Palm-Wine Drinkard* where logic, space and time assume fantastic dimensions and differ substantially from our understanding of their functioning.

But let me return to the question of border (and border crossing) with the implicit presupposition of the co-existence of two neighbouring realms or worlds, a co-existence along the temporal axis depending on whether both worlds are located in the 'here-and-now', in the present and the past or in the present and the future. It would be quite exceptional to encounter them exclusively in the past <u>and</u> the future, which in turn underlines the importance accorded to the present in fantastic writing: an option that suggests that past or future are imagined extensions of the 'here and now'. Spatially speaking, the coexistence of the two worlds may be as closely distanced as noted in *The Lord of the Rings* or as far away as outer space or the imagined-'underworld'. Finally, a special type of spatial coexistence is to be found in the bordering of our state of consciousness with our subconscious mind.

Now, as far as border crossing goes the fantasy writer has the choice of several narrative and dramatizing strategies usually at the same time. He might devise one or several fictitious characters to voluntarily set out and pursue a particular aim thereby creating one or more active agents. But the story's actors might also turn out to be the means or tools of their creator meant to achieve a certain end. Finally, their actions may be enforced on them by the power of an 'invisible hand' that leaves them little room to act other than by being driven to it. Freely stepping across a frontier sets in motion the dramatic action in Amos Tutuola's *The Palm-Wine Drinkard and His Dead Palm-wine Tapster in the Deads' Town* (1952), in Chitra Banerjee Divakaruni's *The Mistress of Spices* (1997), Amitav Ghosh's *The Calcutta Chromosome* (1997), or in Witi Ihimaera's *Sky Dancer* (2003). Yet it is on the suggestion of a guiding power that James Cook enters the underworld in Robert Sullivan's poem *Captain Cook in the Underworld* (2002). The protagonists in Bessie Head's *A Question of Power* (1973) and Boman Desai's *The Memory of Elephants* (1988) are forced to step into the world of their subconscious while the young photographer in Mukul Kesavan's *Looking through Glass* (1995) finds himself back in the historical consciousness of his nation.

As to what fantasy writing is supposed to achieve, opinions range from the view that it attempts to "compensate for a lack resulting from cultural restraints: it is a literature of desire, which seeks that which is experienced as absence and loss", as Rosemary Jackson states,[2] or Claude Lévi-Strauss who talks of the fantastic as a compensation man provides for himself, "at the level of imagination [...] for what he has lost at the level of faith",[3] to finally, Jean Paul Sartre for whom it functions as transforming man's world.

Irrespective of the reasons for choosing a specific narrative strategy, however, the more basic question that interests me here is why these and other novelists of the New Literatures in English have moved into the world of the fantastic. Are they merely subjectively inclined to imaginatively create a world removed from their own immediate experience? Or are they keen to attract their readers' curiosity for the unknown, the mysterious and wonderful, the magical and the horrible? And do they do so to introduce us to their own culture-bound material — legends, myths, fairy tales — to awaken or reawaken interest in their own perhaps suppressed or forgotten culture, thus implicitly constructing their discrete 'imagiNations'? Here then they would part company from realist narrativation that had been part of the colonial baggage so many writers had been burdened with as the literary mode and model to follow.

These and more suggestions offer themselves when we focus our attention on fantasy writing in the New Literatures in English, examples of which we encounter mainly in the novel, but also in stories and plays and at times even in poetry. Some of them, especially more recent publications, have been paid critical attention under the rubric of magic realism, while a few texts have been categorized as signifying a "postmodernism of resistance",[4] postrealist[5] or dystopic writing .[6]

Preceding these latter notions, Stephen Slemon suggested earlier to work out a clearer concept of magic realism in a post-colonial context in order to perhaps establish a basis for comparing texts from separate post-colonial cultures.[7] For my purpose several of his findings and conclusions

2 Ibid., 3

3 Ibid., 18

4 Juniper Ellis, "A Postmodernism of Resistance: Albert Wendt's *Black Rainbow*", *Ariel* 25, 4 (1994), 101–114; here 194

5 Elizabeth DeLoughery, "Towards a Post-Native Aiga: Albert Wendt's *Black Rainbow*", eds. James N. Brown and Patricia M. Sant. Commock, *Indigeneity: Construction and Re/Presentation*, N.Y.: Nova Science Publications 1999, 137–158; here 150

6 Ibid., 153, 158

7 Stephen Slemon, "Magic Realism as Post-colonial Discourse", *Canadian Literature* 116 (1988), 9–24; here 10

are useful because they might be confirmed in my broader approach of looking at fantasy writing generally of which magic realism is one of several sub-genres. Thus it will be interesting to see, first, whether it is generally true that we are dealing here with a post-colonial discourse where silenced voices are recuperated, where marginalized presences "press in toward the centre" so that the site of a text "is a localized region that is metonymic of the post-colonial culture as a whole."[8] Yet as such references to post-colonial culture presuppose the existence of texts written in English in "cultures situated at the fringes of mainstream literary traditions", and accordingly perceive of magic realism "as a literary practice [that seems] to be closely linked with a perception of 'living on the margins'",[9] I would like to ask whether under conditions of globalization we can still conceive of the New Literatures in English along the trajectories of the binary model of centre and margin. In fact, Sudeep Dasgupta has argued that

> [g]lobalization [...] involves a retheorization not just of the 'location of culture' (Bhabha 1994), but [sic!] the very onto-epistemological foundations that conceptualized 'culture' according to the binarisms of East/West, Self/Other, Civilized/Barbarian.[10]

I suggest then to place these literatures into the context of the transglobal multiple exchanges of global and local factors that encompass economic, social and political aspects as much as cultural ones. Their coming together, for example, in the formation of creolized texts, texts I prefer to call 'glocal', will hardly permit us any longer to decipher a dialectic process of central pressure and marginal resistance,[11] let alone, its specific version of 'writing back to the centre'. Let us then leave behind, abandon, the term post-colonial and conceive of the New Literatures in English as glocal literary discourse from where I would like to set out and probe into

8 Ibid., 20

9 Ibid., 10

10 Sudeep Dasgupta, "Topologies of Nationalism: Constructing the 'Native' Between the Local and the Global", eds. James N. Brown and Patricia M. Sant. Commock, *Indigeneity: Construction and Re/Presentation.*, N.Y.: Nova Science Publications 1999, 77–94; here 91

11 For further references to theoretical reflections on glocal culture and glocal literary discourse cf. Dieter Riemenschneider, " Contemporary Māori Cultural Practice: From Biculturalism Towards a Glocal Culture", eds. Dieter Kastovsky, Gunther Kaltenböck, Susanne Reichl, *Anglistentag 2001 Wien: Proceedings*, Trier: Wissenschaftlicher Verlag 2002, 133–145; and Dieter Riemenschneider, "'Nga tipuna ki mua. Ko tatou kei muri — The ancestors in front, we are behind', Māori Contemporary Theatre: Witi Ihimaera: *Woman Far Walking* (2000)", eds. Hans-Ulrich Mohr and Kerstin Mächler, *Extending the Code: New Forms of Dramatic and Theatrical Expression*, Trier: Wissenschaftlicher Verlag 2004, 211–223

specimens of fantasy writing, literary representations that transcend the realist mode, the mimetic, to differing degrees, either by leaving it totally aside or by mixing, juxtaposing or contrasting it with the fantastic mode.

Before exploring a few examples, an important reservation should be made to avoid the erroneous conclusion that all New English language texts fall under this category. On the contrary. As mentioned briefly, the narrative mode of its large majority, especially during the initial phases of setting up discrete national literatures, has been realist to a degree that critics at the time, admittedly, taking up an extreme position, have either castigated for its all too obvious descriptive-ethnological or its non-literary political-propagandist nature or, in reverse, praised for its unequivocal anticolonial and national cultural stance.[12] More recently, however, Georg Lukács's theoretical reflections on the bourgeois novel seem to have reappeared on the scene, though indirectly and modified from the angle of postmodernist thinking. Elizabeth DeLoughery, for example, argues in her analysis of Albert Wendt's novel *Black Rainbow* (1992) that "for a writer invested in recovering suppressed histories, the genre of realism may limit this effort due to its similarity to capitalist teleology."[13] Whether we speak of "similarity" here or of Lucien Goldmann's 'homology', the interesting point is that DeLoughery suggests the employment of an 'other' than the realist narrative mode to pursue the recovering of one's own history outside the capitalist framework.

Could considerations of this nature then serve us as a guiding principle in our investigation of fantasy writing in the New Literatures in English? I leave the question unanswered at this point and instead turn to a few examples chosen at random from among more recent publications of Māori and Indian writers. What are their fantastically imagined worlds, what are their fantasy narratives like? Who are the agents crossing over into the other realm and what effects have their actions there on the realistically represented world of the 'here and now' that usually also plays its part in constituting the literary discourse? And finally, does the fantastic narrative mode construct 'imagiNations' of a transnational nature? In other words, does it form part of a glocal literary discourse as a post post-colonial literature? It may not be coincidental that we come across quite a few

12 Lucie Armitt's remark that "literary modes which are anti-realist and pro-fantastic have often been considered more frivolous than the mimetic" (2) may very well apply here, especially under the aegis of constructing an anti-colonial national literary discourse. Examples are indeed rare among early Indian, Caribbean or African writing in English. See Wilson Harris, *Palace of the Peacock* (1960), G.V. Desani, *All about H Hatterr* (1948), or the writing by Amos Tutuola in the 1950s and 1960s. See Lucie Armitt, *Theorising the Fantastic*, London: Arnold 1996

13 DeLoughery, *op.cit.*, 153

examples of a sustained fabulist or fantastic narrative mode in Māori and Pacific writing on the one hand and literature of the diaspora on the other, and I would venture to maintain that in both cases the need to construct 'imaginary homelands' is stronger here than for writers who are living 'at home'. Do Māori and Pacific authors then not live at home? Yes and no, as their fantastic writings document.

The main action in Witi Ihimaera's most recent novel *Sky Dancer* (2003) is fantastically transferred to the world of birds and centres on the violent struggle fought out between sea and land birds for the dominance of the land and the forest, rivers and lakes. A Māori couple, Skylark and Arnie, are sent by two *kuia*, old women guardians of the forest, to assist the land birds. Thanks to magic and their technical acumen they succeed in entering the fantastic world and in defending the land birds' right to claim their territory, with one of the old guardians sacrificing her human existence in the act of rescuing Skylark from being 'bird eaten' alive and humanity in general, by pulling the ripped sky together and thus preventing sea birds from ever re-entering the fantastic realm of the land birds.

Space does not permit me to go into the dense texture of this story with its multiple shifts of mode and tone, its well-structured dramatization and manifold intertextual references to Māori myths as well as to canonized Western texts like the Bible and the medieval epic or to globally disseminated media events such as musicals and action-films. From the beginning the fantastic mode runs through the realist narrative as the uncanny threat of the sea shags to kill Skylark, whom they identify as the potential saviour of the land birds according to a prophecy they have come to know. Yet we are not dealing with a Māori version of the uncanny in the sense of repressed subjective anxieties and drives as in Hitchcock's film *The Birds* but with a subgenre Tzvetan Todorov has called "the fantastic uncanny".[14] It presents itself as the metamorphosed historical struggle where the owners of the land, Aotearoa, are threatened by invaders from across the sea. While the former have to atone for their vanity that had dismayed their guardian god Tane, Māori Lord of the Great Forest, the latter are driven by avarice and the quest for domination, embodied in their leader of the sea shags, Kawanatanga.[15]

The crossing of the border into the fantasy world of the birds thus is

14 Tzvetan Todorov, *The Fantastic. A Structural Approach to a Literary Genre*, tr. by Richard Howard, Cleveland/London: The Press of Case Western Reserve University 1971, quoted in Jackson, *op.cit.*, 4

15 A term coined in the early 19th century and used in the Treaty of Waitangi, 1840, signifying the British 'governor's rule' in New Zealand, by contrast to the term 'rangatiratanga', or chiefly sovereignty, which the Māori believed they did not yield to the British Crown in the document

a morally motivated, rational and wilful act aimed at self-preservation because saving the world of the land birds means saving humanity. The metamorphosis Skylark and Arnie undergo, their change into birds once they have entered the other world through the Time Portal, and the ensuing bird battle they participate in, turn the story into a heroic fantasy that allegorizes the historical Māori-Pākeha struggle endowing it with a teleological purpose. More importantly, the human-bird agents possess the capabilities of cyborgs moving and manoeuvring like spacecrafts through a spectral region of the fantastic that is intrinsic to the world of science fiction and thus informed and constructed by globally shared fantasy imaginations. Multiple references at the realist level of the story, on the other hand, firmly anchor all characters, with the possible exemption of the two *kuia*, to the everyday world with all its modern and globally available technical and media gadgets, attitudes and views, where a discrete Māori culture has vanished even in small town settlements like Tuapa, somewhere on the South Island. In this sense, Māori are indeed no longer 'at home', yet as the fantastic story testifies, their striving for 'home', or more precisely, enacting their close relationship to the land results in re-establishing their tangible and spiritual 'home' when Skylark takes over the guardianship from her aunts. However, it is now a place where asserting their own culture stands for accepting the trusteeship of the land not merely as a national ethnic task but a global ecological responsibility. Here then Skylark and Arnie's excursion into the fantasy world shows its bearings on the real world where local priorities transform into and assume a glocal dimension by fusing them with global concerns thus creating what I like to call a transnational imagiNation.

Is it through fantasy writing, then, that *the tangible glocality of culture* is given more adequate literary representation than the realist literary discourse can achieve? DeLoughery's thesis of the "realist, nation-building novel",[16] I believe, has to be reconsidered in the light of *Sky Dancer* and other literary texts where both literary modes are employed and where we must ask what different functions they serve within the narrative as a whole. In Ihimaera's novel the fantastic section, though it makes up only a third of the story, dominates, and so it does in Wendt's *Black Rainbow*. Perhaps even more unequivocally so as DeLoughery convincingly expounds. Yet what about diaspora writing, for example Chitra Banerjee Divakaruni's *The Mistress of Spices* [17] or Amitav Ghosh's *The Calcutta Chromosome*?

16 DeLoughery, *op.cit.*, 152

17 Chitra Banerjee Divakaruni, *The Mistress of Spices*, London: Doubleday 1997

Being asked about her first novel, Divakaruni obviously reverted to Salman Rushdie's rejoinder to the critique of *The Satanic Verses* in the late 1980s that it was the novelist's duty to take risks, to push boundaries; boundaries that separate communities and people, as Divakaruni says, and that we create in our own lives. Indeed, to overcome them is the novel's central concern; this rules Tillottoma's life and her relationship with her customers, among whom we meet people from India, the Caribbean, Afro-Americans and Native Americans. Yet though *The Mistress of Spices* is dominantly a realist story about everyday life in a part of Oakland, the Indian protagonist is deeply anchored to the fantastic world of "the island of spice" situated somewhere in the wide expanse of the globe's ocean world. Here she arrived as a young woman who had partly willed voluntarily to run away from home through the power of her "calling thought"[18] that "had set into motion a juggernaut wheel whose turning even I could not arrest"[19] and made her join those pirates that had devastated her home village and killed its inhabitants. And yet, tired of her life as the pirates' queen after a few years and encountering the fantastic sea serpents who tell her about the island and how to find it, it is again her own decision to move there because "it seemed that I had finally found a name for my wanting."[20]

As with *Sky Dancer* a fantasy strain runs through the whole narrative, yet it is not tangibly co-present but evoked through the first person narrator's memories and the occasional words, mainly of warning, spoken by the inner voice of the Old One who had taught Tillottoma and other young women about the healing power of the spices their customers were to administer, to whom they would sell turmeric, cinnamon, fennel or pepper corn. Thus it is the bearings the spice mistresses' acquired knowledge have on the 'here and now' that are foregrounded with the purpose of healing, that is, of transcending the manifold boundaries that separate human beings. In contrast to Ihimaera and Wendt's novels where a temporary rapprochement appears to have been achieved — although a utopian world is by no means envisaged — Divakaruni's story relegates the fantasy world eventually to the background because its perfect moral nature cannot be reconciled with the imperfect world the mistresses of spices are working in. Symptomatically, Tillottoma's human desires, falling in love, thinking of her own happiness and removing herself from the power of the spices, testify to the unbridgeability of the real world and

18 Ibid., 17
19 Ibid., 19
20 Ibid., 24

the fantastic paradise. Her new name Maya encapsulates the "[i]llusion, spell, enchantment, power that keeps this imperfect world going day after day"[21] and it is a multicultural imagiNationed world that she will continue to help overcome its boundaries and fissures. In this sense the fantastic world of the island of spices has served its function of teaching her "that some things are more important than one's own joy".[22]

As a rather different approach to fantasy writing Amitav Ghosh's *The Calcutta Chromosome*[23] presents us with an intellectually challenging text where border crossing into the world of fantasy takes the form of multiple metamorphoses among a group of characters. Their identity remains as fluid as the purpose of their actions eventually remains a matter of speculation, as suggested by the protagonist Murugan whose own enigmatic disappearance sets off the story. Again, I cannot delve into the intricate wealth of the action set variously in the New York flat of Antar, a retired Egyptian computer employee of the International Water Council on 20 and 21 August in the first decade of the new millennium and in Calcutta on the very same days in 1995.[24] While Antar's story of solving the riddle of Murugan — his former colleague who has disappeared from Calcutta — is situated at the realist narrative level, Murugan's quest for the Calcutta chromosome increasingly incorporates fantastic elements. I want to mention only the repeated and uncanny appearances of a young man, the role that a mysterious railway station, its station master and a night train play at a desolate place some 300 miles outside Calcutta that is obviously connected with the disappearance of several people; further, an eerie night ritual in a derelict house or the unannounced and sudden removal of Murugan's landlady who disappears with her tenant's belongings.

21 Ibid., 317

22 Ibid., 315. It may not be inopportune here to comment briefly on Witi Ihimaera's play *Woman Far Walking* , Wellington: Huia Publishers 2000, with its reversal of the fantastic as presence and the past as real, enacted by the 160 year old Tiriti and her younger alter ego Tilly — the fantastically ancient metamorphosed Tiriti (or Treaty) of Waitangi and her similarly metamorphosed guilt feelings — who are made to dramatically present the history of Māori people under colonialism, including their own complicity in the violent colonizing process. The re-enactment of key experiences at the fantastic level of the play's presence cleanses Tiriti's mind in order to overcome her grief and accept her own guilt: A reading of *Woman Far Walking* that underlines the power of the fantastic imagination to question the binary of 'them' and 'us' and accept their coming together in the sense that Tiri's son of a Pākeha father had joined both sides. See Riemenschneider, *op.cit.*, 2004

23 Amitav Ghosh, *The Calcutta Chromosome*. New York: Avon Books 1997

24 A similar juxtaposition of the future and the past serves Ruchir Joshi in his dystopian historical novel *The Last Jet-Engine Laugh*, London: Harper Collins 2001, to thematize quite the opposite of Ghosh's vaguely optimistic outlook by insisting that there are no more new helpful prayers. Story telling is merely to show "ki unhone kya kya, kya kya nahi kio."

Hints towards an understanding of these and other strange goings-on, I believe, are conveyed through Murugan's speculations about the existence of a group of Indian people pursuing, he feels, a counter-science whose first principle is secrecy. They would refuse direct communication about their research on malaria and on a "technique of transmission, the crossover from one soul to another, a technology for interpersonal transference", as Sandra Ponzanesi puts it.[25] In other words, they would refuse communication with others because to put ideas into language "would establish a claim to know which is the first thing a counter-science would dispute."[26] This is an idea Murugan connects with his own investigation into the development of malaria research in the 19th century.

For our purposes of enquiring into the nature of the fantastic world, its agents and the bearings their actions have on the 'here and now', I propose, first of all, that it is Murugan's assumption of the existence of a secretive counter-science in India that compels the story's narrator to endow the characters his protagonist meets in Calcutta as well as incidents that befall both of him and them with a fantastic aura of secrecy and indeterminacy which implicitly relativizes the certainty of knowledge obtained rationally and technologically. Secondly, and more importantly, I believe, that Murugan's thesis "that to know something is to change it, therefore in knowing something, you've already changed what you think you know so you don't really know it at all: you only know its history",[27] relates to the Hindu philosophical concept of silence and the word or truth and non-truth. The truth, in words only graspable by defining it negatively as 'not this not that', *neti neti*, becomes its opposite, that is non-truth, when silence is translated into sound. Thus, to name is to know, but to know is not to know the truth and in that sense knowledge has changed the truth.[28]

If this is a tenable reading of the novel's subtext, then its narrativistic representation must necessarily exclude closure: a conclusion not altogether wrong when we look at the unresolved though surmised riddle of what the Calcutta chromosome is actually all about. Urmila, a young woman who is increasingly drawn into Murugan's quest, wonders about her own role which constrains him to admit that he neither knows what 'they' want

25 Sandra Ponzanesi, "Diasporic Narratives@Home Pages: The Future as Virtually Located", ed. Gerhard Stilz, *Colonies — Missions — Cultures in the English-speaking World*, Tübingen: Stauffenburg Verlag 2001, 396-406; here 403

26 Ghosh, *op.cit.*, 195

27 Ibid., 105

28 Thomas Huttunen argues similarly on 'silence' though not with reference to Hindu thinking. See Thomas Huttunen , "Narration and Silence in the Works of Amitav Ghosh"; *WLWE* 38, 2 (2000), 28-43; here 37–38, 41–42

to change and why nor which role he and the young woman and perhaps others are made to play in 'their game'. At the most, Murugan suggests, you can only assume that they will disclose their knowledge when a new technology has arrived "to deliver their story."[29]

Is this the case when the story is brought to an end, returning us to Antar in front of his computer where Murugan suddenly materializes cybernetically in identically the way he had turned up in Calcutta in 1995 and addresses Antar who is suddenly surrounded by voices telling him: "you're not alone; we'll help you across"?[30] We don't know because we are not told, and thus the question whether the Calcutta chromosome has been discovered remains open. The fantastic mode employed here to "interrogat[e] single or unitary ways of seeing",[31] challenges our attempts at gaining the truth scientifically, even with the help of such highly developed technology as the AVA/IIe systems (4) Antar uses to search into the furthest recesses of virtual space reality to track down information, find answers to questions and solve puzzles. Yet at the same time the fantastic that enters Murugan's life and is mediated through technology does not simply bring us back into our reality because the very existence of voices breaking the silence hints ambiguously at the promise of perhaps eventually finding the chromosome or naming the truth.[32] The truth, I would argue, is presently being conceived of only philosophically as one-ness, as non-duality but perhaps one day made factual. The fantastic mode in *The Calcutta Chromosome* functions to explore the technological possibility of crossing the boundary between individual selves (as the narrative quite clearly manifests)[33] in a way that would erase constructs of individual and supra-individual identities; it thus postulates the creation of a glocal imagiNation.

I want to round off this short presentation with a few observations on a poetry collection and a long poem by the Māori writer Robert Sullivan. *Star Waka* (1999) with its one hundred poems unfolds the *waka*, the Polynesian boat, as their central metaphor that crosses the boundaries of time and space in manifold ways. Here, the poems create a poetical world where

29 Ghosh, *op.cit.*, 219

30 Ibid., 311

31 Bakhtin quoted in Jackson, *op.cit.*, 36

32 See Ponzanesi, *op.cit.* Though I do not disagree, Ponzanesi's use of the postcolonial writing-back paradigm ignores the novel's sub-text which lends its fantastic mode a decisive role, thus underlining the powerful global function of imagiNation

33 For example, with Laakhan as Romen Haldar, Mangala as Mr. Aratouninan, Urmila as Tara or Sonali as Maria

global and local cultural elements no longer exclude each other. "waka 46", for example, takes on board the purpose of travelling into outer space in the space-*waka* to set up a fantastically imagined world of reconciliation among nations and people,

> no longer subject to peculiarities
> of climate the political economies
> of power and powerless
>
> a space waka
> rocketing to another orb
> singing waiata to the spheres.[34]

In *Captain Cook in the Underworld* (2002), representing the human endeavour of imagining the world of the dead, the voice of the poet is replaced by an interchange of chorus, crew and captain, historian and islanders and finally, Orpheus and Maui, as the text was originally commissioned as a libretto. Its first part foregrounds James Cook's voice reconstructed from his journals describing his and his crew's Pacific voyages. After his violent death he is then made to cross the boundary into the spirit world of the dead, joining "Orpheus at the lyre"[35] who helps him enter the world of souls, who according to Polynesian mythology are made to journey further on the earth before they can enter the next world. On their way they might encounter bad spirits, demons and the souls of others, as Sullivan's poem indeed brings home. Subsequently the poet collapses the Greek and Polynesian mythic figures of Orpheus and Maui and relates Cook's enforced journey through the South and North islands of New Zealand to the purgatorial journey in the *The Divine Comedy*.[36] However, its goal is not redemption but a challenge: the offer of "integrity by chance",[37] or in other words: the chance for Cook to learn "so that your soul will stop its journeying."[38] Having been confronted with the soul of a murdered Māori chief, Cook says that he understands his wrongdoings; however, he cannot make undone what has been done.

Captain Cook in the Underworld can be read as a postcolonial text in that it aims at recuperating from a Polynesian perspective the historical encounter of Cook and Polynesia, of the 'disciplined' British colonizer

34 Robert Sullivan, *Star Waka*, Auckland: Auckland University Press 1999, 50. See Riemenschneider 2002, 138–140, for a more extended reading of this poem

35 Robert Sullivan, *Captain Cook in the Underworld*, Auckland: Auckland University Press 2002, 34

36 See also the poem's intertextual references to *The Inferno* (and, incidentally, S.T. Coleridge and Derek Walcott) facing the acknowledgement page

37 Sullivan, *op.cit.*, 2002, 36

38 Ibid., 45

and "these almost men."[39] Yet its portrayal of Cook's learning process that will redeem him, not from his guilt but from his non-knowledge of Polynesia, transforms the text's recuperative nature into an imagined rapprochement that crosses cultural boundary lines. Cook is not punished for his deeds, as both traditions would have it, the Christian exemplified in *The Divine Comedy* and the Māori that demands *utu* for the loss of his *mana*. Rather Orpheus/Maui let his spirit fly away into the next world admonishing it as much as conveying this lesson to the reader "to know this thing [... k]now anything!"[40] The fantasized discursive exchange between the collapsed mythic guide-figure and the Western explorer who has come to know — and is even revered in Polynesia as "divine Lono"[41] — represents a glocal representation of a transcultural imagiNation: a literary discourse, as Sullivan's poem and the other examples from the South Pacific and the Indian diaspora illustrate, that forms an essential part of the New Literatures in English. It distances it from the postcolonial literary discourse in a globalized world that is increasingly suffused with *glocal cultural representations* that cross national boundaries and challenge strategies of conceptualization along national borders.

Works cited

Novels and Poetry

DESAI, Boman, *The Memory of Elephants*, London: André Deutsch 1988

DESANI, G.V., *All about H Hatterr*, London: Francis Aldor 1948

DIVAKARUNI, Chitra Banerjee, *The Mistress of Spices*, London: Doubleday 1997

GHOSH, Amitav, *The Calcutta Chromosome*, New York: Avon Books 1997

HARRIS, Wilson, *Palace of the Peacock*, London: Faber & Faber 1960

HEAD, Bessie, *A Question of Power*, London: Davis-Poynter 1973

IHIMAERA, Witi, *Woman Far Walking*, Wellington: Huia Publishers 2000

—, *Sky Dancer*, Auckland: Penguin 2003

JOSHI, Ruchir, *The Last Jet-Engine Laugh*, London: Harper Collins 2001

KESAVAN, Mukul, *Looking through Glass*, New York: Farrar, Straus & Giroux 1995

SULLIVAN, Robert, *Star Waka*, Auckland: Auckland UP 1999

—, *Captain Cook in the Underworld*, Auckland: Auckland UP 2002

TOLKIEN, J.R.R., *The Lord of the Rings*, London: Allen & Unwin 1954

TUTUOLA, Amos, *The Palm-Wine Drinkard and his dead Palm-wine Tapster in the Deads' Town*, London: Faber & Faber 1952

WENDT, Albert, *Black Rainbow*, Auckland: Penguin 1992

39 Ibid., 29

40 Ibid., 50

41 See Anne Salmond's summarizing remarks in "Our Ancestor Captain Cook" (425–430) on Polynesian reverence of Cook that was brought to an end by American missionaries only during the 1840s and 1850s, in: Anne Salmond, *The Trial of the Cannibal Dog: Captain Cook in the South Seas*, London: Penguin Books 2004

Critical Studies

ARMITT, Lucie, *Theorising the Fantastic*, London: Arnold 1996

DASGUPTA, Sudeep, "Topologies of Nationalism: Constructing the 'Native' Between the Local and the Global," eds. James N. Brown and Patricia M. Sant. Commock, *Indigeneity: Construction and Re/Presentation*, N.Y.: Nova Science Publications 1999, 77–94

DELOUGHERY, Elizabeth, "Towards a Post-Native Aiga: Albert Wendt's *Black Rainbow*," eds. James N. Brown and Patricia M. Sant Commock, *Indigeneity: Construction and Re/Presentation, op.cit.*, 137–58

ELLIS, Juniper, "A Postmodernism of Resistance: Albert Wendt's *Black Rainbow*," *ARIEL* 25, 4 (1994), 101–14

HUTTUNEN, Thomas, "Narration and Silence in the Works of Amitav Ghosh," *WLWE* 38, 2 (2000), 28–43

JACKSON, Rosemary, *Fantasy: The Literature of Subversion*, London & New York: Methuen 1981

PONZANESI, Sandra, "Diasporic Narratives@Home Pages: The Future as Virtually Located," ed. Gerhard Stilz, *Colonies — Missions — Cultures in the English-speaking World*, Tübingen: Stauffenburg Verlag 2001, 396–406

RIEMENSCHNEIDER, Dieter, "Contemporary Māori Cultural Practice: From Biculturalism Towards a Glocal Culture," eds. Dieter Kastovsky, Gunther Kaltenböck, Susanne Reichl, *Anglistentag 2001 Wien: Proceedings*, Trier: Wissenschaftlicher Verlag 2002 133–45

—, "'Nga tipuna ki mua. Ko tatou kei muri — The ancestors in front, we are behind'. Māori Contemporary Theatre: Witi Ihimaera, *Woman Far Walking* (2000)," eds. Hans-Ulrich Mohr and Kerstin Mächler, *Extending the Code: New Forms of Dramatic and Theatrical Expression*, Trier: Wissenschaftlicher Verlag 2004, 211–23

SALMOND, Anne, *The Trial of the Cannibal Dog: Captain Cook in the South Seas*, London: Penguin Books 2004

SLEMON, Stephen, "Magic Realism as Post-colonial Discourse," *Canadian Literature* 116 (1988), 9–24

TODOROV, Tzvetan, *The Fantastic: A Structural Approach to a Literary Genre*, trans. Richard Howard, Cleveland / London: The Press of Case Western Reserve University 1971

Crossing National Borders

The Indian English Novel since the 1990s

AS AN AVID READER OF INDIAN NOVELS written in English I have been impressed again and again by the vitality, vivacity and broad range of themes and styles of a literary genre that for Uma Parameswaran once seemed "destined to die young [… with] A.D. 2000 as the dirge date for Indo-English literature".[1] Fortunately, her hope that "time proves this prediction wrong"[2] has been fulfilled, so much so that even an optimistic reader at the time would not have expected this to happen during the following three decades. A spate of younger writers, keen to narrate their stories in 'that' language, have continued to shape, bend and transform it into ever so many varieties of 'Indian English' which the founding fathers of the novel would have applauded. Mulk Raj Anand, Raja Rao or Bhabani Bhattacharya experimented with it from the 1930s onwards.

It is not my intention to add to a critical discourse that to my mind has long ago run its course, become repetitive and stale. Nor do I want to respond to Makarand Paranjape's (2000) and Tabish Khair's (2001) discourse on the poetics of Indian English fiction, which I have briefly commented upon elsewhere,[3] but I'd like to look at what strikes me as comparatively recent modifications or even additions to the thematic concerns of a literary genre that had begun to step across national boundaries as long ago as with several novels of the forerunners of today's so-called diasporan writing. Among them I would count Anand's *Across the Black Waters* (1940), G.V. Desani's

1 Uma Parameswaran, *A Study of Representative Indo-English Novelists*, New Delhi: Vikas 1976, 2

2 Ibid., 6

3 Dieter Riemenschneider, *The Indian Novel in English: Its Critical Discourse 1934-2004*, Jaipur: Rawat Publications 2005, 38–41

All About H. Hatterr (1948), Raja Rao's *The Serpent and the Rope* (1960) and Kamala Markandaya's *The Nowhere Man* (1973). While these writers returned to India, if not always in person then in their writing, others of the following generation like Dilip Hiro, Santha Rama Rau or Sasthi Brata stayed away. Their 'example' in turn was followed by authors born a few years before or after independence: Farrukh Dhondy, Salman Rushdie, Rohinton Mistry, Firdaus Kanga, Bharati Mukherjee, Meena Alexander, Shashi Tharoor, Chitra Banerjee Divakaruni, Sunetra Gupta or Ravinder Randhawa. Among this group of 'diasporan' authors other novelists can be counted as well though they would return to India or move between countries and continents: Anita Desai, Gita Hariharan, Amitav Ghosh, Vikram Seth, Amit Chaudhuri or Boman Desai. It is an impressive array of names which a close observer of the Indian literary scene would certainly enlarge by also including poets like A.K. Ramanujan, R. Parthasarathy, Sudeep Sen or Sujata Bhatt and one or the other writer-cum-critic like Tabish Khair.

Recalling not merely the titles of their work but their thematic preoccupations, we can draw some provisional conclusions. With a few exceptions stories revolve around Indian characters living in the late 20th century though not necessarily in India. As is almost to be expected, the topic of living away from their home country triggers off problematizing cultural clash, identity and alienation and the search for place and home. Further, these narratives are usually told in a realistic manner that allows little room to the modes of allegory, fantasy and satire or to the kind of 'Hatterrese' mix that empowered Desani's novel with such an exceptional grasp of the reality of the diasporic Indian. Finally, employment of the realistic mode in the bulk of Indian English story telling has also held back diasporan writers from experimenting with linguistic registers even though Desani or Rushdie have shown that English is a rich medium of communication because of its close contact with Indian languages and their colloquial or dialect varieties on the one hand and their own inventiveness and courage to exploit it.

No doubt, all this is not news to the connoisseur of Indian English writing and is mentioned here only by way of raising the question whether we come across recent novels that leave what I would term the beaten tracks of the 'national' and the 'diasporan' experience. In other words, texts that take a more holistic look at today's world by crossing the line that encircles the 'Indian' experience as perceived along national and diasporic trajectories, be they of a thematic or an idealized nature as discussed in Khair and Paranjape's studies. I'd like to answer this question in the affirmative and am thinking of Vikram Seth's *An Equal Music* (1999) and *Two Lives* (2005), Amitav Ghosh's *The Hungry Tide* (2004), Salman Rushdie's *Shalimar the Clown* (2005) or Kirin Nagarkar's *God's Little Soldier* (2006). Though their subject matters differ, it is not just India the reader encounters here, let alone Indianness we are lured into. No doubt, the location in *The Hungry Tide* is the Sundabarns and substantial events of Rushdie and Nagarkar's stories occur in Kashmir and Bombay respectively, while one of the 'two lives' in Seth's novel is that of the Indian dentist Shanti Behari Seth. Still, I would argue that both, events and characters in these works are to be placed within a larger than an Indian referential frame. Let me illustrate what I mean.

Seth's *An Equal Music* is exceptional in that it is so far removed from the Indian context that it stands quite apart while its composition gives reason to speculate on the emergence of a discrete subgenre of the Indian English novel. If the reader had no idea about its author the text would not offer the least clue because neither action nor character, neither theme nor language and style fit into perceived patterns of writing we readily identify with the tradition of Indian English fiction. It is a very private story told through the highly subjective voice of the English musician Michael whose main interest lies in talking about himself as the member of a famous string quartet and as a man who loves Julia, also a musician who, as he finds out, is gradually turning deaf. Both had met as students in Vienna a decade before and fallen in love but had lost contact of each other after he had abandoned her quite unexpectedly and rather ruthlessly. Running into each other coincidentally in London after so many years, both resume their relationship though Julia is married and has a son, only to once and for all part again because of yet another failure on Michael's part to honour their relationship.

However, far more exciting than this love story of sorts is the musical story with its exquisite presentation of details pertaining to examples of classical European compositions, in particular by Schubert and Bach, and its disclosure of the group dynamics of the four members of the Maggiore Quartet, including the portrayal of their differing personalities. Here we must acknowledge Seth's profound immersion into and sensitive understanding of a European art as a narrative stance we have not come across in Indian English writing. It suggests his deep love for a musical tradition totally different from his own which he celebrates in a novel where the love story narrated by a high-strung, egomaniac and ever so indifferent male recedes into the background. The total exclusion of Seth's own culture in *An Equal Music* does not even allow us to speak of it as a transcultural text but to see it as a contribution to the European music story tradition. It is, indeed, an exceptional 'Indian' novel where the epithet 'equal' might suggest that European classical music matches its Indian counterpart.

By contrast, Ghosh's *The Hungry Tide* is unambiguously located in India, or more precisely and like several of his previous works, in his home state of Bengal. Yet in spite of the impressive local colour the Sundarbans are painted in with their intricate waterways and its tides, its myriad islands and sandbanks that are forever shifting, its vegetation and animal world, its storms and, last but not least, its dense population of fishermen and peasants, the author's principal motif, I believe, lies elsewhere. The story of a few days in the lives of the young Indian cetologist Piyali Roy having arrived to observe a subspecies of dolphin, of the Delhi-based translator Kanai and his aunt Mashima, and finally, of the fisherman Fokir and his family, revolves around an issue of global dimension. What should have precedence in the modern world, the subtext asks: the care for survival of an ecologically balanced biotope like the Sundarbans or settling impoverished and homeless refugees in their fertile surroundings to ensure their survival? It is a question the novel does not answer, or rather, the answer given is twofold. Years ago the Bengal government had stepped in and forcibly removed the settlers from the land they had illegally taken possession of. Now, the task lies with people like Piyali, Kanai and Mashima who devote their lives to create bearable living conditions for the original people of the Sundarbarns.

The plot structure reveals itself as multiple-layered depicting the various characters' relationships as they develop. Most impressive is the Piyali-Fokir relationship embedded in the natural world of water and islands that is counterpoised by local myths and legends. Both motifs are bundled together in a text that forms part of, as much as it contributes to issues of eco-literature, a new kind of writing that has evolved in recent years and has been met with increased attention by writers and readers. *The Hungry Tide* thus points towards a new direction in Indian English fiction which in the past has paid but scant attention to nature and instead has privileged topics relevant to the urbanized middle-class of the big cities.

This preoccupation with city life serves as a usable starting point from which to approach Seth's latest novel, *Two Lives*, which like *An Equal Music*, at least for its greater part, is located in London. Shanti Behari Seth settled here in the 1930s and in 1951 married the German Jewish refugee Henny Gerda Caro who had escaped the Nazis just before the outbreak of the war. The novel thus portrays an unusual pair of 'exiles' whose lives draw our attention to an aspect of diasporic writing we have hardly ever come across, and certainly not in Indian fiction in English. At the same time, the book's unusual amalgam of biography, memory, documentation and essay-like excursions into European history and national psychogrammes highlights how unstable the borderlines of traditional literary genres have become. What is particularly noteworthy in this respect is Seth's approach as an erstwhile uninformed outsider who is anxious to explore the truth of Germany's historical role in the 20th century and here especially the fate Germans meted out to its Jewish community under Nazi rule. The initial motif of reconstructing his granduncle's life thus becomes incorporated into the story of the fractured lives of two people that leads us to understand European history as part of modernity, scrutinized here for the first time from an Indian angle. *Two Lives* brings home the message of looking back at experiences of people in the 20th century in order to understand the present with its allegedly global cultural wars, the increasing chasm between 'us' and 'them', the 'pure' and the 'impure', true and false Christians, and last but not least, the West and the Muslim worlds. This 'twist' of the narrative and its final appeal to "eschew group hatred" and to trust in "humane logic and perhaps, in due course, love"[4] (499) takes me straight to my next example, to Rushdie's *Shalimar the Clown*.

The multi-layered story winds its way geographically from America to Europe, to Kashmir and back to America while in time it moves from the present to the past and back to the present. The seemingly irresolvable tangle of love and hatred motivating the actions of individuals as well as of groups of people sworn to enforce their own version of racial and religious truth on others give rise to a truly global scenario of violence and terrorism that has characterized Nazism in the past as much as it does the ongoing conflict in Kashmir. Rushdie's sombre story of the Muslim Shalimar and his Hindu wife Boonyi, French-born American Max Ophuls and his English wife Margaret and Max and Boonyi's American-Indian daughter Kashmira or India reminds us of *The Moor's Last Sigh* (1995) with its pessimistic outlook into the future, yet a future that in this novel encompasses much more than the fate of an Indian family. A parallel though can be drawn between the inextricable convolutions of personal passions and political and ideological convictions that drive people on in both novels. This holds true in particular of Shalimar's actions that are motivated not so much by his own and his Muslim conspirators' ambition to free Kashmir from Indian rule and set up a Muslim state but from his desire to revenge Boonyi's betrayal of leaving him, of becoming Max's lover and the mother of their child.

4 Vikram Seth, *Two Lives*, London: Little, Brown 2005, 499

I believe that it is precisely Rushdie's intention to unmask man's lust for power that motivates the main agents on three continents and in different historical periods to perpetrate inhuman atrocities: the Nazis in occupied France who succeed in eradicating the Jewish community including Max's family; the Indian military in Kashmir who suspect anyone to side with their adversaries, that is, several Muslim guerrilla parties, who in turn do not only fight the unbelievers from outside but also each other and even kill civilians they suspect to support 'the others'; and finally, those hard-core, totally non-political criminals in California whom the authorities can hardly keep in check. Violence though is legitimate in the case of Nazi terrorism, as Max's involvement in La Résistance in France proves; not however any longer in the self-opinionated and factional power game in Kashmir, and certainly not at all in Shalimar's personal revenge. He murders Boonyi, sent back to Kashmir where she is ousted by her family and lives in isolation, traces and kills Max in Los Angeles and finally confronts Kashmira/India in her father's house. Being all set to defend herself the outcome of their encounter remains as open-ended as the Kashmir conflict.

Like its tightrope dancing protagonist, *Shalimar the Clown* presents us with a world dancing on the rope and threatening to plunge to its death. It is a world in which terrorist acts in India form but part of a conflict that has assumed global dimension. As national boundaries do not any longer count, the writers' responsibility and courage are asked for to respond to the frightening international scenario of terrorism that has begun to affect the lives of more and more people at the beginning of the 21st century. It is a response very much at the heart of Kiran Nagarkar's *God's Little Soldier*.

Having portrayed the dense and convoluted network of power politics, religion and art in 17th century Rajasthan in his impressive novel *Cuckold* (1997), he now draws a similarly lively picture of the complex interplay of present day global politics, religion and morality, the sciences and the arts, economics, finance and ecological concerns. The exuberant story whose main plot, subplots and innumerable details, intertextual references and shifting points of view cannot even be summarized here, narrates the fate of Zia and Amanat, two brothers of the Bombay Muslim family of Khan. Raising the perennial question of man relating to the world, Zia represents active man, Amanat contemplative man. Profoundly concerned with the creation of a better world, Zia pursues this goal restlessly by assuming different names and identities, living for a time with Trappist monks in France and assisting them in renovating their monastery. Discovering his gift as a stockbroker he subsequently supports fundamentalist Americans like them as 'God's little soldier' to create healthy surroundings for the young by pushing for legislation against premarital sex, abortion and homosexuality. Yet doubting their evangelical goals he reverts from his adopted Christian faith to Islam, joins the Taliban in Afghanistan and after their defeat becomes an international arms trader. Betrayed and fearing for his life; he opts to hide underground — and makes his exit from the novel. Driven by his quest for the one and only truth worthwhile to be accomplished, the moral aspect of using such doubtful means as terrorism, brain wash, nuclear and biochemical warfare is subordinated to the aim of creating a better world for future generations. Zia though, and this may explain his chameleon-like transformations, is never really sure about what is the truth and whether his actions may not be motivated by selflessness and altruism but rather by his wish for personal salvation. Nor is Amanat of much help with his admonishing letters, his stories and plays that convey a moral stance vis-à-vis the world 'out there'. Neither one nor the other religious belief nor the active involvement in the world of economics and finance, politics or warfare, neither moral contemplation nor the artist's representation, Nagarkar's novel suggests as "a fable for our times", offers a final answer to the true nature of God. In this sense each of us must beware of playing the role of God's little soldier.

I hope to have shown how the modern Indian novel in English has yet again been set on a new course that may have had Rushdie's *The Satanic Verses* (1988) as its starting point at the end of the 1980s. A concern with questions of a global dimension and importance marks a departure from predominantly local themes and authorial preoccupations on the one hand and life in the diaspora on the other. No doubt, such writing will continue to engage Indian authors at home and abroad as an abundance of publications easily testifies. Here, the vicissitudes of the Indian middle-class family continue to command much attention as in Akil Sharma's *An Obedient Father* (2000), Rohinton Mistry's *Family Matters* (2002) and Shashi Deshpande's *Moving On* (2004); or the tribulations of a working life as in Githa Hariharan's *In Times of Siege* (2003) or Anurag Mathur's *Scenes from an Executive Life* (2001). The same writer's *The Inscrutable Americans* (1991) and Boman Desai's *Asylum, USA* (2000) enlarge the canvas of diasporan writing while Shashi Tharoor's *Riot* (2001) and Allan Sealey's *The Brainfever Bird* (2003) centre on the meeting if not confrontation of Indian and foreign characters. No doubt, all these novels make interesting reading, yet what I am asking is, who else will join Ghosh, Nagarkar, Rushdie and Seth to take their readers to new destinations?

Works cited

Novels

ANAND, Mulk Raj, *Across the Black Waters*, London: Jonathan Cape 1940
DESAI, Boman, *Asylum, USA*, New York: Harper Collins 2000
DESANI, G.V., *All about H Hatterr*, London: Aldor 1948
DESHPANDE, Shashi, *Moving On*, New Delhi: Penguin 2004
HARIHARAN, Githa, *In Times of Siege*, New Delhi: Penguin 2003
MARKANDAYA, Kamala, *The Nowhere Man*, London: Allen Lane 1973
MATHUR, Anurag, *The Inscrutable Americans*, New Delhi: Rupa 2004 [1991]
—, *Scenes from An Executive Life*, New Delhi: Penguin 2001
MISTRY, Rohinton, *Family Matters*, London: Faber & Faber 2002
NAGARKAR, Kiran, *Cuckold*, New Delhi: Harper Collins 1997
—, *God's Little Soldier*, Delhi: Harper Collins India 2006
RAO, Raja, *The Serpent and the Rope*, London: John Murray 1960
RUSHDIE, Salman, *The Satanic Verses*, London: Viking Penguin 1988
—, *The Moor's Last Sigh*, London: Jonathan Cape 1995
—, *The Ground Beneath Her Feet*, New York: Henry Holt 1999
—, *Fury*, London: Jonathan Cape 2001
—, *Shalimar the Clown*, London: Jonathan Cape 2005
SEALEY, Allan, *The Brainfever Bird*, London: Picador 2003
SETH, Vikram, *An Equal Music*, London: Phoenix House 1999
SHARMA, Akil, *An Obedient Father*, New York: Farrar, Strauss & Giroux 2000
THAROOR, Shashi, *Riot*, New Delhi: Viking 2001

Critical Literature

KHAIR, Tabish, *Babu Fictions: Alienation in Contemporary Indian English Novels*, New Delhi: OUP 2001
PARANJAPE, Makarand, *Towards a Poetics of the Indian English Novel*, Shimla: Institute of Advanced Study 2000

Nature and Landscape

An Evolutionary Psychological Analysis of Raja Rao's Writing

SINCE S. MENON MARATH'S brief reference to *Kanthapura* in 1948[1] more than five hundred critical studies[2]—book reviews, essays and books — have been published on Raja Rao's literary oeuvre manifesting the writer's important contribution to Indian English writing during the second half of the 20th century. As I have shown elsewhere,[3] critical studies have been overwhelmingly concerned with the Indian writer's engagement with the Hindu philosophical school of Advaita Vedanta and possibilities of its literary-narrative representation both through the genre of the novel and an adopted language, English. Yet, the question which role nature and landscape play in Rao's writing has never been asked seriously although the foregrounding of localities in titles like *Kanthapura* or *On the Ganga Ghat* suggests connotations beyond mere naming. No doubt, critical silence has been so because the modern Indian English novel in general has not been particularly attentive to the representation of nature or landscape, and only a few examples come to mind: an important scene in G.V. Desani's *All about H Hatterr*,[4] Saleem Sinai's experience of the Sundarbans in Salman Rushdie's *Midnight's Children*,[5] or Amitav Ghosh's respect for and engagement with ecological concerns in *The Hungry Tide*.[6] But these are exceptions and Raja Rao's work confirms the rare occurrence of passages focusing on nature and

1 S. Menon Marath, "Three Indian Novelists", *Life and Letters* 59 (1948/49), 187-92

2 See Dieter Riemenschneider, "Bibliography", *The Indian Novel in English: Its Critical Discourse 1934-2004*, Jaipur: Rawat Publications 2005, 346-375

3 Riemenschneider, "Literature as Sādhāna: The Reception of Raja Rao's Novels," *op.cit.*, 289-380

4 G.V. Desani, *All about H Hatterr — a gesture*, London: The Saturn Press 1949, 100-101; 104-106

5 Salman Rushdie, *Midnight's Children*, London: Picador Edition 1982, 360-366

6 Amitav Ghosh, *The Hungry Tide*, Delhi: Ravi Dayal Publishers 2004

landscape. However, the ones we encounter are sufficiently significant to deserve being studied more closely; the more so since to my knowledge only Gerhard Stilz's "Return to the Jungle? Colonial and Post-colonial Landscapes in Indian English Literature"[7] has focused on this topic from a cultural perspective which I would like to question for this very reason. Judging the function of nature in *Kanthapura* (and in Mulk Raj Anand's *Two Leaves and a Bud*), he says: "Indian writers do carry on presenting Indian nature in the colonialist tradition with its culturalists concerns"[8] — a judgement echoing his earlier conclusion that "the colonizers were both physically and mentally threatened by the colonized and his, her or its dark nature. Landscape, climate, flora and fauna have come to play a dominant role in the impersonal variants of this conflict."[9]

I shall not address the culturalists concerns in *Kanthapura, The Serpent and the Rope, The Cat and Shakespeare* and *On the Ganga Ghat* but would like to pursue my thesis that the perception and creative representation of landscape in literature — as in the arts generally — is also grounded in genetically evolved adaptations of man facing his environment. Studies in Social Biology and Evolutionary Psychology have proposed that *homo sapiens*, for ever on the move and in search of an environment that grants him survival and protection, has learned to discern landscape features that promise him safety and nourishment from those that do not. For example, discussing habitat selection theory and "environmental aesthetics from an evolutionary and ecological perspective",[10] Gordon H. Orians and Judith H. Heerwagen[11] as well as Jay Appleton[12] have pursued the question of why certain stretches of nature or landscapes strike the observer as beautiful or ugly or evoke mixed feelings. They propose the thesis substantiated by research[13] that savanna-like habitats evoked positive responses in *homo*

7 Gerhard Stilz, "Return to the Jungle? Colonial and Post-Colonial Landscapes in Indian English Fiction", eds. Hena Maes-Jelinek and Geoff Davis, *A Talent(ed) Digger*, Cross/Cultures, vol. 20, Amsterdam/Atlanta G.A.: Rodopi 1995, 324-334

8 Ibid., 330

9 Ibid., 334

10 Jerome H. Barkow, "Environmental Aesthetics", ed. Jerome H. Barkow, *The Adapted Mind: Evolutionary Psychology and the Generation of Culture*, New York/Oxford: OUP 1992, 551-553; here 551

11 Gordon H. Orians and Judith Heerwagen, "Evolved Responses to Landscapes", ed. Jerome H. Barkow, *op.cit.*, 556-579

12 Jay Appleton, *The Symbolism of Habitat: An Interpretation of Landscape in the Arts*, Seattle and London: University of Washington Press 1990

13 Stephen Kaplan, "Environmental Preferences in a Knowledge-Seeking, Knowledge-Using Organism", ed. Jerome H. Barkow, *op.cit.*, 581-598; here 586

sapiens by offering unimpeded views, easy orientation and movement as well as trees to protect him and grant him a lookout. Accordingly, habitat selection theory postulates that such a preferred environment affected human responses and became part of our genetic make-up; a condition that has survived over millennia till the present and in spite of man's transformation from nomadic to sedentary life during the 'Neolithic Revolution' around 10 000 years ago.[14] To these critics then the study of human responses to nature and landscape went along studying the evolution of aesthetic tastes as well. Landscapes, seascapes, even urban scapes and architecture, they say, evoke emotional and, subsequently, cognitive responses due to our genetic heritage. As Orians and Heerwagen maintain, "evidence of aesthetic responses attuned to the savanna environment can be found in our manipulations of landscapes for aesthetic purposes,"[15] and they point at landscape features such as hills and mountains, rivers, valleys and open spaces, the sea and the horizon, as having been used by painters, photographers, landscape (!) gardeners, architects and writers to evoke and/or manipulate our sensation and our perceptions.[16] However, both authors qualify their thesis by warning us that the evaluation of the artistic achievement of landscape representations merely from "an evolutionary-adaptive approach to environmental aesthetics", must not be considered self-sufficient, let alone inclusive, yet it will invigorate our interpretation. Besides, it will make us aware of a cross-cultural universal in spite of the fact that "ecological signals have been transformed, over time"[17] into culture specific events and artefacts.

Similarly, in his study *The Symbolism of Habitat — An Interpretation of Landscape in the Arts*, the British geographer Jay Appleton has also argued — and illustrated his thesis with examples taken from literature — that human beings experience landscape in ways that are based on our environmental adaptations, an "environment visually perceived"[18] and composed of single features such as hills, mountains, rivers. Singly or as a 'composition', these ecological signals evoke emotional as well as cognitive responses, sensations and perceptions which Appleton relates to three "features that increase the likelihood of survival" he calls prospect, refuge and hazard. Prospect allows us to survey the environment from

14 Allan H. Simmons, *The Neolithic Revolution in the Near East: Transforming the Human Landscape*, Tucson: The University of Arizona Press 2007

15 Orians, Heerwegen, 551

16 Ibid, 570

17 Ibid., 571

18 Appleton, 22

an elevated place, refuge to find protection and hide; and hazard "stirs a feeling of being threatened and of wanting to escape."[19]

How would Rao have responded to the concept of environmental aesthetics? I imagine having discussed it with him during one of our early morning constitutionals at C.D. Narasimhaiah's Dhvanya Loka in Mysore. Visualizing him raising a polite eyebrow and remarking quietly that man's realization of the world quite generally was to be understood less along the hypothesized evidence of a doubtful scientific discipline such as Evolutionary Psychology than along those lines of thinking put forward by his narrator Rama in *The Serpent and the Rope*. In answer to Madeleine, his wife's question, "what is it separated us, Rama?" he responded: "India believes that to prove the world as being real or unreal is being really objective". And that is the actual meaning of

> hav[ing] a scientific outlook. [...] The world is either unreal or real — the serpent or the rope [...], there is no in-between-the-two — and all that's in-between is poetry, is sainthood. (332)

Man's cognition of the real world is achieved when he comes to know that the "actual, the real has no name [because] [t]he rope is no rope to itself." (332) Rama's, and by implication Rao's understanding of nature and landscape then could be defined as arriving at a point of unnaming what has been named/ is being named, and thereby of having been made actual; in other words: to recognize the world from a metaphysical instead of a natural scientific angle. If so, does Rao's creative literary handling of nature and landscape bear this out?

Kanthapura is an old woman's story about the fate of her village and its inhabitants in the political turmoil of the 1930s; and in spite of the author's sophistication (unmistakeably conveyed through his "Foreword"), he succeeds in creating a credible, simple-minded narrator. Here *Kanthapura* clearly differs from Rao's later work where learned, sophisticated, even puzzling minds tell their stories and demonstrate their varying approaches to landscape and its features. The opening scene of *Kanthapura* is not merely memorable for the old woman's story-telling style but also for possessing almost all the ingredients of landscape presentation that are taken up again in the course of the narration. For example, by merely naming topographical features of the village surroundings such as mountains, forests, gorges, valleys and roads, the narrator largely refrains from embellishing, let alone from ascribing metaphorical or allegorical

19 Appleton, cover flap blurb

meaning to the landscape. Further, once the environment has been re-created imaginatively, it is made to serve as the setting for action: carts and lights move, voices, singing and cattle bells can be heard as well as "the soft hiss of the Himavathy:" (*Kanthapura*, 1) The scene is rounded off by the narrator's remark that people believe, "the Goddess of the River plays through the night with the Goddess of the Hill", and with an invocation to the goddess to be blessed. All in all then, a perception of landscape is transmitted where the villagers are supplied with their means of survival: that is, products to be traded, peace ruling among the people and protection guaranteed by the goddesses. The landscape of Kanthapura is painted as a safe habitat, and the more so when the narrator details its mythological genesis emitted through Kenchamma hill and its red colour. Not only will it remind the villagers of a demon's bloody defeat by the goddess but the choice of a hill as battleground is itself significant in terms of evolutionary psychology since an elevation in nature offers man the chance to survey his surroundings as well as to protect him.

Rao's narrative procedure then consists of listing physical features of a landscape; relate them to movement, to human life, and embed both of them in their mythological context. It is a pattern we encounter again when the carts that had earlier left the village return (42–43), or when Moorthy's mother Narsamma dies outside the village by the river (46), and finally when the villagers experience the rains in the month of Vaisakh. (114)

A similarly patterned landscape description also assumes the meaning of a hazard, and here we come across examples when the villagers' fate has turned around, when they are dropped on the Ghats and feel like being in a jungle and are only relieved when "on the top of the hill we see the dangling light of a cart" (136); or when we turn at Kanthapura's opponent: the partly cultivated, partly uncultivated landscape of the Skeffington Coffee Estate, and here especially during the rainy season. Nature is perceived as an unsafe place with its snakes (52-53), its lack of protection against the rain (54-55) and ensuing illness and death. (57) Initially though, the Estate had seemed to offer an abode to the coolies because its landscape features held this promise (48-50) evoked by the old woman's description of the landscape and the movement of people. Yet in comparison to Kanthapura it lacks two essential elements: people's free choice of a habitat and its divinely guaranteed protection. Economic need enforces the coolies' choice of their habitat and in place of Kenchamma there is the unlikely god-like figure of the Sahib, "a tall, fat man with golden hair." (50)

Rao's radical move from a political to a philosophical perspective finds expression also in his landscape presentation in *The Serpent and the Rope*. Here, infrequent references basically relate to five or six topographical clusters, i.e. rivers, mountains, sea, regions, cities, and the world, but rarely to specific features such as a rock, a tree or a road. We do not encounter extended, detailed, let alone poetically rendered representations. Importantly though, as Rama travels in France, India and England, his sensitive experiences of local landscapes — Mont Sainte-Victoire, The Pyrenees, the Alps, the Himalayas, Ganges, Cam, Thames and Rhone — and cities — Benares, London, Paris, Aix — gradually merge into and create a comprehensive understanding of nature that foregrounds the general — the mountain, the river, the sea, the city and finally, the land. In the end, his travelling through space and time mirrors the narrator's increasing awareness of his need for a guru and an early return to India. The function of landscape, I would like to propose, lies in permitting Rama to affirm the existence of the world both as a tangible and a transcendental reality. How then does Rao invoke landscape and evoke responses of an aesthetic nature in his narrator?

At the end of his stay in Europe Rama's often quoted words, "India is not a country like France is, or like England. India is an idea, a metaphysic" (*The Serpent and the Rope*, 376), summarize his experiences of Europe, including its landscapes, in comparison to those of his homeland. Yet it is important to note that both equally evoke positive responses throughout. At the most, mountains and rivers are awe inspiring but never hazardous, let alone threatening. It is their beauty and their power, their age and continuity that impress the mind, the safety they promise and the nourishment and sustenance they provide that assures man. Looked at from an evolutionary angle, these landscapes promise man an abode — and yet they differ by degree as a comparison between European and Indian mountains illustrates:

> one saw on a day of the mistral the beautiful Mont Sainte-Victoire [...] clear as though you could talk to it. The mistral blew and blew so vigorously: one could see one's body float away, like pantaloon, vest and scarf, and one's soul sit and shine on the top of Mont Sainte-Victoire. (14)

And further:

> Mont Sainte-Victoire itself. There was sainthood about that elevation of the mountain [...] because the good Cézanne saw it day after day; and it carried such a message of strength, and of the possible, that it was something of a Kailās for us. (54)

As to the "noble Pyrenees", "you could look at [them] and know to be strong one must be pure as snow" (95), while the

> marital air of the mountains, the convexity of spring; the anemones and the blue irises of the Alps; the lavender, the thyme and the rosemary; they seemed like death become white, like blood in the limbs and freshness in one's eyes. (364)

The sensual perception of Mont Sainte-Victoire, the Pyrenees and the Alps proves less of an aesthetic than a cognitive experience that indicates the speaker's outer and inner distance, a detachment conveyed through relativizing comparisons — "as though you could talk", "something of a Kailās", "they seemed like death" — , or assumptions: "one could see", "you could look." The observing subject and the observed object remain apart, an insight that questions the function of the mountain as an abode advantageous to man's survival. The references to "sainthood" and "Cézanne" underline Mont Sainte-Victoire's "in-between-the-two"-status referred to earlier. The closest to transcend this subject-object split occurs at the time of Madeleine's forty-one day fast when "one heard strange musical sounds [...] and as each sound ended another more powerful one rose as if creating mountains, rivers, seas, roads, man." (323–4) Indeed, the assumed birth of such tangible objects from sound takes us to Rama's experience of India's landscape, especially the Himalayas.

From the train window on his way to Hardwar Rama watches "the birds and the deodhars of the Himalayas, [...] a whole tribe of deer [that] jumped across the pools of the forest", and the parrots with "very lovely yellow rings round their throats", and he feels "the Himalayas shone above them, simple, aware, vibrant with sound." And he concludes that somewhere "between the interstices of those trees, somewhere in the movement of the hinds, in the mountain stillness of Hardwar did I feel a new knowledge. I felt *absence* [...]. The mountain echoed an absence that seemed primordial, a syllable, a name." (40–41) Years later and one night in Paris Rama recollects virtually the same landscape to which he wants to return now, to the "deodhars of the Himalayas, [...] the deer in the forests, [... and] the keen call of the elephant in the grave ocellate [sic!] silence of the forests." (376) Here, landscape is experienced — and recreated in the mind — through details in nature that merge into a living entity where sound and stillness, presence and absence conflate and create "a new knowledge". From the perspective of evolutionary psychology the Himalayas are experienced as the observer's transcendental home or abode, a place which does not so much guarantee man's physical than his spiritual survival in the sense of leading him to *moksha*.

Having so far focused solely on Rama's experiences of mountains I should add that rivers often are part of them with the Ganges being of prime importance. Again, his responses are always positive and his descriptions consist of merely a few (topographical) features combined with reading them or reflecting upon their meaning. The Ganges with its flowers, fish and logs the boat occasional hits is a "grave and knowing river" (23) that invokes Rama the observer's worship. The experience of such unequivocal subject-object relationship is not yet overcome when he speaks of her motherliness, of her "who had born the sorrows of our sorrowful land" and of the impurity "we made her bear." (33) Yet, the "ashes and bones let down into the Ganges in Benares" letting her know of "our secret" and patrimony shifts the subject-object relationship towards the river's ability to merge presence and absence, much the same way the Himalayas do. Finally, Rama's own dipping into the Ganges makes him realize her knowing, her wisdom and a feeling of purity. It is an act of expiation for the "kidnapped and forsaken [...] and for the dead" that lets him conclude that there "is no absence if you have the feel of your own presence" (41); the duality of subject and object has been realized as non-duality. Again, the river does not so much stand for man's physical protection or his sustenance, but it is a transcendental abode; and everlasting at that, since the Ganges waters flow into the sea, return as snowflakes that melt and turn again into Ganges water. (170) Recollected many years later in Paris, Rama is anxious to return to India hoping and wishing "I could be a river, a tree, an aptitude of incumbent silence". (376)

By contrast, European rivers like the Cam, the Thames or the Rhône fail him, the first because it is embedded in time, in history, while the Rhone — not unlike Mont Saint-Victoire — "somewhere [...] must know the mysteries of Mother Ganga." (245) But it does not and instead takes up that in-between position that separates Petit Avignon and Avignon des Papes, preventing us to cross "the broken bridge of Saint-Bénézet." (377) At the most you can evoke Mother Rhône to go to India. (389) Finally, Cam and Thames remain mere tangible objects, the one silent, self-reflective and outside history, teaching you "that history is made by others and not by oneself" (168), the other imperial, mature with a knowledge of herself that occasionally makes history so intimately connected with the river, and stop to look at itself when "two lovers hooked arm to arm" look at it. (199)

Throughout, Rama projects his meanings on the landscapes he encounters, seemingly anthropomorphizing them but in reality conceiving of his European mountains and rivers as tangible objects and of his Indian ones as the transcendental abode he wishes to make his home. Yet there can be no doubt that his culturally moulded aesthetic sensation and cognitive perception of landscape is rooted in man's perception of his environment as a result of his adaptation to a habitat that offers him the chance to survive.

Thematically and in its narrative manner Rao's novella *The Cat and Shakespeare* relates to the *Serpent and the Rope* and has evoked perhaps even more disparate critical reactions than his novel. Not unlike Rama, its first-person narrator Ramakrishna Pai is an inward-looking, self-centred and highly speculative person also preoccupied with love, woman and truth, but for him landscape plays a minor role if we perceive of it in its natural state. However, as indicated already, landscape features have been employed by man to create parks, gardens and buildings, and it is here where Pai's repeated references especially to house but also to wall and garden come in. Attended to briefly at the beginning of his narrative they gradually accumulate weight and eventually merge in a revelatory experience that basically closes the story. The author employs very much the same manner of describing and creating a landscape as in his previous writing. Having been instigated on the idea of building a house of three stories by his neighbour Govindan Nair (*The Cat and Shakespeare*, 10), Pai looks at the boundary wall which, tile-covered, bulging and obstreperous, runs along, dips and rises "on its wild, vicarious course." (11) Characteristically, observations of movement and life complement the picture: leaves are falling, fruit is dropping and cattle are rising. And again, a reflection and an invocation round it off: "Purity is so near, so concrete. Let us build the house. Lord, let me build the house." (11) This by now familiar manner of drawing a landscape recurs when Pai imagines the house he will give Shanta, "a house three stories high", with a tamarind tree in the back yard, dahlias, a mango tree with fruit and a koel singing and mango fruit ripe like Shanta's womb "that has grown round." (51) Having eventually built "a house two stories high [to prove the world is]" (108), Pai then wishes to add the third storey "so that I could see up to the end of the sea" (111): a notion now laughed at and rejected by Nair who had originally spoken of three stories. Yet Pai realizes the truth of his neighbour's reaction once he has crossed the wall, walked through a garden landscape of plants and people — again drawn in simple terms — and steps up inside a house where he does not see the sea "but eyes seeing eyes seeing" (113); where "if I go on seeing a point, I become the point"; where opposites cease and subject and object coalesce. It is an experience that once and for all tells Pai to "never build a house three stories high." (116)

Analysed from the perspective of evolutionary psychology, climbing to the top of the house promises man, not unlike climbing the tree in the savannah or the top of a mountain, prospect: to see, explore and understand his surroundings and to safeguard himself against danger. For Rao and his narrator the cultural transformation of this genetically evolved adaptation to one's environment lies in man's realization of his and the world's transcendental non-dual nature. Nair's "third storey" initially taken literally by Pai, reveals itself as a metaphor of the elevation you have to climb to see not "up to the end of the sea", or in the words of Rama, the horizon falsely taken for the rope from the angle of the serpent, but for what language cannot name and what Pai calls "nose (not the nose) and eyes seeing eyes [...] love yet knew not its name but heard it as sound ...." (113) Unlike Rama who arrives at this truth cognitively, Pai experiences it, confirming K.R. Srinivasa Iyengar's view that Rao has moved from *jñana* in *The Serpent and the Rope* [...] on to *bhakti-prapatti* in *The Cat and Shakespeare.*"[20]

The most important landscape scene in the final text, *On the Ganga Ghat*, occurs at the very end of the last story and here it is less the narrator's sensual-aesthetic sensation of the river than his cognitive perception of its flowing that triggers his philosophical reflections upon flowing and unflowing, death and truth, place and time. Asking whether death has a meaning, the Ganga answers that death is as much of a superstition as the probability of the river growing dry. What one must learn though is to see through movement as no movement, through space as no space in order to understand that "where there is no end there is no beginning" (*On the Ganga Ghat*, 127), and that this is the simple truth "if only we listen to ourselves." Eventually returning to his sensation of the river he concludes, "if you dare have a deep look on the Ganges evenings, and see the Ganges unflowing, then you know there is no Ganges. Water is just water..." (127) As we have noted often, Rao's landscape representation ends with an aphorism and an invocation, a paradoxical one as it seems, when the speaker pleads with Mother Ganga, "please be gracious, and, — flow." (127) It is his admission of being able only to take the in-between-stance of the poet who needs words to speak to express the unsayable. Yet such culturally evolved perception is grounded in the genetically evolved adaptation to a habitat that signals safety and survival to the mind of the viewer both in the sense of his material and his spiritual well-being.

20 K.R. Srinivasa Iyengar, "Literature as Sadhana: A Note on *The Cat and Shakespeare*," *Aryan Path* 40, 6 (1969), 301-305; here 305

In substance landscape representations in Rao's works do not change. Their features are neither sensed negatively nor are they without bearing on the perceiver. Judged from a cultural perspective these sensory signals are cognitively perceived as embedded in the specific memetic heritage of Brahminic India, yet viewed from an evolutionary psychological angle they are also grounded in man's genetically evolved responses to his habitat — and thus cross-culturally significant as universals of human nature.

Works cited

Novels

DESANI, G.V., *All about H Hatterr*, London: The Saturn Press 1949

GHOSH, Amitav, *The Hungry Tide*, Delhi: Ravi Dayal Publisher 2004

RAO, Raja, *Kanthapura*, New Delhi: OUP, 19th ed. 2006

—, *The Serpent and the Rope*, New Delhi: Orient Paperbacks, 3rd ed. 1995

—, *The Cat and Shakespeare*, New York: Macmillan 1965

—, *On the Ganga Ghat*, New Delhi: Vision Book 1989

RUSHDIE, Salman, *Midnight's Children*, London: Picador Edition 1982

Critical Studies

APPLETON, Jay, *The Symbolism of Habitat: An Interpretation of Landscape in the Arts*, Seattle and London: University of Washington Press 1990

BARKOW, Jerome H. et al, eds., *The Adapted Mind: Evolutionary Psychology and the Generation of Culture*, New York/Oxford: OUP 1992

BARKOW, Jerome, H., "Beneath New Culture is Old Psychology: Gossip and Social Stratification", eds. Barkow et al., *op.cit*, 625–638

IYENGAR, K.R. Srinivasa, "Literature as Sadhana: A Note on *The Cat and Shakespeare*", *Aryan Path* 40, 6, (1969), 301–305

KAPLAN, Stephen, "Environmental Preference in a Knowledge-Seeking, Knowledge-Using Organism", eds. Barkow et al., *op.cit.*, 581-598

MARATH, Menon, "Three Indian Novelists", *Life and Letters* 59 (1948/49), 187–192

ORIANS, Gordon H. and Judith H. Heerwagen, "Evolved Responses to Landscapes", eds. Barkow et al, *op.cit.*, 556–579

RIEMENSCHNEIDER, Dieter, "'Bibliography", *The Indian Novel in English: Its Critical Discourse 1934-2004*, Jaipur: Rawat Publishers 2005, 346–376

—, "Literature as Sādhāna: The Reception of Raja Rao's Novels, *op.cit.*, 289–380

SIMMONS, Alan H., *The Neolithic Revolution in the Near East: Transforming the Human Landscape*, Tucson: The University of Arizona Press 2007

STILZ, Gerhard, "Return to the Jungle? Colonial and Post-Colonial Landscapes in Indian English Fiction", eds. Hena Maes-Jelinek and Geoff Davis, *A Talent(ed) Digger*, Cross/Cultures, vol. 20, Rodopi: Amsterdam/Atlanta, GA 1995, 324–334

‘The Train has Moved On’

R.K. Narayan’s *The Guide* and Literary History[1]

THE CRITICAL RECEPTION OF R.K. NARAYAN’S fourteen novels over a period of more than half a century has established him as the most popular of the three founding fathers of the modern Indian novel in English. Nearly 900 publications — monographs and essay collections, contributions to learned journals and magazines, reviews of single works in diverse media, and filmed versions of at least two works — exceed by far the attention paid to Mulk Raj Anand, or Raja Rao’s achievement. They testify, besides, to the sustained interest in Narayan’s narrative oeuvre that ranges from *Swami and Friends* (1935) to *The World of Nagaraj* (1989). An overview will give an idea of the number of critical responses during the periods 1935-1970, the 1970s, the 1980s, and 1990-2004. Besides, it will permit a close look at *The Guide* (1958), Narayan’s most popular novel. Its literary innovative features will show that this story, though embedded in the intermediate period between the late colonial and the early independence years in India, is a forerunner of the post-1980s Indian novel in English.

Literary criticism understood as textual analysis and evaluation is intimately intertwined with parameters of quality and much less with those of quantity. Still, statistical figures arrived at by looking at the overall critical reception of a writer’s oeuvre, the attention paid to his early and/ or mature works and the ranking of individual texts offer insight into his achievement and certainly intellectual pleasure to the mathematically-minded observer. To start with, I would like to pick up on this idea and

1 This is a slightly revised version of my essay published in the ejournal *ASIATIC* 3, 2 (December 2009), 88–100. See www.asiatic.iiu.edu.my

investigate the critical reception of R.K. Narayan's work from this angle, and in particular the response to *The Guide* (1958). Thereafter I shall relate my findings to a selection of critical-analytical insights presented by his literary critics. What do figures collected and assembled from a period of six decades (1934-2004), tell us, and where do they take us with regard to a qualitative assessment of the writer's overall achievement, and of his *The Guide*?

My own comprehensive Narayan bibliography[2] (2005) contains 858 publications, including 134 reviews, written by approximately 600 authors and thirty anonymous reviewers. 180 of the 600 critics, or three of ten, are foreigners: a considerable percentage, which documents Narayan's international reputation. Concomitantly, I noticed that Narayan criticism proper set in only twenty-five years after the publication of his first novel, *Swami and Friends* (1935), and after nine of his fourteen works had already been available, first from well-known English publishers, and then from an Indian publishing house, the author's own Indian Thought Publications in Mysore. With the appearance of *The Guide* however, critics appear to have woken up suddenly, and as their increasing attention from the 1960s onward testifies, they have never since lost sight of the novelist's work. This, his eighth novel, has remained the author's most popular work. In 1961, it was honoured by the Sahitya Akademi in New Delhi, as the first Indian novel in English to win the Akademi's national award. Statistically speaking, it has been scrutinised, analysed, and written about more often than any other Narayan novel, which virtually invites us to establish a connection between quantitative and qualitative criteria of assessment. Eighty-four essays and books on *The Guide* by far outnumber the thirty critical responses to *The Man-Eater of Malgudi* (1961), the novel that comes next in popularity — not to mention the two essays on *Mr. Sampath* (1949), for many critics the author's least convincing novel. Very much the same can be said about reviews: twenty-five on *The Guide*, or nearly double the number than on *The Financial Expert* (1952), a novel obviously very much appreciated by American reviewers. Furthermore, we must not overlook the numerous analyses of *The Guide* contained in general essays on Narayan's oeuvre, or in comparative studies that relate his work to other Indian or to international novelists writing in English. Naturally, these figures must be related to the number of years a book has been on the market. Even so, *The Guide* takes an impressive lead, with a factor of 2.43 that arises from

2 Dieter Riemenschneider, *The Indian Novel in English: Its Critical Discourse: 1934–2004*, Jaipur: Rawat Publishing 2005, 230–279

the number of critical essays and books divided by the number of years the novel has been in print. Here *The Bachelor of Arts* (1937) with a factor of 0.12 makes up the 14th and last position.

Let us now have a look at characteristic features of Narayan's writing during the four periods into which I have subdivided the reception process, starting with the years 1935 to 1970, and followed by the 1970s, the 1980s and the 1990s and after. About ninety more or less brief publications, complemented by about 100 reviews appeared during the initial period. Basically, the essays attempt to present us with an overall-view and a general evaluation of Narayan's works, not unexpectedly summarising and commenting upon their plots and characters, their themes and narrative modes and the author's use of English. Already now, references to *The Guide* figure prominently, with the remarkable number of twenty-one reviews published in 1958, the same year as the book. Altogether in a positive vein — which was an exception among Indian critics of the time when commenting upon their compatriots' writing in English — the writer's story-telling talent is as much lauded as his gentle humour and simple language, his sharp focus on the Indian middle-class, and his refraining from commenting upon his stories and from preaching. Characteristics, as William Walsh remarked, that defined his "Indian sensibility"[3], and caused C.D. Narasimhaiah to praise his writing as "truly Indian",[4] and K.R. Srinivasa Iyengar to speak of the author's "thoughts and feelings, the stirrings of the soul … all of the soil of India, recognizably autochthonous."[5]

Overall, textual analysis or close reading is the preferred method of interpretation, which reflects both, a critical awareness of the need to introduce Narayan to his new readers, and the predominant methodology of the time, the school of New Criticism. Still, apart from focusing on the text qua text, we also come across comparative studies meant to explore common themes and narrative structures, and to contextualise Narayan's writing from a literary historical, a psychological or an ideological angle. Iyengar, for example, takes his cue from the town of Malgudi, the novels' exceptional setting, and suggests, "that Malgudi is the real 'hero' of the eleven [sic! nine] novels and many short stories."[6] The novels' characters,

3 William Walsh, "The Intricate Alliance: The Novels of R.K. Narayan", *Review of English Literature* 2, 4 (1961), 91–99; here 92

4 C.D. Narasimhaiah, "R.K. Narayan's *The Guide*", *The Literary Criterion* 4, 4 (1961), 63–92; here 66

5 K.R. Srinivasa Iyengar, "R.K. Narayan", *Indian Writing in English*, Bombay: Asia Publishing House 1962, 273–301; here 280

6 Ibid., 284

on the other hand, "seem to achieve some sort of transmigration from body to body and name to name." (ibid.) "Narayan," he argues, "seems to see the world as a mere balance of forces," and focuses on "the miracle of transcendence and the renewal of life, love, beauty, peace."[7]

As it would prove over the next four decades, Iyengar's judgement was almost taken as the final word on Narayan and was hardly ever questioned seriously, not the least, I believe, because it appeared so strikingly true to Indian critics on the one hand, while an international critical discourse on the Indian novel in English was to develop only gradually, with the reception of Narayan's work abroad and 'non-Indian' critical approaches to a comparatively 'new' genre of the novel. For example, Walsh, Narayan's first serious British critic, broadens Iyengar's character analyses by placing these figures against their social and cultural background, and he also invites our attention to the fact that non-Indian readers will not immediately understand the novels' cultural references: a sine qua non, as a look back at the critical misjudgement of the East German Walter Ruben's Marxist-Orientalist approach demonstrates. Calling the portrayal of Raju, "ein untypisches kleinbürgerliches Einzelschicksal" — "a single individual's atypical petit bourgeois fate,"[8] betrays Ruben's ideologically blinkered view as much as his non-knowledge of India.

Walsh, Iyengar, and Ruben — to whose names we can add James Dale (1965) and K. Venkatachari (1969) — look at Narayan's whole oeuvre, but they also pay much attention to *The Guide,* while Narasimhaiah and Satyanarain Singh (1968) offer extended analyses of the novel. However, their estimate of its thematic concerns and character portrayals — Singh, for example talks about "crisis and resolution" — does not fundamentally differ from their colleagues' conclusions.

A look at the writer's achievement in the 1970s suggests a reversal of the previous period, a creatively most productive phase in Narayan's career, since he published just one novel, *The Painter of Signs* (1976). Yet these were no barren years, because they witnessed the publication of three collections of short stories, a travelogue, an autobiographical account and the condensed prose versions of *The Ramayana* (1973) and *The Mahabharata* (1978). At the same time and luckily, the long break between *The Vendor of Sweets* (1967) and *The Painter of Signs* (1976) appears to have invited many critics to take stock and assess the novelist's achievement

7 Ibid., 301

8 Walter Ruben, *Indische Romane: Eine ideologische Untersuchung*, Bd. II & III, Berlin: Akademie-Verlag 1967, Bd.III, 154

up to that point; an altogether promising task, as it proved, since by now his eleven novels had become easily available, both in India and abroad. 140 critical responses, including ten reviews, demonstrate that Narayan had begun to establish himself as a writer worthwhile reflecting about and writing upon.

The 1970s experienced the publication of four books on the author and two on *The Guide*. Besides, we now also encounter a widening interest in Indian writing in English and concomitantly, a growing number of general studies of the Indian novel in English, quite a few of which would contain separate chapters on Narayan's works or relate them to those of others. To mention only a few and more original publications: Meena Shirwadkar's *Image of Woman in the Indo-Anglian Fiction* (1979) is a first step towards Indian feminist studies and pays more attention to the author's women characters than earlier critics have done, whereas Uma Parameswaran's *A Study of Representative Indo-English Novelists* (1976) takes existing Narayan criticism as her point of departure, thus creating an awareness of the methodology of reception aesthetics. Looking at the author's narrative talent often praised by others, she considers him a weak narrator, since in "seven out of ten novels the plot breaks midway, never quite managing to resolve the incongruence between realism and fantasy which are its main components."[9] Only *The Guide*, she feels, differs because of the story's ambiguous ending with its near perfect unity of realism and fantasy. Besides, Parameswaran's earlier verdict, that Raju "speculat[es] that this risk [of death or survival] pays dividends," and that he will recover to accept a glucose-saline injection and his light will shine brighter than ever for his devotees",[10] certainly strikes a new note when compared to other critics' morally-veiled judgement of the guide's sacrifice and/or redemption.

The very question of narrative mode also brought into play by Parameswaran is pursued by several of her colleagues who comment upon the comic, the parabolic, the symbolic or the mythic mode. For Keith Garebian Narayan's vision of life in its totality, a characteristic Indian attitude, is best served by a comic impulse, which is most convincingly presented parabolically and episodically. M. Sivaramkrishna (1978) foregrounds the symbolic mode and feels that in *The Guide*, symbolically speaking, cave and temple are structuring devices. Thus, Raju, Rosie, and Marco become equally 'guilty' as they conceive of the temple, respectively, as a tourist

9 Uma Parameswaran, "Native Genius: R.K. Narayan", *A Study of Representative Indo-English Novelists*, New Delhi: Vikas 1976, 42–84; here 46

10 Uma Parameswaran, "Rogues in R.K. Narayan's Fiction", *Literature East & West* XVIII (1974), 203–15; here 214

item, as "part of what [Rosie] regards as an ignoble past," and as a "curio cerebrally cut off from the rest of life."[11] However, Raju's gradual insight into the true meaning of this building does not only restore 'order' — Iyengar's category — but appears to redeem him. Parabolically speaking then, he mutates from sinner to saint, or as Goyal (1977) and vanden Driesen (1979) have entitled their articles, respectively, "From Picaro to Pilgrim", and "From Rogue to Redeemer."

As a final example of original thinking, Vijay Misra's (1979) philosophical handling of the dialectic of maya and Indian literary texts takes recourse to the philosopher Shankara's idea of structuring the relationship between Brahman (the Real) and the phenomenal world as "metaphysical encounters." Misra refers to them as "meta-text I." Discussing *The Guide* vis-à-vis this perception, its text proper, called "text II," reveals itself as patterned along the tension of nartaki (Rosie), the self (Raju) and bhakti (Raju's escape from samsara); which leads Misra to conclude that the Indian novel cannot get away from the weight of the construct, the "meta-text II." That is to say, "Indian literary texts carry within themselves theories about Indian literature"[12]: the knowledge of perceptions articulated in Indian aesthetics helps the critic towards placing even a text in English within his own literary-philosophical tradition.

Approximately 240 critical studies, including more than half a dozen monographs and four comprehensive essay collections, written by 150 critics, of whom fifty are from outside India, appeared in the 1980s. More urgently than hitherto, such heightened attention paid to the author, whose last three novels had appeared between 1983 and 1989, makes us ask about the relationship of quantity and quality. Do we encounter criticism that more or less and necessarily repeats and summarises insights the discerning reader has already come across? Do essays in collections and journals depart, if not altogether, then at least to some degree, from well-trodden paths? And finally, do we encounter more recent methods of investigation, say Sanskrit aesthetics or feminist theory, or fresh ones like the 'new' trends of postmodernist or postcolonial theorising? The answer would be: usually not, but at times, yes. The narrative mode continues to attract critics, for example, U.P. Sinha who discusses the idea of a 'mythic' novel, which when successfully put into practice, presents "the mythic element of

11 M. Sivaramkrishna, "The Cave and the Temple: Structural Symbolism in *The Guide*", *Osmania Journal of English Studies* 14, 1 (1978), 71–79; here 77

12 Vijay Misra, "The Dialectic of Maya and the Principles of Narrative Structure in Indian Literature", *ACLALS Bulletin* 5th Ser. 2 (1979), 47–60; here 56

Indian sensibility in a creative grapple with reality."[13] As Sinha maintains, the status of mythic can be bestowed upon Narayan's work because of the author's "mythic consciousness"[14] that makes the world of Malgudi "simultaneously temporal and timeless."[15] D.V.K. Raghavacharyulu returns to comedy, which he says, can "evoke pity and terror, and through them work towards an appropriate katharsis",[16] brought about, for example, in *The Guide*. Such a reading, he says, brings to light that facet of the Indian aesthetic tradition that "stresses on [sic!] sama-drishti as the capacity to view suffering and sorrow... as but an integral part of the ontological situation."[17]

S.P. Ranchan and G.R. Kataria contribute to the feminist discourse by employing C.G. Jung's idea of the Feminine, which causes them to reject a traditional reading from a Hindu-philosophical angle of the male protagonist's transformation, for example in *The English Teacher* (1945), in favour of one "brought about by the Feminine." It is "radically different from the kind of transformation sought after by most religions through meditation or visualization."[18] Similarly, Raju comes to the Feminine not through Rosie but through the "descending force of the Feminine which is symbolized in the descent of the rain in the distant hills."[19] Both critics differ from Ram Dial's psychoanalytical approach, who argues that it is the interaction of Raju's anima and Rosie's animus that furthers their development towards Self: a Self eventually realized when Raju is transformed "through his interaction with the collective psyche into the living archetype of a Wise Man."[20] Regrettably, Ram Dial drops Rosie somewhere on the way to her realisation of Self — as does the author: a relapse from psychoanalysis into Advaita Vedanta.

Attention paid to a single Narayan novel is one of the outstanding quantitative features of the 1980s, and here every third of roughly seventy essays focuses on *The Guide*, with *The Man-Eater of Malgudi* (1961) coming

13 U.P. Sinha, *Patterns of Myth and Reality: A Study in R.K. Narayan's Novels*, Delhi: Sandarbh Publishers 1988, 1

14 Ibid., 2

15 Ibid., 6

16 D.V.K. Raghavacharyulu, "Small-Scale Reflections on a Great House of Fiction: R.K. Narayan's Chronicles of Malgudi", ed. M.K. Naik, *Perspectives on Indian Fiction in English*, New Delhi: Abhinav 1985, 21–48; here 29

17 Ibid., 30

18 S.P. Ranchan and G.R. Kataria, "Transformation via the Feminine in R.K. Narayan's Krishnan, Raju, and Jagan", *Journal of South Asian Literature* 22, 2 (1987), 5–15; here 5

19 Ibid., 12

20 Ram Dial, "The Anima-Animus Interaction in *The Guide*", ed. Atma Ram, *Perspectives on R.K. Narayan*, Ghaziabad: Vimal Prakashan 1981, 168–77; here 150

second, but boasting merely a dozen critical responses. Among the more exciting readings, we come upon differing analyses of the psychological make-up of characters in *The Guide*. For K.M. Chandar (1984), Raju suffers from an inferiority complex, which explains his partly successful, yet eventually failing attempts at over-compensation. Escape from over-anxiety as a last resort complements the picture of such a mental disposition, with the novel's protagonist finally accepting his fate, not because of his insight, but because of his weakness brought about by fasting. Jai Dev (1987) looks at Raju's childhood, a period totally controlled by his elders, which foreshadows his need to be supported by his community — as Velan does, holding him literally up in the river. It is a view not shared by G.S. Amur (1985), to whom Raju's end symbolizes transcendence, while Viney Kirpal (1988) insists on varnashrama: Raju journeys through the four stages of life to Self-realisation. Finally, O.P. Mathur (1982) considers the ambivalent make-up of all major characters as culturally determined by their traditional world, into which the West has entered and created a "grey twilight world of contemporary life quivering hesitatingly between tradition and modernity, East and West, inextricably mixed up in the minds of individuals."[21]

Considering Narayan's advanced age and surmising that *The World of Nagaraj* (1989) would perhaps be his final novel, it was to be expected that criticism from the 1990s onward might turn more often towards attempting an overall assessment of his literary achievement. Indeed, the impressive number of twenty-seven book-length publications between 1990 and 2004 testifies to this development, especially when compared with the previous decade. Similarly pertinent is the observation that eighty essays deal with a single novel, which might be partly attributable to the fact that the number of 'first-time' Narayan critics had grown faster than ever before, most of them, of course, being academic newcomers who would naturally choose to focus on just one work. Indeed, of the 600 authors listed in my book, about every fourth scholar's name makes its first appearance during these years. Still, and in spite of the spate of these publications, a close look at them betrays an imbalance between quantity and quality, if the latter is to be understood as bringing about original insights and thus adding to and widening our understanding and appreciation of the writer's literary output. More often than not, old traces are being followed by young academics, many of them from university departments of English, who

21 O.P. Mathur, "*The Guide*: A Study in Cultural Ambivalence", *The Literary Endeavour* 3, 3–4 (1982), 70-79; here 71

seem to be not always aware of existing scholarship, perhaps innocently so because of the lack of resources. Remarkable again is the supreme role *The Guide* plays during these years, so is the 'resurrection' of *The Dark Room* (1938) and *Swami and Friends* (1935) after their long slumber in limbo and due to feminist studies and an increased interest in children and young adult literature. *The Guide* though continues to set critics on the track of character analysis, with Raghavendra Narayan Singh (1994) and R. Ramachandra (1994) drawing our attention to the neglected aspect of their loneliness. For Narayan Singh, they battle their condition in a gender-specific manner: males by resorting to their amorous instincts, women by turning to artistic occupations.[22] Michael Gorra (1994) and K. Meera Bai (1994) reject such simplistic notions and point to the influence of Hindu perceptions of man and woman, while contrasting views on the figure of Rosie-Nalini are offered by Balbir Singh, Lakshmi Holmstroem and Gayatri Chakravorti Spivak. Singh relates the Jungian idea of human beings' desire for immortality as a "primordial affirmation," and its realisation in the collective unconscious, to the Indian ideal of conveying "a sense of timelessness."[23] Holmstroem contextualises Rosie by foregrounding the social aspect of her 'development': a "deliberate ambiguity in [her] portraiture",[24] attributable to the woman's presentation from a male narrator's angle, which mirrors "the bafflement of a traditional, largely male society, in its face-to-face encounter with new notions of selfhood and particularly, of womanhood."[25] Spivak addresses the figure of Rosie from a postcolonial angle and calls her the "remote instrument of Raju's enforced sanctity," and "the nautch (dance) girl... a cliché of the imagining of British India",[26] who eventually "is not needed in the last phase of the book: the phase of ethnicity over culture. India is folk kitsch."[27]

A further critical approach to *The Guide* deals with story-construction although character 'development' continues to play its part here too. For Patrick Swinden the "only change [in life and character] is in the

22 Raghavendra Narayan Singh, "R.K. Narayan: Artist of Uniform Sensibilities", ed. A.L. McLeod, *R.K. Narayan: Critical Perspectives*, New Delhi: Sterling 1994, 147–55; here 154

23 Balbir Singh, "Theme of Art and Immortality in R.K. Narayan's *The Guide*", *The Literary Criterion* 25, 2 (1990), 36–46; here 38

24 Lakshmi Holmstroem, "Women as Markers of Social Change: *The Dark Room*, *The Guide* and *The Painter of Signs*", ed. C.N. Srinath, *R.K. Narayan: An Anthology of Recent Criticism*, Delhi: Pencraft International 2000, 102–13; here 102

25 Ibid., 102–3

26 Gayatri Chakravorti Spivak, "How to Teach a 'Culturally Different' Book", ed. Donna Landry and Gerald MacLean, *The Spivak Reader*, New York/London: Routledge 1996, 237–66; here 244

27 Ibid., 245

recognition of the unchanging",[28] due to parameters of Hindu philosophy playing an important role in the novel. On the surface, Raju appears to change, an impression brought about by the writer's use of Western story-telling techniques, such as changing the point of view and time-shifts. Yet Narayan's employment of Hindu myths and traditional narrative patterns, Swinden maintains, forces us to read Raju as a saint and a trickster, a personality not unlike a hero taken from an Indian epic, such as the Ramayana.[29] Chitra Sankaran too emphasises the writer's "instinctive assimilation of his native literature"[30] and draws on storytelling elements of "the ancient Sanskrit genre, the katha or tale"[31] with its insertion of different stories into a single narrative, its movement back and forth between past and present, and accordingly, its employment of different narrative tones. Likewise, characterisation is also dictated by traditional considerations:[32] Raju is the "trickster sage" of Hindu mythology, acting as a link between the Gods and humans.[33] Nonetheless, to this critic *The Guide* is not a myth but a novel where Narayan succeeds in "making it feasible to interpret Raju's fate in both these lights."[34]

A final cross-cultural reading of the book highlights hybridity as the catchword of its 'postcolonial scenario' in Monika Fludernik's comparative study. Hybridity links Raju to postcolonialism in that his lack of self-confidence is a direct outflow of the dependency the colonial power had forced upon its subjects. Further, accepting his role as a sadhu, might not only "signal a kind of token nationalist and traditional revival"[35] but also "constitutes the major instance of hybridity in the text… in that Raju appropriates traditional signifiers for his own decidedly secular ends."[36] Other phenomena of hybridity, Fludernik proposes, are Marco, the "blind" colonial usurper, who is tricked by the crafty native, and Raju's commercialisation of Indian culture in his role as guide and impresario.

28 Patrick Swinden, "Hindu Mythology in R.K. Narayan's *The Guide*", *The Journal of Commonwealth Literature* 34, 1 (1999), 65–83; here 66

29 Ibid., 78

30 Chitra Sankaran, "Patterns of Story-telling in R.K. Narayan's *The Guide*", *The Journal of Commonwealth Literature* 26, 1 (1991), 127–50; here 127

31 Ibid, 128

32 Ibid., 133

33 Ibid., 134

34 Ibid., 148

35 M. Fludernik, "Colonial vs. Cosmopolitan Hybridity: A Comparison of Mulk Raj Anand and R.K. Narayan with Recent British and North American Expatriate Writing", ed. M. Fludernik, *Hybridity and Postcolonialism: Modern Indian Literature*, Tübingen: Stauffenburg 1998, 263-92; here 270

36 Ibid., 271

The Guide then "illustrates a pattern of postcolonial hybridity," where the traditional wins over the modern, but "only after having been hybridized by the influence" of the Western world.[37]

My summarising account of the critical discourse on Narayan's novels and particularly on *The Guide* shows a prevalence of a particular critical approach at a given period, which reflects, or is apt to mirror, the then dominating influence of a critical school. Further, the choice of certain questions directed at a text is motivated by what critics feel to be uppermost in a writer's mind. Applied to Narayan, it is his interrogation of the make-up and fate of his character(s) — and to tell their stories appropriately. With *The Guide* the large number of (differing) analyses of the story's open ending reflects their preoccupation with Raju's identity not only in his role as the teller of his own tale but also as the projection of the third-person narrator. In this respect and against the background of the Indian English novel written between the 1930s and 1950s *The Guide* holds a special position which, I would like to argue, indicates the novelist's doubt about the concept of identity as well as about the scope and truth of realistic story telling.

Yet it was to be a younger generation of Indian writers who really opened new vistas of story-telling a few decades later. Though sharing their concern for contemporary Indian man and woman with Narayan their novels engage much less with the role of tradition in modernity than with the repercussions of modernity upon Indians in a world they increasingly conceive of in global terms; a world where India's national borders become more and more porous as, among other factors, the spread of Indian diasporas testifies. If Raju the guide's predicament could be read as the writer's examination of the concept of guru,[38] Indian English novelists of the late 20th century predicate their character portrayals in their fictional constructions of modern man and woman quite generally on the fluidity of the term identity; a venture, incidentally, that entails experimentation in narrativization as a result of questioning the meaningfulness of the realistic mode. They are wary of the narrator's reliability or the need to round off his or her story; they distrust the truth of a master narrative, and they have created a post-modern pastiche of modulated narrative bits and pieces that offer the reader an astounding range of thematic references and diverse variants of what happened. To mention but a few examples that deserve a more detailed analysis than can be undertaken

37 Ibid., 273

38 See Makarand Paranjape, "The Reluctant Guru: R.K. Narayan and *The Guide*", www.makarand.com [2005]

here. In Ruchir Joshi's *The Last Jet-Engine Laugh* (2001) the seventy year-old narrator Paresh delves into his past and that of his family under the motto, "ki unhone kyakya, kyakya nahi kio", "what he did do and did not do" — a maxim, incidentally, that had motivated Raju to tell his life-story to his listener Velan; or Hari Kunzru's main character in *The Impressionist* (2002), appearing under an array of different names — Pran, Rukhsana, Pretty Bobby, Jonathan, "an eight-anna" — who takes us even further by creating a multiple identity for himself.[39] And to add: these characters are made to live in a fictitious world where the realistic narrative mode does not 'rule supreme', on the contrary: magic realism, fantasy writing or science fiction have made inroads as narrative strategies that underpin the post-modern constructedness of these narratives as well as they direct our attention to many writers' agnostic attitudes. Epistemologically, *The Guide* has not exactly 'shown the way', but behind the author's back the novel has indicated the direction into which a substantial number of Indian novels in English would move in the future. Indeed, the first sentence of a fictitious story Narayan supposedly had written down a long time ago, "The train had just arrived at Malgudi", could be complemented by Railway Raju, voice over: "and has since moved on to new destinations."

Works cited

Novels

CHATTERJEE, Upamanyu, *English, August*, London: Faber & Faber 1988
DESANI, G.V., *All about H Hatterr — a gesture*, London: The Saturn Press 1949
GHOSH, Amitav, *The Circle of Reason*, London: Hamish Hamilton 1986
GUPTA, Sunetra, *The Glassblower's Breath*, London: Orion 1993
JOSHI, Ruchir, *The Last Jet-Engine Laugh*, London: Harper Collins 2001
KUNZRU, Hari, *The Impressionist*, London: Hamish Hamilton 2002
NARAYAN, R.K., *The Guide*, Chennai: Indian Thought Publications, 61st reprint 2006
RUSHDIE, Salman, *Midnight's Children*, London: Jonathan Cape 1981

Critical Studies

AMUR, G.S., "A Saint for Malgudi: A New Look at R.K. Narayan's The Guide", ed. M.K. Naik, *Perspectives on Indian Fiction in English*, New Delhi: Abhinav 1985, 49–57
BALBIR SINGH, "Theme of Art and Immortality in R.K. Narayan's *The Guide*", *The Literary Criterion* 25, 2 (1990), 36–46
CHANDAR, K.M., "R.K. Narayan's *The Guide*: A Psychological Study", *The Journal of Indian Writing in English* 12, 1 (1984), 8–13

39 To name a few more protagonists in post-1980s writing who can be added here: Saleem Sinai in *Midnight's Children*; Alu in Amitav Ghosh's *The Circle of Reason*; Agastya in Upamanyu Chatterjee's *English August*; or the anonymous female in Sunetra Gupta's *The Glassblower's Breath*

DALE, James, "The Rootless Intellectual in the Novels of R.K. Narayan", *The University of Windsor Review* 1 (1965), 128–37

DEV, Jai, "The Importance of Being a Child: A Note on Two Details in Narayan's *The Guide*", *The Journal of Indian Writing in English* 15, 2 (1987), 11–15

DIAL, Ram, "The Anima–Animus Interaction in *The Guide*", ed. Atma Ram, *Perspectives on R.K. Narayan*, Ghaziabad: Vimal Prakashan 1981, 168–77

FLUDERNIK, M., "Colonial vs. Cosmopolitan Hybridity: A Comparison of Mulk Raj Anand and R.K. Narayan with Recent British and North American Expatriate Writing", ed. M. Fludernik, *Hybridity and Postcolonialism: Modern Indian Literature*, Tübingen: Stauffenburg 1998, 263–92

GAREBIAN, Keith, "Narayan's Compromise in Comedy", *The Literary Half-Yearly* XVII, 1 (1976), 77–92

GORRA, Michael, "History, Maya, Dharma: The Novels of R.K. Narayan", ed. A.L. McLeod, *R.K. Narayan: Critical Perspectives*, New Delhi: Sterling 1994, 42–52

GOYAL, Bhagwat S., "From Picaro to Pilgrim: A Perspective on R.K. Narayan's *The Guide*", ed. K.K. Sharma, *Indo-English Literature: A Collection of Critical Essays*, Ghaziabad: Vimal Prakashan 1977, 141–55

HOLMSTROEM, Lakshmi, "Women as Markers of Social Change: *The Dark Room*, *The Guide* and *The Painter of Signs*", ed. C.N. Srinath, *R.K. Narayan: An Anthology of Recent Criticism*, Delhi: Pencraft International 2000, 102–13

IYENGAR, K.R. Srinivasa, "R.K. Narayan", *Indian Writing in English*, Bombay: Asia Publishing House 1962, 273–301

KIRPAL, Viney, "Moksha for Raju: The Archetypal Four-stage Journey", *World Literature Written in English* 28, 2 (1988), 356–63

MATHUR, O.P. "*The Guide*: A Study in Cultural Ambivalence", *The Literary Endeavour* 3, 3–4 (1982), 70–79

MEERA BAI, K., "R.K. Narayan's *The Guide*: From 'Vanaprastha' to 'Sannyasa': A Transition Fraught with Ambiguities", ed. R.K. Dhawan, *Indian Literature Today*, vol. 2: *Poetry and Fiction*, New Delhi: Prestige 1994, 141–46

MISRA, Vijay, "The Dialectic of Maya and the Principles of Narrative Structure in Indian Literature", *ACLALS Bulletin* 5th Ser. 2 (1979), 47–60

NARAYAN SINGH, Raghavendra, "R.K. Narayan: Artist of Uniform Sensibilities", ed. A.L. McLeod, *R.K. Narayan: Critical Perspectives*, New Delhi: Sterling 1994, 147–55

NARASIMHAIAH, C.D. "R.K. Narayan's *The Guide*", *The Literary Criterion* 4, 4 (1961), 63–92

PARAMESWARAN, Uma, "Native Genius: R.K. Narayan", *A Study of Representative Indo-English Novelists*, New Delhi: Vikas 1976, 42–84

—, "Rogues in R.K. Narayan's Fiction", *Literature East & West XVIII* (1974), 203–15

PARANJAPE, Makarand, "The Reluctant Guru: R.K. Narayan and *The Guide*", www.makarand.com [2005]

RAGHAVACHARYULU, D.V.K., "Small-Scale Reflections on a Great House of Fiction: R.K. Narayan's Chronicles of Malgudi", ed. M.K. Naik, *Perspectives on Indian Fiction in English*, New Delhi: Abhinav 1985, 21–48

RAMACHANDRA, R., "Breaking the Borderline: A Note on R.K. Narayan's People", *The Literary Criterion* 29, 2 (1994), 18–24

RANCHAN, S.P. and G.R. Kataria, "Transformation via the Feminine in R.K. Narayan's Krishnan, Raju, and Jagan", *Journal of South Asian Literature* 22, 2 (1987), 5–15

RIEMENSCHNEIDER, Dieter, *The Indian Novel in English: Its Critical Discourse: 1934–2004*, Jaipur: Rawat Publishing 2005

RUBEN, Walter, *Indische Romane: Eine ideologische Untersuchung*, Bd. II & III, Berlin: Akademie-Verlag 1967, Bd.III

SANKARAN, Chitra, "Patterns of Story-telling in R.K. Narayan's *The Guide*", *The Journal of Commonwealth Literature* 26, 1 (1991), 127–50

SHIRWADKAR, Meena, *Image of Woman in the Indo-Anglian Fiction*, New Delhi: Sterling 1979

SINGH, Satyanarain, "*The Guide*: Crisis and Resolution", *Indian Literary Review* 1, 3 (1968), 9–23

SINHA, U.P., *Patterns of Myth and Reality: A Study in R.K. Narayan's Novels*, Delhi: Sandarbh Publishers 1988

SIVARAMKRISHNA, M., "The Cave and the Temple: Structural Symbolism in *The Guide*", *Osmania Journal of English Studies* 14, 1 (1978), 71–79

SPIVAK, Gayatri Chakravorti, "How to Teach a 'Culturally Different' Book", ed. Donna Landry and Gerald MacLean, *The Spivak Reader*, New York/London: Routledge 1996, 237–66

SWINDON, Patrick, "Hindu Mythology in R.K. Narayan's *The Guide*", *The Journal of Commonwealth Literature* 34, 1 (1999), 65–83

VANDEN DRIESEN, Cynthia, "From Rogue to Redeemer: R.K. Narayan's *The Guide*", *International Fiction Review* 6 (1979), 166–70

VENKATACHARI, K., "R.K. Narayan's Novels: Acceptance of Life", *Osmania Journal of English Studies* 7, 1 (1969), 51–65

WALSH, William, "The Intricate Alliance: The Novels of R.K. Narayan", *Review of English Literature* 2, 4 (1961), 91–99

Glocality and its (Dis)contents

The Future of English Language Literatures Studies[1]

Abstract

The following reflections on the future of English Language Literatures (ELL) as an academic discipline in the Humanities in the 21st century are directed at two aspects. First, the role they can play as texts of a glocal nature challenging the tendency of an increasingly globalized world to subsume academic research and teaching in tertiary institutions to such economic parameters as competition, efficiency and profitability. Second, the possible function of ELL within an institutionalized transnational network to be set up in future and to challenge both, the homogenizing cultural and educational agendas of transglobal corporates and trends towards nationalist reductionism. An analysis of the interplay of global and local cultural forces that have led to investigations into their hybridization or glocalization undertaken in cultural and social studies is followed by comments on constitutive differences between English Literature (EL) and ELL. The paper is rounded off with a discussion of the glocal nature of Shashi Tharoor's novel Riot as representative of recent ELL texts and their contribution to what Ulrich Beck has called a "cognitive map."

Global Challenges and English Literary Studies

WHAT CHALLENGES WILL THE HUMANITIES have to face in the process of global changes? And by challenges I mean questions raised as to their

1 The title of my paper refers back to Joseph E. Stiglitz's *Globalization and Its Discontents*, New York & London: W.W. Norton 2003, but plays with the double meaning of 'contents' and its relationship to 'glocalization'

content, their organization and their goals vis-à-vis the globalization process that has begun to encompass and affect all spheres of human activities, their economic and fiscal transactions, political rule and social organization but also mankind's cultural activities, and along with them, those processes of self-reflexivity that constitute modernity and the content of the scholarly disciplines of the Humanities. What is at stake here is the ongoing and above all renewed pursuit of our interpretation and of making sense of what Max Weber has called the "double constitution [or composition] of reality": its social, economic, political and cultural conditions on the one hand, and their interpretation on the other, through which we create "images of the world" that guide our actions, "crystallizations of religious and cultural ideas that claim to interpret the world adequately and regulate man's behaviour on the basis of norms and values."[2]

Now, it would be presumptuous to address myself to the large field of the Humanities in their totality as I am neither an expert in most of its disciplines nor would I venture to reflect here on their future from the more generalized angle of cultural or social history. Rather, I would like to focus on literature and literary studies, or more precisely, on the literatures in English and their academic-institutional organization in the university. To rephrase my question then and to apply a more compact though not necessarily unequivocal term, I want to ask <u>what</u> English literary studies are meant to encompass. <u>How</u> should they be organized, and what <u>objectives</u> are they to pursue and possibly to achieve in the future?

Further and for obvious reasons, my observations will be restricted to the German university scene of the last quarter of the last century with its more or less radical changes of gradually substituting an open and flexible four-year course system and affecting the near total independence of professors as scholars and teachers under the heading of 'university reforms'. It is the perhaps third or fourth agenda drawn up since the early 1970s and after the student revolt against ossified academic structures, but it appears that this time the agency of 'reform' will have to be taken very seriously when compared with past attempts that by hindsight have, with the exception of the early 1970s effected cosmetic rather than radical changes. At the same time, the process of dealing with the proposed measures has certainly always been very time- and energy consuming and more often than not has had negative repercussions on the quality of research and teaching of those academics who had felt that they had to critically co-operate with

2 Hans-Ulrich Wehler, *Konflikte zu Beginn des 21. Jahrhunderts*, München: C.H. Beck 2003, 144

the state and university administration in order to maintain their identity and not be overruled by technocratic concerns. Yet, such engagement, it appears, is even more necessary at present because of the much more far-reaching consequences the proposed reform measures will have under the pressure of globalization with its guiding 'values' of economic growth and profit-orientation, national and international competitiveness and ranking; the latter having itself established as a kind of university world cup fought out not at an interval of four years but continuously, alas, without a set of generally agreed-upon rules. This indeed casts doubts on the meaningfulness and sense of the various ranking systems employed.

University scholars and teachers in virtually all disciplines ranging from Economics to Social Studies and the Humanities have been alerted to address globalization and have set out to analyse its agents, to assess its working and, quite generally, to make transparent a process that has been called inevitable while concomitantly it has begun to affect every human being in one way or the other. Among them Masao Miyoshi, Professor of Comparative Literature at the University of California in San Diego, may be cited here with his assessment of the changes introduced into the Humanities departments of his and other American universities. In his essay "'Globalization', Culture and the University", he draws on his own and his colleagues' experiences and argues that the state has lost power to transnational corporations who have begun to determine university politics. From their point of view, cultural productions are profitable commodities to be marketed, and it is the task of the university to transform their academic programmes accordingly. To serve their purposes, parameters to be introduced, like course enrolment, student-teacher ratio or the number of majors in a department, are to be geared towards a system of ranking which in turn establishes the reputation of a university and the value of its products in a national and international competitive market. Excellence, Miyoshi, says, is to be achieved for the sake of excellence, and professors who once presumably "professed [...] are now merely professionals, entrepreneurs, careerists, and opportunists, as in the corporate world."[3]

It is a bleak picture he paints. However, I believe it does not describe the situation universities generally find themselves in already, but it certainly

3 Masao Miyoshi, "'Globalization', Culture, and the University", eds. Frederic Jameson and Masao Miyoshi, *The Cultures of Globalization*, Durham & London: Duke University Press 1998, 247–270; here 267. See also Miyoshi's essay "Ivory Tower in Escrow", eds. Masao Miyoshi and H.D. Harootunian, *Learning Places: The Afterlives of Area Studies*, London and Durham: Duke UP 2002, 19–60

highlights the pressure exerted on them by the prevailing ideology of market economy pursued by transnational corporations. The question then is how can English literary studies resist or redirect and usefully transform this pressure — unless we totally subscribe to it. And such is the trend, unfortunately, experienced by Miyoshi and, I am sure quite a few among us. Can we create a forum that evades the danger of our departments being turned into service stations functioning under industrial management? How can we safeguard, to once more quote Miyoshi, research independent from industrial needs?

Global / Local and Glocalization

I think that we have to look for answers by first understanding one of Weber's "images of the world," that is "nationalism," and here more precisely, nationalism in its present global context. Talking about "Nationalismus und der Nationalstaat heute" ("Nationalism and the Nation State Today)," the German historian Hans-Ulrich Wehler[4] refers to its creative power that has brought about the nation, which in turn has found its 'housing' in the nation state. Though nationalism, he says, has led — and we could very well add here, continues to lead — to devastating 'achievements,' it has nevertheless proved flexible and has indeed survived. The nation state, on the other hand, has come under serious attack by global processes of transformation[5] that have led towards the emergence and gradual formation of, for example, new economic regions in South East Asia or on the North American continent, and to an economic-political supranational structure like the European Union.

Of prime importance for us here are the cultural implications of such new supra-national formations because to be able to function politically they necessarily have to accommodate the diversity of different national cultures whose discrete images of themselves, grown over a long period

4 Wehler, "Nationalismus und der Nationalstaat heute", *op.cit.*, 112–125

5 There are, of course, two camps: those who believe that the nation state will survive and who point at the emergence of new states after the end of the cold war, and their opponents who are convinced that it is unable to survive under the onslaught of globalization. Michael Hart and Antonio Negri (*Empire*, Cambridge, Mass: Harvard University Press 2001) represent this latter group but hold that the nation state will not survive in its old form [my emphasis] as a juridico-economic structure. They argue that, "the globalization of production and circulation, supported by this supranational juridical scaffolding [e.g., GATT, WTO, IMF, World Bank] supersedes the effectiveness of national juridical structures." (336) On the other hand, Edgar Grande ("Globalisierung und die Zukunft des Nationalstaat", eds. Ulrich Beck und Wolfgang Bonß, *Die Modernisierung der Moderne*, Frankfurt: Suhrkamp 2001, 261-275), joins those who believe in a 'middle path', the possibility of a combination of nation states and transnational collectives co-operating to solve globalization pressure, especially in its economic dimension.

of time and deeply ingrained in the psyche of their people, are resilient and continue to define their respective national identities or 'images of the world.' No supra-political unit, no European Union will be able — at least for a long time to come — to abolish, either through democratic or autocratic means, a German, an Italian, a Frenchman or an Englishman's rootedness in his own national culture. And that is to say that nationalism perceived of as a cultural construct will indeed have to be reckoned with now and in future when we address the problematic of our own scholarly discipline.

However, to return to the nation state, the gradual loss of its sovereignty vested in its prerogatives of managing its own affairs that range from politics, economy and finance to education may go hand in hand with its increasing and eventually total submission to the laws of the global market economy and its regulations, thus leaving little chance for the survival of diverse national cultures. Are there then no prospects of survival? Thus, investigations in cultural studies have given no reason for Miyoshi's pessimism while we find ourselves indeed and objectively in a position to redefine our tasks. However, we have to remind ourselves of two points. We must distinguish between what a national culture can achieve, qualitatively speaking, by handling the impact of globalization, and how national and supra-national agents of its institutionalization will react. And we must not overlook that as scholars and teachers we are part of the system, tied down by the administrative and fiscal set-up of the university. Where then do our chances lie of constructively responding to globalization?

Cultural studies and cultural practice prove that neither an 'emptying out' of the local occurs, a 'dissolution of cultural identities,' nor a total submission to the 'one world of commodities.' Rather, we observe processes of hybridization or creolization "with respect to cultural forms as 'the ways in which forms become separated from existing practices and recombine with new forms in new practices.'"[6] With reference to Roland Robertson[7] I prefer to use the term 'glocalization' instead of creolization because it points at the interplay of <u>global</u> and <u>local</u> factors in an emergent global society[8] and indicates that combined processes of globalization and localization occur, lending new emphasis to the local, which however is

6 Jan Nederveen Pieterse, "Globalization as Hybridization", eds. Mike Featherstone, Scott Lash and Roland Robertson, *Global Modernities*, London: SAGE 1995, 45–68. Quoted in Dieter Riemenschneider, "Contemporary Māori Cultural Practice: From Biculturalism towards a Glocal Culture", *Journal of New Zealand Literature* 18/19 (2001), 139–160

7 Roland Robertson, "Glocalization: Time-Space and Homogeneity-Heterogeneity", eds. Featherstone, Lash, Robertson, *op.cit.*, 25–44

8 Claus Leggewie, *Die Globalisierung und ihre Gegner*, München: C.H. Beck 2003

not identical with its renaissance. Glocalization, in other words, manifests a compulsion to re-localize de-traditionalized traditions within the global context through translocal exchanges, through dialogue and even through conflicts, as Ulrich Beck suggests in his summary of Robertson's position.[9]

Apart from Robertson, I'd also like to mention Arjun Appadurai (1990), Arif Dirlik (1996), Stuart Hall (1991) or Ulf Hannerz (1996) and their contributions to the discourse on glocalization that have influenced my own critical engagement with contemporary Māori cultural practice from Aotearoa / New Zealand, that is, my more recent work on poetry, drama and the novel, painting and film: research revealing the glocal dimension of 'texts' whose specificity results precisely from the creative response of the local to the global with both being embedded in the process of globalization.[10] This entails though the need to look more closely at the exact meaning of 'local', 'global' and 'glocal'. The first, 'local', I think, can be grasped quite easily when we remind ourselves of, for example, handed-down traditional Māori beliefs, customs, rituals and quite generally, cultural and literary practices. 'Global', on the other hand, is a much more diffuse term because in its most generalized form it includes any idea, any human practice introduced from the outside world into a culture that is primarily perceived in local terms. My use here is restricted to signifying cultural ideas and forms practiced elsewhere outside the realm of the Māori locality, although eventually I cannot circumscribe it in its entirety — at least not here and now. As to the 'glocal' nature of cultural products, it is necessary to keep in mind differing local cultural specificities. In other words, the glocality of contemporary Māori poems in Robert Sullivan's Star *Waka* (1999) differs from, let us say, the Caribbean Derek Walcott's *Omeros* (1990) because of their discrete local references and contextuality.

9 Ulrich Beck, *Was ist Globalisierung?* , Frankfurt: Suhrkamp 1998, 85–87. See also Thomas L. Friedman's proposal of "multiple filters to prevent [...] cultures from being erased by the homogenizing pull and push of global capitalism." (Friedman, *The Lexus and the Olive Tree*, New York: Random House, Anchor Book Edition 2000; ed. 2003, 204). Talking about the most important filter, the ability to "glocalize", that is, absorbing influences that "naturally fit into [a culture and to] resist those things that are truly alien," (295) I feel that Friedman's argument is too narrowly tied into a binary opposition between global and local, or in his own words "a culture and other strong cultures", the one and the alien that encounter each other.

10 For example, "Of Warriors, a Whale Rider, and Venetians: Contemporary Māori Films", eds. Anke Bartels and Dirk Wiemann, *Global Fragments: (Dis)-Orientation in the New World Order*, Amsterdam/New York, NY: Rodopi 2007, 139–151

English Literature and English Language Literatures

After these brief and indeed very general comments on the complex network of globalization and national transformation, national culture and cultural glocalization, I would like to look at its implications and its bearing on our own engagement as scholars and teachers of English literature — or to be more correct, of English literatures in their plurality since we cannot really speak any longer of one unified, let alone monolithic corpus of English literature but only of a multiplicity of English language literatures in a world-wide modern context. This does not, of course, mean to be blind to a literary tradition from England that has preceded the emergence of English language literatures on almost every continent, but it compels us, to begin with, to distinguish among different cultural traditions from which they have emerged and to whose formations they continue to contribute. The essential difference between the one — I would like to call EL — and the others — ELL — I believe, lies in their differing degrees of glocalization. English literature (EL), embedded in a local-national culture that has been challenged more basically only after the arrival of millions of immigrants to Britain since the mid-20th century and by their literary production, has only recently begun to develop towards a glocal literature. English language literatures (ELL), on the other hand, have by their very foundation as colonial literatures been shaped by specific localities. In the case of the so-called settler colonies/cultures of Australia, Canada or New Zealand these included initially mainly the physical factors of new geographical surroundings combined with the experience of otherness and migration. With African or Asian writing, on the other hand, specific historically grown cultural contexts accounted for distinct differences to EL right from the beginning. Here, incidentally, I would go further than postcolonial theorizing has suggested, by not perceiving of these literatures as postcolonial since such conceptualisation reduces the multiple cultural interplay between the local and the global to a dialectic and primarily politically-engendered exchange between colonizer and colonized, centre and margin. It may be true that in their initial stages English language literatures conformed more clearly to the postcolonial paradigm but at their latest stages and with the appearance of globalizing processes their distinctive features as 'glocal' can no longer be overlooked.

If these methodological considerations are tenable, objectives and methods of researching and teaching English language literatures as glocal texts will have to differ to some extent from those of English literature — excepting perhaps, as indicated, its latest phase. Although one can of course argue that cultural products have always been hybrid and, as Claus Leggewie reasons, "the emergence of a global culture is just another grade of 'hybridization' of in any case 'hybrid' cultures,"[11] I disagree because the grade of hybridization is not just a matter of form but one of content, as a randomly chosen example will illustrate. Arnold Wesker's *Trilogy* (1960) certainly incorporates global features such as the resistance to fascism, a critical engagement with international Marxism and a concern with global solidarity against capitalism, but the cultural conflict Wesker's figures experience is an aesthetically conceived representation of internal (English) social differentiation rather than one perceived as a clash of the local and the global. On the other hand, Witi Ihimaera, the Māori playwright's *Woman Far Walking* (2000) clearly dramatizes this juxtaposition by drawing together Māori historical-psychological experiences — their colonization — and modern self-reflexivity derived from globally practiced thinking on history and nation-building on the one hand and psychology on the other.[12] Similarly and as to its dramatic form, *The Wesker Trilogy* is firmly rooted in contemporaneous European (or Western) naturalist-realist conventions whereas *Woman Far Walking* incorporates features derived from Māori dramatic acting on the *marae*, music and dancing, as well as dramatic and dramaturgical devices from the globally practiced art of epic theatre. Ihimaera's colleague Roma Potiki's plea that "Māori theatre must deal honestly with what has happened and is happening to Māori people — the joy and the hell that we, as survivors of the damage of colonialism, have learnt to live with and live through," but that it should also realize that "it is not a rigid form [because] Māori are living within a social context that is global,"[13] illustrates the modern self-reflexivity I have spoken of.

This example must suffice to demonstrate the basic constitutive differences between EL and ELL that have to be taken into consideration in our pursuit of English Literary Studies. While the former has been much more concerned with the aesthetic representation of an imagined national community — incidentally also pursued in Australian, Canadian and New Zealand creative writing from the middle of the 20th century onwards — ELLs' concerns, for example in Anglophone African, Caribbean or Indian

11 Leggewie, *op.cit.*, 41

12 For details refer to my "Māori Contemporary Theatre — Witi Ihimaera: *Woman Far Walking* (2000)", eds. Hans-Ulrich Mohr and Kerstin Mächler, *Extending the Code: New Forms of Dramatic and Theatrical Expression*, Trier: Wissenschaftlicher Verlag 2004, 211–223

13 Roma Potiki, "Confirming Identity and Telling the Stories: A Woman's Perspective on Māori Theatre", eds. Rosemary Du Plessis, Phillida Bunkle, *Feminist Voices: Women's Studies Texts for Aotearoa / New Zealand*, Auckland: Oxford University Press 1992, 153–162; here 162

English literature, have circled more around their hyphenated cultural nature and status.

Contextual Universalism: Shashi Tharoor's Novel "Riot"

Let me focus now on the potential contributions of English Language Literatures towards a study programme and research projects that could shape teaching and scholarly pursuits on a global scale, relating university departments across national boundaries to a sort of supra-national or transcultural educational unit that reflects the general political trend towards such structures as mentioned above, that may assist us in understanding transcultural conflicts and contribute towards setting up programmes of global studies to come to grips with the multidimensionality of glocal life and actions.[14] Naturally, I do not want to be misunderstood here as a utopian dreamer who conveniently and for argument's sake effaces the powerful efficacy of globalism as the neo-liberal ideology of market dominance. Yet I believe that the glocal nature of English Language Literatures offers us one referential frame to understand how globalism works and could be responded to by opening windows for intercultural communication and co-operation with the final aim of creating a cognitive map that will lead us to a global civil society.[15]

Ulrich Beck's model of "intercultural critique"[16] might be helpful here. Commenting upon the two mutually exclusive epistemological camps of the universalists and the contextualists (or relativists), he proposes "contextual universalism" as an epistemological foundation from where we can set out, first to inquire into the 'truth' of one's own culture, setting up individual norms valid only for ourselves, but secondly, allows to be critiqued by others: "Contextual universalism means", he says, "[that] one has to open up what one holds holiest to the critique of others", which philosophically, morally and politically is a step taken from certainty to truth on the terrain of universalisms.[17]

14 Beck, *op.cit.*, 1998, 231

15 Wehler, *op.cit.*, 80–89

16 Beck, *op.cit.*, 1998, 141–149

17 Ibid., 149. Beck rejects both 'universalist universalism' and 'universal contextualism', because they claim universal validity either of perceived norms and 'truths' or of their absolute relativity. 'Contextual universalism' on the other hand, is based on the assumption that non-interference with another culture is impossible. To quote an example: "contextual universalism" does not prevent us from accepting the violation of human rights in a culture different from ours but it is wary of super-imposing our version of these rights. Instead it asks us to understand those rights as they are perceived from the angle of the other culture and then enter into a dialogue about how to realize the validity of human rights per se." (148)

The random sample of an Indian English novel wonderfully illustrates this model and shows how an ELL text disturbingly intervenes in the kind of global discourse on culture exemplified by Samuel Huntington's untenable thesis of an 'intercultural war' in his controversial book *The Clash of Civilizations and the Remaking of World Order* (1996). While he — and he is not alone, of course — conceives of cultures as essentialist units, bound to a definite territory and being the result of local processes of learning, with each group, society or nation having its own and differing culture that has neither changed over the centuries nor is it going to do so, I identify with a concept of culture as a dynamic, open-border, translocal process of learning that, incidentally, by no means is lacking in internal contradictions.[18]

Shashi Tharoor's novel *Riot* (2001) thematizes the political development in India since the early 1990s with its broadly advertised trend of the BJP and other right-wing parties and movements towards purifying the country's culture of 'foreign' elements in order to establish *Hindutva* or *Ram Raj*: the supreme rule of Hinduism in all spheres of life — from which, as I was told, education at all levels has not been exempted, as the re-writing of text books or the re-organization of courses testify. Tharoor's story centres on such attempts in connection with the rebuilding of the Ram Mandir in Ayodhya after the destruction of the Babri Masjid built by the Moghuls on the supposed site of Ram's birth. In the town of Zalilgarh Hindus agitate for the collection of tiles to contribute to this religious task. Yet their efforts to enforce, even by violent means, the truth of their religious convictions are not only controlled and kept in check by the local District Commissioner and the police but are subtly questioned in a parallel narrative strand. Here, a young American woman is engaged with field work studying Indian women's self-help groups and actively supports the policy of birth control, much against the resistance of men who consider her activities as interfering with their culture. The connecting link between the chain of public events and her personal narrative, namely the extra-marital relationship between her and the D.C., interests us only marginally here though its failure attracts some attention to culturally differing perceptions of the man-woman relationship. However, this aspect so central in the earlier Indian English novel beset by the cultural problematic of the East-West encounter, for example in Raja Rao's *The Serpent and the Rope* (1960) or Balachandra Rajan's *The Dark Dancer* (1958), has been replaced in *Riot* by interrogating the definition of culture as such.

18 See Dieter Senghaas , *Zivilisierung wider Willen*, Frankfurt: Suhrkamp 1998, 140; Beck, *op.cit.*, 1998, 118

Remarkable here is its very thematic and narrative foregrounding. The story is not told by a first person narrator as in Rao's novel or through the consciousness of Rajan's protagonist but constructed from a number of different perspectives like letters and diary entries, newspaper reports and interviews, political speeches, memories and reflections and finally, through realistically presented scenic action and dialogue from the narrator's point of view. Such a range of different versions of the events does not permit us to gain insight into what really happened in the town or to the main actors but conceals the truth that lies hidden in the web of public and personal views and convictions conveyed to the reader. We are not told why the American woman is murdered and by whom. Nor whether the establishment of *Hindutva*, to which a specific understanding of the man-woman relationship as well as the rejection of birth control measures are intimately linked, finds the support of all sections of the Hindu population, including its intellectual elite and, last but not least, of the narrator himself. Or finally, whether globally promoted ideas of the equality of men and women, of birth control and the establishment of NGOs like women's self-help groups represent <u>the</u> truth. What *Riot* however achieves is to convey its textual glocality both in content and form, the one by bringing together local and global views and convictions that demonstrate that the exegesis of cultural sources is not so much motivated by their defenders' belief in their 'truth' but by considerations of power politics. Formally, the novel's multi-perspectivism relates it to one of the globally practiced post-modern narrative strategies that *ipso facto* negates the truth claim of the 'grand récit', replacing it by fragmentary narrations with their provisional claims of the truth. Nonetheless, I would not equate the uncertainty of truth in Tharoor's novel with postmodernism's radical scepticism but would relate it to Beck's notion of "universal contextualism", that is to say, to the text's invitation to the reader to intervene in the discourse on globalism by acknowledging the glocality of culture.

The Challenge of English Language Literatures

If this and other examples of English Language Literatures then permit us to speak of their glocality, which in turn offers us the possibility of restructuring our literary studies, two questions remain to be answered. Which role would English literature *qua* national literature play here? And will agencies of globalism with their threat of economic control and cultural homogenization not feel called upon to counteract a discursive practice and its possible institutionalization that threatens to subvert its own strategies?

My own experience has not given me reason to believe that the introduction of ELL studies has threatened the existence of EL studies at all — nor has it, regrettably, proved relevant to the methodological discourse on literary studies. One of the reasons for this is to be found in the traditional framework of academic independence that grants an appointed and tenured professor near total freedom of research and teaching that has served my purpose of introducing and establishing ELL studies and besides has encouraged me to support similar efforts at other German universities. After a quarter of a century the co-operation of colleagues has resulted in creating a national network of ELL study programmes whose degree of institutionalization naturally differs from one university to the other, but it functions and has certainly also survived because it has never threatened EL studies 'proper' by questioning its role.[19] It is perhaps needless to add that I would have wished EL studies to reflect on its research and teaching objectives and to perhaps co-operate with ELL studies by developing strategies of dealing with globalism. Yet, apart from a few instances of personal commitment this has not been the case.

The need to do so, however, may soon become more pressing when German state and university education policy will more clearly join the march begun already elsewhere, for example in New Zealand where I notice a high degree of delight on the part of university vice-chancellors and quite a few heads of departments to be ranked highly in the national competition for academic gold medals, hopefully in all disciplines. Needless to say that not each and every academic, for example at Auckland University, has joined the choir of jubilation sung recently on the pages of the university's official organ, *News*, and celebrating that the university has "emerged as the country's leading research university on 'virtually any measure' in the Performance Based Research Fund assessment."[20] Here, it would be necessary to go into details of research projects to assess on what grounds excellence has been acknowledged and financially rewarded, apart from also analyzing those parameters of assessment that have formed the basis for national comparison. In this context it strikes one as somewhat paradoxical that New Zealand's vice-chancellors objected to the Tertiary Education Commission's original plan of comparatively assessing New Zealand and British universities as being untenable since differing systems

19 One should also mention the various learned societies that have been set up in the wake of ELL studies, for example the German Association for the Study of the New Literatures (ASNEL) founded in 1989, or the international Association for Commonwealth Literature and Language Studies (ACLALS), founded as early as in 1964

20 *The University of Auckland News* 34, 4 (May 2004), 3

would be confined on the Procrustean bed. Still, whatever opposition generally as well as under specific circumstances may exist among academics concerned, their voices are neither heard nor listened to or they have fallen silent for whatever reasons.

The assessment fever, as we all know, has spread like the Spanish influenza and has also infected German academics who fight it by inoculating themselves, or by filling in questionnaires and submitting reports on their research and teaching activities that are to be assessed and graded by outsiders. It appears that there is no way out for the education sector to counter market requirements but submit itself to its objectives and regulations. An enforced choice compounded by the response of national and supra-national corporations to a survey that chances to find a job are small for graduates in the Humanities. According to the weekly *Der Spiegel*, 63% of them replied that they would not employ German and Romance literature or history graduates. English literature graduates, one would assume, would fare slightly better because of their language qualifications. A market requirement that has already led towards a split between cultural and literary studies programmes and language teaching in the university and even to the departmentalization of language studies in separate language schools.

Where do we go from here then, short of resigning ourselves to a global trend of serving the research needs of the industry or, alternatively, of constructing more or less utopian models of survival? Suggestions offered in English and German publications on globalization and its educational implications I have consulted have either — and perhaps out of sheer necessity — restricted themselves to a description of the *status quo* or suggested measures that would require governments to rethink their policy. Ulrich Beck devotes the last part of his book *Was ist Globalisierung?* [*What is Globalization?*] to "Antworten auf Globalisierung" ["Responses to Globalization"][21] where he briefly discusses such counter measures as international co-operation, the transnational state, the new orientation of education policy, new cultural-political-economic objectives, a social contract against exclusion and Europe. Though all of them bear the mark of self-reflexivity and are grounded in a realistic assessment of present-day economic, political and cultural conditions, they do not, and indeed cannot go beyond expressing desiderata, hopes, expectations and suggestions clothed in the grammatical garment of the subjunctive mode. Nor do Hans-Ulrich Wehler's sceptical remarks, expressed in the indicative mode,

21 Beck, *op.cit.*, 1998, 217–268

that the nation state is incapable of dealing with globalization, multinational corporations and war lords in dissolving states, refrain from eventually also using the subjunctive mode when he pleads that "the power bearers of globalization should be subjected to an internationally valid system of rules that would [my emphasis] legally control and expropriate arbitrarily appropriated rights."[22] And whether Michael Hardt and Antonio Negri's conclusion in their voluminous and ambitious study *Empire* (2001) is more than wishful thinking that the multitude must organize itself, act politically and confront the repressive operations of the Empire, remains an open question. It is difficult though to imagine that the multitude becomes an active political subject even under such favourable global conditions as the complete deterritorialization of communication, of education and culture and in spite of, as the authors maintain, this 'new proletariat' having already begun to articulate itself through NGOs. In the end both writers are forced to admit, "[t]he only event that we are still awaiting is the construction, or rather the insurgence, of a powerful organization," and to concede, "we do not have any models to offer for this event. Only the multitude through its practical experimentation will offer models and determine when and how the possible becomes real."[23]

As far as the future of ELL studies goes as a discipline of the Humanities, I believe that the project outlined above deserves serious attention because it will help in setting up the cognitive map Ulrich Beck envisages. Institutionalized within a framework of transnationally co-operating departments, it will create possibilities of challenging political and cultural practices, both of narrowly conceived national, if not to say nationalist culture studies and of globally promoted homogenizing trends of an economically determined and defined education policy: by foregrounding the increasing glocalization of societies and cultures and the concomitant need for people to obtain full rights of citizenship.[24]

Works cited

Creative Writing

IHIMAERA, Witi, *Woman Far Walking*, Wellington: Huia 2000

RAJAN, Balachandra, *The Dark Dancer*, New York: Simon and Schuster 1958

RAO, Raja, *The Serpent and the Rope*, London: John Murray 1960

SULLIVAN, Robert, *Star Waka*, Auckland: Auckland University Press 1999

THAROOR, Shashi, *Riot*, New Delhi: Viking 2001

22 Wehler, *op.cit.*, 197

23 Hardt/Negri, *op.cit.*, 411

24 Ibid., 400

WALCOTT, Derek, *Omeros*, London: Faber & Faber 1990
WESKER, Arnold, *The Wesker Trilogy*, London: Jonathan Cape 1960

Critical Studies

APPADURAI, Arjun, "Disjuncture and Difference in the Global Cultural Economy", *Public Culture* 2, 2 (1990), 1–24
BECK, Ulrich, *Was ist Globalisierung?* Frankfurt: Suhrkamp 1998
DIRLIK, Arif, "The Global in the Local", eds. Rob Wilson and Wimal Dissanayake, *Global/Local: Cultural Production and the Transnational Imaginary*, Durham & London: Duke University Press 1996, 21–45
FRIEDMAN, Thomas L., *The Lexus and the Olive Tree*, New York: Random House, Anchor Book Edition 2000
GRANDE, Edgar, "Globalisierung und die Zukunft des Nationalstaats", eds. Ulrich Beck und Wolfgang Bonß, *Die Modernisierung der Moderne*, Frankfurt: Suhrkamp 2001, 261–275
HALL, Stuart, "1. The Local and the Global: Globalization and Ethnicity", ed. Anthony D. King, *Culture, Globalization and the World-System*, Houndmills and London: Macmillan Education 1991, 19–39
HANNERZ, Ulf, *Transnational Connections: Culture, People, Places*, London: Routledge 1996
HARDT, Michael and Antonio Negri, *Empire*, Cambridge, Mass: Harvard University Press 2001
HUNTINGTON, Samuel, *The Clash of Civilizations and the Remaking of World Order*, New York: Simon & Schuster 1996
LEGGEWIE, Claus, *Die Globalisierung und ihre Gegner*, München: C.H. Beck 2003
MENZEL, Ulrich, *Globalisierung versus Fragmentierung*, Frankfurt: Suhrkamp 1998
MIYOSHI, Masao, "'Globalization', Culture, and the University," eds. Frederic Jameson and Masao Miyoshi, *The Cultures of Globalization*, Durham & London: Duke University Press 1998, 247–270
—, "Ivory Tower in Escrow", eds. Masao Miyoshi and H.D. Harootunian, *Learning Places: The Afterlives of Area Studies*, London and Durham: Duke UP 2002, 19–60
PIETERSE, Jan Nederveen, "Globalization as Hybridization", eds. Mike Featherstone, Scott Lash and Roland Robertson, *Global Modernities*, London: SAGE 1995 45–68
POTIKI, Roma, "Confirming Identity and Telling the Stories: A Woman's Perspective on Māori Theatre", eds. Rosemary Du Plessis, Phillida Bunkle, *Feminist Voices: Women's Studies Texts for Aotearoa / New Zealand*. Auckland: Oxford University Press 1992, 153–162
RIEMENSCHNEIDER, Dieter, "Contemporary Māori Cultural Practice: From Biculturalism towards a Glocal Culture", *Journal of New Zealand Literature* 18/19 (2000/1), 139–160. (A slightly different version in: eds. Dieter Kastovsky, Günther Kaltenböck, Susanne Reichl, *Anglistentag 2001 Wien: Proceedings*, Trier: Wissenschaftlicher Verlag 2002, 133–146)
—, "Māori Contemporary Theatre: Witi Ihimaera, *Woman Far Walking* (2000)", eds. Hans-Ulrich Mohr and Kerstin Mächler, *Extending the Code: New Forms of Dramatic and Theatrical Expression*, Trier: Wissenschaftlicher Verlag 2004, 211–223
—, "Of Warriors, a Whale Rider and Venetians: Contemporary Māori Films", eds. Anke Bartels and Dirk Wiemann, *Global Fragments: Dis-Orientation in the New World Order*, Amsterdam/Atlanta: Rodopi 2007, 139–151
ROBERTSON, Roland, "Glocalization: Time-Space and Homogeneity-Heterogeneity", eds. Mike Featherstone, Scott Lash and Roland Robertson, *Global Modernities*, London: SAGE 1995, 25–44
SENGHAAS, Dieter, *Zivilisierung wider Willen*, Frankfurt: Suhrkamp 1998
STIGLITZ, Joseph E., *Globalization and Its Discontents*, New York & London: W.W. Norton 2003
WEHLER, Hans-Ulrich, *Konflikte zu Beginn des 21. Jahrhunderts*, München: C.H. Beck 2003

The Persistence and Creation of Internal Borders

India in Aotearoa New Zealand

> *A more cautious view is that stereotypes, whether specially directed at Chinese and Indians, or more generally at Asians, still persist within contemporary New Zealand [...] These may not be the insulting caricatures of the earlier Hindoo or Chinaman, but continued resistance remains in some quarters to New Zealand's localized Asian identity.*[1]

> *People might have their own very different and complex ideas about nation and nationalism, about language and religion, about 'identity' and cultural meanings or symbols, and about their personal relationships to all these categories. This is what public discourse and certain kinds of diaspora studies overlook or sideline, and what a new kind of scholarship is attempting to retrieve or recuperate.*[2]

These two quotations chosen from recently published studies on Indians and Asians in Aotearoa New Zealand point at two major issues that

1 Manying Ip and Jacqueline Leckie, "'Chinamen' and 'Hindoos': Beyond stereotypes to Kiwi Asians", eds. Paola Voci & Jacqueline Leckie, *Localizing Asia in Aotearoa*, Wellington: Dunmore Publishing 2011, 159–186, here 183

2 Martin Fuchs, Antje Linkenbach, Aditya Malik, "What does it mean to be Indian? A View from Christchurch", ed. Sekhar Bandyopadhyay, *India in New Zealand: Local Identities, Global Relations*, Dunedin: Otago University Press 2010, 81–106; here 105

I want to address in this paper though I will concentrate on the latter. These are the perception of immigrants as the 'other' of a nation's understanding of its own culture, and the immigrant people's self-perception of their identity — as individuals and as members of a community. Both are not necessarily grounded in the "race relations paradigm" discussed by Stuart Hall or Homi Bhabha[3] but in ethnic, geographic, religious, linguistic, gender and generational relations, as will be demonstrated in the course of this paper. At the same time, to speak of 'vanishing borders' in spite of the noticeably increased mobility of Indians in the 'Age of Globalism', appears misleading because a strong tendency prevails of maintaining if not drawing 'internal' border lines between and among Indian settlers in New Zealand. Following a brief historically oriented introduction meant to point out when and how perceptions of one's group identity have evolved over a period of nearly a century of migration and settlement, my paper will focus on the present situation — and on self-perceptions — of Indian settlers in Aotearoa New Zealand. That is, I am less concerned with the critical discourse on migration as addressed by, among others, Robert Cohen (1997), Douglas S. Massey et al (1998), Stephen Castles and Mark Miller (1998) or Adrian Favell (2007)[4] than with the nature of a specific diaspora as a discursive, empirical and aesthetic figure.

India in New Zealand: Local Identities, Global Relations, a collection of a dozen essays edited by Sekhar Bandhopadhyay, contains a wide-ranging bibliography,[5] which however includes references to merely three books, a small number of essays and a few unpublished papers as well as B.A. and M.A. theses written before the mid-1990s on Indians in New Zealand. They are either of an introductory nature or pay attention to single ethnic or religious groups, for example Gujaratis, Punjabis and Muslims, or to regional Indian settlements, e.g. in Christchurch and the Waikato. More comprehensive and analytical investigations started only towards the end of the 20th century. One of the reasons for this scant attention is of

3 Adrian Favell, "Rebooting Migration Theory: Interdisciplinarity, Globality, and Post-disciplinarity in Migration Studies", eds. Caroline Brettell et James Hollifield, *Migration theory: talking across disciplines*, London: Routledge 2007, 259-278; here 265. See also Homi Bhabha, "Culture's in Between", eds. Stuart Hall and Paul du Gay, *Questions of Cultural Identity*, London: Sage 1996, 53–60

4 Robert Cohen, ed. *Theories of Migration*, Edward Elgan: Cheltenham 1996; Douglas S. Massey et al., *Worlds in Motion: Understanding International Migration at the End of the Millennium*, Oxford: Clarendon Press 1998; Stephen Castles and Mark Miller, *The Age of Migration*. London: Macmillan 1998. Adrian Favell, see note 3

5 Sekhar Bandyopadhyay, *op.cit.*, 255–269

a quantitative nature. Although dating back to 1809 and 1814 when a few Indian sailors jumped ship, respectively in the Bay of Islands and Otago Harbour, the first half dozen 'legal' Indian immigrants arrived in 1881. Forty years later, their population counted no more than 671, which increased fourfold to 2 452 by 1951. Yet another thirty years later 15 810 Indians lived in the country. In contrast and according to the 2006 census,[6] the last quarter of the 20th century showed an increase by 660 per cent to a total of 104 582 people of Indian descent. Making up more than two percent of the New Zealand population, Indians had finally become a visible minority[7] and, perhaps not unexpectedly, now the object of a series of investigations and analyses from various research angles. Jacqueline Leckie's pioneering *Indian Settlers: The Story of a New Zealand South Asian Community* (2007) offers a comprehensive history of Indian migration and settlement over more than a century in a book that combines historical documentation from archival resources with narratives by and interviews with a large number of individuals, complemented by reproduced photographs, many of which were contributed by her interviewees. As the most knowledgeable scholar in the field, Leckie also co-edited with Paola Voci a volume of essays entitled *Localizing Asia in Aotearoa* (2011). Focusing on "micro or local histories and cultural spaces", these essays, as the editors claim, are intended to contribute to "understand diversity not just via an examination of cultural belongings that are defined by macro-national entities"[8]: a pertinent reference towards a methodological negotiation that sets out to interrogate conceptions of cultural community on the one hand and identity on the other. As it becomes immediately obvious, this shift from the macro to the micro level of immigrant/diasporan studies is basically grounded in the increasingly multi-ethnic character of New Zealand in the 21st century, and more specifically in Indians constituting a large and heterogeneous group.[9]

As Sekhar Bandyopadhyay remarks in his "Introduction" to *India in New Zealand: Local Identities, Global Relations* (2010): 'Kiwi-Indians' do not only constitute the southernmost group in the Indian global diaspora,[10] but this group's internal cultural diversity includes intergenerational differentiation

6 Arvind Zodgekar, "Indian Presence: A Demographic Profile", ed. Sekhar Bandyopadhyay, *op.cit.*, 65–78; here 66

7 Jacqueline Leckie, *Indian Settlers: The Story of a New Zealand South Asian Community*. Dunedin: Otago University Press 2007, 177

8 Paola Voci & Jacqueline Leckie, "Introduction: Beyond nations and ethnicities: Localizing Asia in New Zealand", eds. Paola Voci & Jacqueline Leckie, *op.cit.*, 7–23; here 9

9 Leckie, *op.cit.*, 2007, 177–178

10 Bandyopadhyay, "Introduction", *op.cit.*, 7–20; here 8

as well as different linguistic, religious and cultural backgrounds since Indians "come from practically all the regions of India and from previous destinations of Indian migration"[11]: a statement substantiated by figures of the 2006 New Zealand census. The number of Fiji-born Indians increased from less than one thousand in 1981 to near 20 000 in 2001, a change mainly due to the exodus of the descendants of the Girmitiyas, former indentured Indian labourers, from their home for more than a century[12] after the 1987 and 2000 military coups on the islands. Belonging mainly to business and professional groups, Fiji-Indians moreover added to the social tapestry of New Zealand Indians whose large majority till the 1990s had been made up of petty traders. Leckie equalized the Indian diaspora in the 20th century with retailing, with Pukekohe, a small town south of Auckland, forming the centre of the Indian settlement.[13] Janet McAllister has added that by the mid-1990s eighty-five per cent of Auckland's dairies were owned by Indians.[14]

The diversity of the social set-up of immigrants from Fiji has since been complemented by members of a newly emerging middle class from India that has arrived over the last two to three decades. By 2001 the percentage of Indian retailers had decreased to twenty-four while the number in white-collar occupations had increased to forty-four per cent;[15] and whereas in 1991 only about fourteen per cent of the male Indian population had a university qualification, this figure had more than doubled by 2001 to 29,4 per cent. Indeed, "the Indian community [if one can really employ this term any longer] today is no longer a socially homogeneous group."[16]

Concomitant with these social changes, to which political changes were also instrumental, like the election victory of the Labour Party in 1984 and the passing of the 1987 Immigration Act, the selection of migrants was facilitated according to their professional qualifications and the economic requirements in New Zealand.[17] The religious and linguistic diversity increased while the gender map came to differ radically from the one of the past. The majority of Indians remained Hindu, but the share of Christians and Muslims began to rise. Side by side to the languages of Hindi, Gujarati and Punjabi, still spoken by more than fifty per cent of the

11 Ibid, 11

12 Leckie, *op.cit.*, 2007, 173

13 Bandyopadhyay, *op. cit.*, 53, 55. See also Natasha Hayl, "A Long Diaspora: Indian Settlement", ed. Bandyopadhyay, *op.cit.*, 45–64.

14 Janet McAllister, "Passages from India", *Metro* (November 2002), 68–73; here 70

15 Leckie, *op.cit.*, 2010, 58

16 Zodgekar, *op.cit.*, 70

17 Leckie, *op.cit.*, 2007, 172

Indian population, other Indian languages have made their appearance on the linguistic map, as has 'English Only', spoken by three out of ten Indians, while ninety per cent attest to also speaking the language.

Finally to be mentioned is the increasing role of women with tertiary qualifications.[18] Considering that till the mid-20th century it was mainly males who had migrated — whose arrival had been favoured over women's — the gender imbalance began gradually to shift. Initially, women had mainly remained attached to their families,[19] while figures relating to the time span between 1996 and 2006 bear evidence not only of an increased number of educationally qualified Indian women in New Zealand but also of their faster percentile growth rate in higher education in comparison with European New Zealand women.[20]

I would like to draw several conclusions from my brief survey of these carefully researched statistical figures on Indians in New Zealand — people severally referred to as hyphenated New Zealand-Indians, Indo-New Zealanders, Kiwi-Indians, Indo-Fijians or Fiji-born Indians. (The number of Indian migrants from Africa, the US, Europe, Canada, or even Australia is still too small to have earned them another hyphenated real and discursive existence). First, the historical, social, linguistic, generational, educational, gender and religious diversity as well as the differing geographical/national backgrounds of Indians in New Zealand necessitates reflections on the understanding of the terms 'diaspora' and 'community' since Indian people in New Zealand are closely linked with these variables[21] in locally defined contexts and experiences. The recognition of such specifically coloured meanings of the 'Indian' community and diaspora will avoid generalizations that strain or even distort their lived reality. Second and intimately connected, is the question of cultural identity, a many-layered term that is to be approached both, from the subjective or psychological perspective of an individual's self-perception as a private being, and as someone perceived by others in his/her role as a public person within his/her experiences of meeting /confronting culturally diverse 'worlds'.

As I have mentioned already, these issues have been addressed over the last decade in essays and in interviews conducted by historians, sociologists, anthropologists, educationists as well as by scholars of cultural, media and community studies — not to forget, also by artists living or residing in New Zealand. I shall briefly summarize the main points they have arrived at

18 Zodgekar, *op.cit.*, 73; Leckie, *op.cit.*, 2007, 172

19 Leckie, *op.cit.*, 2007, 109–123

20 Zodgekar, *op.cit.*, 73

21 Voci/Leckie, *op.cit.*, 9

before turning to several — and as yet very few — literary representations of Indian migrants in Mallika Krishnamurthy's novel *Six Yards of Silk* (2005) and the theatre plays written and performed by Jacob Rajan and Justin Lewis.

Jacqueline Leckie calls the Indian settlement "a long diaspora" and wonders whether the term diaspora is at all "applicable to the complex waves of Indian settlement and re-settlement"[22] — a development which I have already referred to. And she appears receptive to Carmen Voigt-Graf's distinction between diaspora and transcultural community, the former characterized solely as a migrant community with "sentimental and symbolic ties to the ancestral homeland", while the latter also includes its material and real links to the homeland.[23] These modifications are backed up by other scholars who prefer to distinguish "between 'labour', 'trade', 'cultural' and 'imperial'" as well as 'victim' diasporas, because the notion in the present discourse, they argue, has assumed a form of essentialism and has become the "carrier of ideas and cultural continuity *across* national boundaries ... [evoking] images of a transnational bond."[24]

Field work or micro studies conducted in New Zealand thus illustrate how problematic the term diaspora is when examined at the micro level or 'from the inside'. In contrast, to the Indian historian Sekhar Bandyopadhyay Pakeha-New Zealand attitudes to the country's Indian population appear to be determined by an essentializing definition of diaspora. Having been ruled — and continue to be ruled — by the country's global or imperial connections (to the erstwhile Western, imperial 'motherland'), these attitudes are shaped, he says, largely though not exclusively "by a postcolonial public discourse on underdevelopment and backwardness that owed its origins to imperial stereotypes [...] of India."[25] As a piece of documentary evidence Bandyopadhyay quotes the headline of an issue of the *The New Zealand Herald* proclaiming, "They are hungry but they have the bomb", and he also relates to responses of interviewees who complained that professional qualifications from abroad are not recognized, nor had Bandyopadhaya's informants ever been promoted in New Zealand.[26] Concluding, that over a period of more than eighty years the situation for many Indian migrants does not appear to have changed significantly (168),[27]

22 Leckie, *op.cit.*, 2010, 61

23 Ibid., 47

24 Fuchs/Linkenbach/Malik, *op.cit.*, 82

25 Bandyopadhyay, *op.cit.*, 169; Bandyopadhaya, "In the Shadow of the Empire: India-New Zealand Relations since 1947", Bandyopadhyay, *op.cit.*, 167–185

26 Ibid., 168

27 "Stereotypes [...] still persist within contemporary New Zealand [... and] continued resistance

he blames Pakeha New Zealanders for still being unable to understand "middle India."[28] Which is to say that they simply fail to take note of and grasp the scale of global social and economic changes as also those in the field of education that have occurred in India over at least the last two decades. In many quarters in New Zealand there exists an unwillingness, Bandyopadhyay feels, to revise the outdated postcolonial discussion on underdevelopment and backwardness.

The insights presented here and gained from studying Indian diasporan and community structures in New Zealand are, of course, based on a large number of individual case studies centring on the issue of Indian people constructing their selves and of grappling with an understanding of their cultural identities. As has been pointed out, defining oneself in New Zealand occurs much less at a national or ethnic level — although this also happens, of course — than in local contexts with multiple cultural surroundings and social, religious, generational, gender and educational variables. Bandyopadhyay comes to the conclusion that "Indianness" in New Zealand means different things to different people within the community, and that identities are negotiated by individuals on an everyday basis.[29] This is to say that we come across a wide range of self-perceptions marked at one end by collapsing one's individual cultural identity with tradition-guided agencies which, for example, insist on caste-marriage, strict loyalty to the regional-linguistic-cultural world of one's family and its background, and accordingly on the feeling of belonging to a specific socio-cultural network: a network often in the guise of a regional-ethnic (Auckland Marathi Association) or merely ethnic association (Sikh Society). However, researchers have more frequently come across the experience of an in-between position of identity construction; for example, the belief that one's efforts in having made New Zealand your home had enriched one's life and enabled you to enjoy "a double identity";[30] or, in more problematic terms, relating one's self to two worlds that were inextricably intertwined and perhaps even uncertain.[31] Interlocked with such sentiments is the conviction of many interviewees and respondents,

remains in some quarters to New Zealand's localized Asian identity", Ip/Leckie, *op.cit.*, 183. The term Asian, incidentally, points at the authors' essay on "Chinamen" and "Hindoos"; see Bandyopadhaya, *op.cit.*, 168

28 Ibid., 185

29 Ibid., 12

30 Fuchs et al., *op.cit.*, 99

31 Amanda Gilbertson, "Choosing Indian and Kiwi Identities: The Ethnic Options of New Zealand-born Gujaratis", Bandyopadhyay, *op.cit.*, 123–140; here 137, 133

of their own agency, of looking at their own attitudes, decisions and actions as determined by an autonomous and choosing self[32] — which turns them, as several scholars have said, into "accomplished artists of *bricolage* [...] of skilfully handling and putting together diverse fragments of culture."[33] And this is done in a pragmatic rather than a programmatic manner.[34] Accordingly, negotiating one's position in a community is discerned as an on-going process which precludes an ultimate definition of an individual's cultural identity.

Observing these processes over a period of time has, besides, given reason to assume that the more often it is noticeable that personal agency is insisted on and executed the more we have reason to speak of people shifting from perceiving themselves in collective and communal terms to identifying themselves in individual terms. National, ethnic and other supra-individual notions of identity are losing ground by shifting towards individual self-portraits,[35] and perhaps even to seeing oneself as global citizen — as one respondent put it: "'I am proud of India, India has developed so much, but it is no longer a place where I can live. I belong neither to India nor to New Zealand — I am in between, I am a global citizen'".[36] Whether they are guided by "certain basic universalist ideas, derived from religion [...] or secular humanist ideas", as Martin Fuchs and his colleagues suggest,[37] remains to be explored further — apart from the neglect of material considerations of an economic nature which certainly also play a role in defining oneself as a global citizen.

Let me now turn first to the novel *Six Yards of Silk* and then to the plays, so I may analyse the creative treatment of Indian diaspora and cultural identity in New Zealand against the findings of the foregoing studies. Thirty-five year old Sharmila, married to the Pakeha New Zealander Keith and mother of three little boys, had emigrated from South India with her parents and younger brother Ramesh when she was still a child. Deeply disturbed after the sudden disappearance of her brother — who, as it turns out, had drowned himself –, she begins to distance herself from her family and her everyday life, becomes more and more depressed and retreats into the world of her childhood and adolescence which she had closely

32 Ibid., 139
33 Fuchs et al. *op.cit.*, 101
34 Gilbertson, *op.cit.*, 138
35 Gurjet Singh and Verpal Singh, "Changing identities among Kiwi Sikhs: Local, individual or world citizenship?", Voci/Leckie, *op.cit.*, 204–217; here 215
36 Fuchs et al., *op.cit.*, 98
37 Ibid., 103

shared with Ramesh. Both had often rebelled against their more tradition-oriented parents' many strictures from which the boy had suffered more than his sister. His absence now means the loss of Sharmila's mainstay which her family obviously cannot immediately replace. The psychological struggle she faces undergoes a cultural turn of events with her aunt's visit from South India. Meant to help and support her with her daily chores, Meenama, her mother's sister, who is deeply rooted in her Indian heritage, reawakens her niece's memories of her childhood and relatives, of the family's Kerala home and its local surroundings with their colours, smells, sounds and bright light, the heat and monsoon rains, the food, clothes and stories — and the traumatic event of her little sister's death by lightning. The past that had receded over the years — exemplified by Sharmila's total neglect of "the gods", the bronze idols in the cabinet on a shelf — gradually gains the upper hand in her mind and causes her to literally shut the present out by spending more and more time in her bedroom. Her cultural identity attained while growing up and having her own family in New Zealand is seriously challenged now with the world of her parents and aunt reasserting itself paradoxically through Sharmila's simultaneous experience of loss and reunion.

By contrast, her brother, very conscious of the culture conflict he found himself in as an adolescent and a young man, becomes increasingly ill suffering from psychosis as the reader learns from Ramesh's thoughts and outbursts conveyed through indirect free speech in untitled chapters strewn through the novel. Both, his parents' traditional ideas of living like a young Indian male forced onto him and the obstacles he had faced during his school days and in the labour market, in other words, the clash between the two worlds Ramesh had grown up in, proves insoluble and finally destroys him.

The issue then of cultural identity in Krishnamurthy's fictional rendering of two young Indian migrants is treated from a gender-differing perspective. Sharmila finally manages to cope pragmatically with the pull of tradition without denying it but Ramesh succumbs to the conflicting pulls of his Indian parents and Pakeha New Zealand's prejudices against migrants. Apart from the cultural side of the siblings' predicament we should not overlook its basically psychological fabric. Both characters are portrayed as highly sensitive and individualized human beings who minutely register 'the world's' demands and attitudes, their own feelings and individual responses and ascribe them existential importance — a configuration of fictional characters to which the writer's own personal make-up and biographical background may have contributed significantly.

General conclusions as to Indian migrants' living in India and the issue of cultural identity thus must not be drawn from merely one literary text. Still, *Six Yards of Silk* certainly reflects the reality and highlights salient points of migrants' predicaments.

Looking at the novel's literary-aesthetic achievement, the Ramesh chapters impress because the single narrative point of view shapes and controls a cohesiveness of content and form, of Ramesh's talking about his sensory hallucinations, the vanishing borders between the internal and external world and the sustained mood of strain and tone of presentation. The 'sari chapters', on the other hand, entitled with references to the garment's parts and ways of dressing in it and wearing it, are less cohesive, at times surprising the reader with unexpected and unwarranted shifts of perspective from present to past and back and from one character to the next (95-106, 108-116, 132-137). Here it seems that Krishnamurthy has not yet found a way of fully integrating the different time levels and character studies into a narrative that unfolds as densely as Ramesh's story.

Jacob Rajan and Justin Lewis's *Indian Ink* (2005), the trilogy of the plays *Krishnan's Dairy* (first performed in 1997), *The Candlestickmaker* (first performed in 2000), and *The Pickle King* (first performed in 2002),[38] proves to be of a very different aesthetic calibre. Though each play is centred on the interaction of a few characters the plots are of very slender proportion and besides focus on different social segments within the Indian diaspora in New Zealand. As the title suggests, Krishnan runs a dairy and he works long hours to just make a living for his small family. Echoing the hard and not always safe life of many lower middle class migrants who, as I've mentioned, continue to make up a considerable proportion of Indians in New Zealand, the play foregrounds their often confrontational existence and echoes violent attacks on them that have occurred from time to time.[39] Though meant with reference to the more recent play *Guru of Chai*, Rajan's words that "the play you are about to see was born of a real life connection,"[40] very well holds true also of *Krishnan's Dairy*.

Compared to the novel, character delineation is sparse and contents itself with roughly sketching the hard working, responsible dairy owner and, in contrast, his more traditionally anchored Indian wife who is full of stories and 'beliefs' and has a sweet tooth. This kind of attribution reveals

38 Two more plays have been performed since: *The Dentist's Chair* (2007) and *The Chai Guru* (2010). See www.indinanink.co.nz

39 Leckie, *op.cit.*, 2007, 174; Leckie, *op.cit.*, 2010, 60

40 See www.indianink.co.nz/Guru of Chai/Reviews

a very characteristic feature not only of this play: introducing humour and a light touch that counterpoints the serious portrayal of characters and events and employs the contrast between two differing cultural identities as a means of comic relief. In *The Candlestickmaker* a similar effect is brought about by the rhetoric of a retired professor of astrophysics facing his aged female servant and cook's sleight-of-hand retorts in Malayalam and broken English. This character constellation bears similarities with the outspoken and business-minded widowed matriarch running a small hotel in *The Pickle King* and the educated and demure heart surgeon who is forced to make his living as the hotel's porter. In this play Rajan and Lewis call attention to the neglect of "precious human capital" not being utilized by New Zealand employers[41] and bemoaned by the young Indian surgeon, who also mentions the case of a Sri Lankan economics lecturer exploited as a cleaner, or the Polish pharmacologist working "in functions."[42]

Altogether, the three plays take a very different course when compared with the novel. Combining the serious side of Indian migrants making a living in New Zealand with comic elements derived from contradictions in character and style, the playwrights do not shun theatre's rationale to entertain. It is furthermore enhanced by the use of theatrical forms like masks (referred to by Rajan as "Indian caricature masks"), thereby drawing on an element of Commedia dell'Arte[43] with its concomitant effects of allegory, but also of Brechtian 'alienation'. (Masks identify the various characters, but in performance are, as a rule, only worn by Rajan who thus plays different roles). Finally, music and various other devices (a duck, for example, manipulated by a puppeteer in *The Candlestickmaker*) add to the entertainment factor of plays that have succeeded in drawing huge audiences in New Zealand over nearly two decades and which have won critical acclaim in both Europe and the US: plays located at the interface of the local, the diasporan and the global and not meant just for a local Indian-New Zealand but an international audience.

Six Yards of Silk and the five plays by Rajan and Lewis indicate the beginnings of yet another literary tradition in English created by one of the more recent migrant groups in Aotearoa New Zealand. It may well contribute new patches, each necessarily bordered, to the patchwork of

41 Zodgekar, *op.cit.*, 76

42 Rajan/Lewis, *op.cit.*, 2005, 122–123

43 Ibid., 19. "I think that Jacob and I are somehow drawn to old theatrical forms and we take great pleasure from rediscovering them in a contemporary context." www.indianink.co.nz/News/On Tour. Besides, the mask "guides the script", as Rajan put it. See Natasha Hayl, "Indian Ink Interview", *The Listener* (June 18, 2011)

the country's modern literature; an increasingly polycultural body of work to which Pacific Islanders, Chinese, European migrants and Indians have added, and because of which the perception of a 'national' literature takes on new meaning. As Jan Kemp in her eponymous poem, "We are all newcomers"[44] puts it:

> On Long Bay beach the languages
> of sky of sea of land, and of the newest
> comers speaking Samoan, Croatian,
> Hindi, Italian, Afrikaans, Arabic, Mandarin
> overheard in just one swim
> from three to seven pines and back—
> in a half hour Maori and English
> made plankton shoaling through
> the incoming whale tide of costumes and custom—

44 Jan Kemp, *Dante's Heaven*, Auckland: Puriri Press 2006, 15

Works cited

Creative Writing

KEMP, Jan, *Dante's Heaven*, Auckland: Puriri Press 2006

KRISHNAMURTY, Mallika, *Six Yards of Silk*, Wellington: Steele Roberts 2005

RAJAN, Jacob & Justin Lewis, *Indian Ink: Krishnan's Dairy. The Candlestickmaker. The Pickle King*, Wellington: Victoria University Press 2005

Critical Studies

BANDYOPADHYAY, Sekhar, "Introduction", ed. Sekhar Bandyopadhyay, *India in New Zealand: Local Identities, Global Relations*, Dunedin: Otago University Press 2010, 7–20

—, "In the Shadow of the Empire: India-New Zealand Relations since 1947", Bandyopadhyay, *op.cit.*, 167–185

BHABHA, Homi, "Culture's in Between", eds. Stuart Hall and Paul du Gay, *Questions of Cultural Identity*, London: SAGE 1996, 53–60

CASTLES, Stephen, and Mark Miller,*The Age of Migration*, London: Macmillan 1998

COHEN, Robert, ed. *Theories of Migration*, Cheltenham: Edward Elgan 1996

FAVELL, Adrian, "Rebooting Migration Theory: Interdisciplinarity, Globality, and Post-disciplinarity in Migration Studies", eds. Caroline Brettell et James Hollifield, *Migration theory: talking across disciplines*, London: Routledge 2007, 259–278

FUCHS, Martin, Antje Linkenbach, Aditya Malik, "What does it mean to be Indian? A View from Christchurch", Bandyopadhyay, *op.cit.*, 81–106

GILBERTSON, Amanda, "Choosing Indian and Kiwi Identities: The Ethnic Options of New Zealand-born Gujaratis", Bandyopadhyay, *op.cit.*, 123–140

HAYL, Natasha, "Indian Ink. Interview", *The Listener* (June 18, 2011)

IP, Manying and Jacqueline Leckie, "'Chinamen' and 'Hindoos': Beyond stereotypes to Kiwi Asians", eds. Paola Voci & Jacqueline Leckie, *Localizing Asia in Aotearoa*, Wellington: Dunmore Publishing 2011, 159–186

LECKIE, Jacqueline, *Indian Settlers: The Story of a New Zealand South Asian Community*. Dunedin: Otago University Press 2007

—, "A Long Diaspora: Indian Settlement", Bandyopadhyay, *op.cit.*, 45–64

MASSEY, Douglas S. et al., *Worlds in Motion: Understanding International Migration at the End of the Millennium*. Oxford: Clarendon Press 1998

MCALLISTERE, Janet, "Passages from India", *Metro* (November 2002), 68–73

SINGH, Gurjet and Verpal Singh, "Changing identities among Kiwi Sikhs: Local, individual or world citizenship?", Paola Voci & Jacqueline Leckie, *op.cit.*, 204–217

VOCI, Paola & Jacqueline Leckie, eds. *Localizing Asia in Aotearoa*, Wellington: Dunmore Publishing 2011

—, "Introduction: Beyond nations and ethnicities: Localizing Asia in New Zealand", Voci & Leckie, *op.cit.*, 7-23

WATSON, Geoff, "'Indians Show the Way': Sport and Localization among Indians in New Zealand", Voci & Leckie, *op.cit.*, pp. 50–67

ZODGEKAR, Arvind, "Indian Presence: A Demographic Profile", Bandyopadhyay, *op.cit.*, pp. 65–78

Translating Cultures

Pictorial and Literary Representation of India in William Hodges's Paintings and Travel Book

DURING THE YEARS MY WIFE AND I lived in New Zealand we travelled quite often and virtually covered the two islands from north to south, from Cape Rainga to Bluff, and enjoyed the often spectacular scenery of the country. Not only was I impressed by the volcanoes in the centre of the North Island and the almost perfectly shaped cone of Mt. Taranaki near New Plymouth, or the glaciers and mountain ranges of the Southern Alps including Mt. Cook, but also by the rolling hills of Northland, the breathtaking views of the large lakes in Southland, the huge basin-like valleys of Central Otago, the intricately shaped Otago Peninsula and the vast outlook over Banks Peninsula. Having experienced these sights, I realized how challenging the New Zealand scenery must have been to the indigenous population and European explorers and settlers and how attractive to artists, poets as well as painters. I began reading about their responses and experiences, made a point of visiting museums and art galleries and became more and more interested in the genre of landscape painting. The range and the variety of thematic and technical approaches chosen to paint the abundant richness of the New Zealand scenery testify to the pleasure a large number of artists had in sketching or painting, on the spot or from memory, the details of a scene that had evoked their aesthetic pleasure and triggered their artistic sensibility and execution.

Among early painters I became particularly fascinated by the English artist William Hodges (1744–1797), who had been commissioned to accompany James Cook on his second voyage on the *Resolution* from 1772 to 1775. Having reached the west coast of the South Island of New Zealand in March 1773, Hodges painted 'The North Entrance to Dusky Bay' in May

The North Entrance to Dusky Bay

and was praised by Cook for his "'very accurate view both of the North and South entrance as well as several other parts of this Bay'". Besides, Cook held that the painter "'hath delineated the face of the country with such judgement as will as once convey a better idea of it than can be expressed by words.'"[1] Cook's appraisal of Hodges's 'delineation of the face of the country,' in other words, his accuracy of observation and representation I shall return to.

What I found of similar if not even greater interest, while having a closer look at Hodges's career as a landscape painter, was the fact that after his return to England he was commissioned again as a painter, and now by the then Governor-General of India, Warren Hastings, to come to India and work there. He arrived in 1779 and the painter's visit was to last for six years. In his book *Travels to India During the Years 1780, 1781, 1782, and 1783*, "printed for the author" in London in 1793, and "one of the earliest published travel accounts by a professional artist",[2] Hodges presented his

1 Roger Blackley, *Two Centuries of New Zealand Landscape Art* , Auckland: Auckland City Art Gallery 1990, 12

2 Beth Fowkes Tobin, "The artist's 'I' in Hodges's *Travels in India*", Jeff Quilley and John Bonehill, *William Hodges, 1744–1797: The Art of Exploration*, Catalogue to the Exhibition at the National Maritime Museum, Greenwich, 5 July–21 November 2004 and the Yale Center for British Art, New Haven, 27 January–24 April 2005, New Haven and London: Yale University Press 2004, 43–48. Tobin also raises the important question as to "the relationship between aesthetics and colonialism" (43) to which I shall return.

readers with detailed reports on his travels, that took him from Calcutta westward along the Ganges river and via the towns of Patna, Benares, Lucknow and Agra to Gwalior, and back again. Besides and obviously asked to do so by Hodges, the printer also included fourteen plates, engravings of pictures many of which he had painted during his travels and on the spot. After his return and having been appointed a member of the Royal Academy in 1787, he exhibited his paintings between 1785 and 1794, and among them not merely Indian landscapes but also pictures of buildings that he had *converted* from original water colour or aquatints into oil. Hodges earned the reputation not only of being the first English painter of 'oriental scenes' but also of being its specialist, since two more books quickly followed *Travels in India*. These were *A Collection of Views in India Drawn on the Spot in the Years 1780, 1781, 1782, and 1783*, and 'executed in aquatinta, in imitation of the original drawings', and *Select Views of India Drawn on the Spot, in the Years 1780, 1781, 1782 and 1783 and extended in aqua tinta (London 1785–88)*,[3] which contains forty-eight prints. The depth of the English painter's dedication to a very different culture at the end of the eighteenth century amply recorded here naturally raises the question as to the extent he appropriated India as a European outsider. Can we, especially from the postcolonial perspective, classify him as an early Orientalist who influenced, perhaps even shared in creating the discourse on Orientalism that was to manifest itself more transparently in the nineteenth century? I shall attempt to find an answer by first asking why Hodges had agreed to Hastings's proposal to visit India, and how he defined the task he had set for himself. Finally, I shall turn to his achievement as the first professional European landscape painter to travel to and document India.

The final pages of *Travels in India* offer an insight into Hodges's motives. After his return with Cook he had complained of the market in England as lacking in paintings of native scenery, and he must have been glad to receive Hastings's invitation to come to India, not the least because travelling in India would, as he put it, "add greatly to our stock of knowledge relative to the Eastern continent".[4] Here, it is the "picturesque beauty of a place [… represented] as a natural object, or as connected with the history of the country, and the manners of the people"[5] that challenged

3 Natasha Eaton repeatedly refers to Warren Hastings's support of Hodges and mentions that he "assisted the painter in finding additional Company [i.e. East India Company] funding for Hodges's aquatint series *Select Views of India (1785–88).*" See Natasha Eaton, "Hodges's Visual Genealogy for Colonial India, 1780–95", Quilley and Bonehill, *op.cit.*, 35–42; here 36

4 William Hodges, *Travels in India during the Years 1780, 1781, 1782, and 1783*, (London) 1793, 152

5 Ibid., 154

the curious and engaged artist in him to make visible a world to his own countrymen known only through reports and descriptions visitors and travellers had written down or left behind. Now however, accurate visual representations of the country's 'face', of its scenery and its buildings, its art objects and people, would convey a truthful picture to the outside world, "to give a more perfect idea thereof, than could be formed from written descriptions only": a view Cook had earlier concurred with.[6] At the same time, Hodges was of course aware of the limits of an artist's imagination as a prerequisite for his task, and he cautioned that it must be under the strict guidance of cool judgement, or we shall have fanciful [my emphasis, DR] representations instead of the truth, which, above all, must be the object of such researches.[7]

He certainly possessed 'the perfect knowledge of his art', having been trained in London as a landscape painter in the Grand Style, but at the same time would also rely on his 'cool judgement', or on acutely precise observations of the subjects chosen for his near-naturalistic paintings. Examples from his journey with Cook illustrate his clinging to this goal, for example when painting geological formations and weather conditions, or manufactured objects and detailed architectural features of the many Muslim buildings he came across while travelling in India.[8] Here, we meet with a representative of the Age of Reason: cool judgement is required to achieve the true representation of the subjects chosen by the painter — no less than by the researcher — whose goal it must be to find out their 'real and natural character', in short: the truth. But apart from such more general, philosophical considerations, Hodges was also interested in 'the history

View in Pickersgill Harbour, Dusky Bay, New Zealand

6 Francis Pound, *Frames on the Land: Early Landscape Painting in New Zealand*, Auckland: Collins 1983, 60

7 Hodges, *op.cit.*, 152

8 See my Note and reference to: < www.racollection.org.uk>

and progress of the arts in India',[9] and his *Travels in India* is no less than an attempt to relate his ideas to his paintings and to refer again and again to the history of Muslim architecture in Northern India.

Finally, the eighteenth century artist was simply curious, as he himself repeatedly points out in his book;[10] an aptitude he shared with many of his contemporaries in search of exotic subject matters and parts of the world, the discovery of which, incidentally, would lay the foundation for modern ethnographic and geographic research. There can be no question that the artistic, the philosophical and the scientific approaches and investigatory methods chosen by such curious people were grounded in the history of the Western rationale of reasoning and aesthetic perceptions. Nonetheless, Hodges's writings and paintings testify to a genuine eagerness to acquire knowledge of the unknown. It was not perceived in the sense of Edward Said's thesis on 'Orientalism', claiming that British travel writing, for example, was implicated in "Western nations having created an 'Other'."[11] This English traveller's paintings of Indian landscapes and buildings and his writing, I argue, were motivated by discovering India for himself and his countrymen. They were neither meant to create an image of an alien, let alone an exotic country, nor to appropriate it in the way the European colonizing mind would begin doing not much later on in the early nineteenth century. William Dalrymple's novel *White Mughals: Love and Betrayal in Eighteenth-Centuy India* (2000) could be cited here as a story based on historical research in late eighteenth century India, clearly demonstrating that the idea of colonial control and the desire for hegemony had not yet taken possession of curious Englishmen in India.[12]

---

9 Hodges, *op.cit.*, 63

10 Ibid., 79, 97

11 Jayati Gupta, "The Poetics and Politics of Travel Writing", ed. Somdatta Mandal, *Indian Travel Narratives*, Jaipur: Rawat Publications 2010, 26–36; here 34

12 In his perceptive, convincingly argued and highly informative study, *The Artificial Empire: The Indian Landscapes of William Hodges*, Richmond, Surrey: Curzon 2000, Giles Tillotson discusses this aspect in the section "Orientalism and the Visual Arts", 100–116. He does not deny that there is a colonial connection to the images painted by Hodges and his contemporaries but proposes to bear in mind that the colonial connection "of such images [...] involves an appeal to historical incidents or ideas" rather than to the manner of representation. In short, one moves away from the picture plane treating the picture only as a reference to something else. (102) Further, Tillotson stresses the point that the use of the picturesque with its "quest for scenery exhibiting dramatic formal variety" generally, but also in Hodges's paintings, was a response to landscape in Britain and continental Europe and not "exclusive to the colonial domain." (103) He sums up his argument with the remark: "We can speak of picturesque images of objects which have Orientalist significance, and we can show how the images might have been understood in that way, <u>but the picturesque itself is not Orientalist</u> [my emphasis]." (103) It would be a mistake then to take representation for perception, since they are not the same.

Bhimbetka Cave Painting

We know that Indian artists did not paint landscapes at the time since no examples of this exist. Hodges had taken note of the country's art and painting traditions, as his frequent references in *Travels in India* show, and he praised specimens of 'Mussulman [...painting ... in miniature... as] highly beautiful in composition and in delicacy of colour',[13] but we miss any remark on representations of nature as such. Art historians have suggested that cave paintings dating from 2000 to 1500 B.C. and discovered in 1957 near Bhimbetka, south of Bhopal, contain one or the other feature of nature, which of course does not permit us to speak of landscape art.[14] And this holds true also of the Moghul painting schools established in the sixteenth century where we do come across details of nature, often stylized, illustrating the written word.[15] By comparison, Rajput paintings from the seventeenth century onward resort more frequently to features of nature — flowers, trees and wooded areas, gardens, hills and mountain ranges, brooks and rivers — , and often also display birds and animals.

13 Hodges, *op.cit.*, 150

14 Arguing that the conception (and visual representation) of landscape requires an evolved subjectivity, it has been pointed out that "there is absolutely no trace of landscapes in cave paintings [... because] landscape is where the subject posits itself in relation to nature [...], where consciousness must distance itself from nature." This consciousness had obviously not evolved at the time cave paintings were created. See Rachael Ziade DeLue and James Elkins, ed. *Landscape Theory*, London and New York: Routlege 2008, 107–8.

15 See J.M. Rogers, *Mughal Miniatures*, London: The British Museum Press 2006, 46

But these are on the one hand embellishments of narratives focusing on single figures or people interacting and on the other, endow the paintings with symbolic meaning; they are "to capture the mood and emotion of the scene portrayed,"[16] but not to represent a landscape per se.[17] Nature serves as a backdrop to court or hunting scenes, or as background in the sense of a *locus amoenus* at a lovers' tryst, and this holds true even in the works of Raja Ravi Varma (1848–1906), the first Indian Western-style painter, for example in 'Shakuntala' (1870) It was not before the 1920s that K. Venkatappa and others, for example Abanindranath Tagore (1871–1951), began adopting the landscape genre to some degree and

Shakuntala Looking Back to Glimpse Dushyanta

16 See Roda Ahluwalia, *Rajput Painting: Romantic, Divine and Courtly Art from India*, London: The British Museum Press 2008, 119

17 Roda Ahluwalia's book offers excellent documentary evidence. Covering the early seventeenth to the early nineteenth century, this collection of illustrations does not contain a single landscape painting that would offer a parallel to the European genre, though it was itself not unknown in India at the time. Among examples, we come across nature made to serve as a backdrop to people or animals, all painted in a near-realistic style (fig. 35 and 36). Besides, there are near-surrealistic (fig. 42) and increasingly, stylized paintings (fig. 62 and 64). Fig. 82 and 103, also stylized, offer in-depth and close to perspective views of nature, with fig. 103 of the late 1770s showing a "lush landscape of undulating hills and forested slopes in muted tones of green." Still, even when perspective was attempted, it "was never given prominence, the ultimate objective being to interpret narrative gently and with heightened lyricism." (155) Cf. also the art critic Jacob Wamberg's *Landscape as World Picture: Tracing Cultural Evolution in Images*. vol. 1, "Early Modernity", Aarhus: Aarhus University Press 2009, where he talks of the "autonomous landscape image [...] as an image whose sole motif is landscape, whose justification is the view across the landscape itself" connects its emergence "with the autonomous concept of art as such" and places it in sixteenth century Europe. (71, 72) Indeed, the idea of art as such, whether in painting, sculpture or music, lay outside the tradition of Indian aesthetics.

Hilly Terrain, Udaka Mandal

for their own, often national-culturally oriented purposes to establish an original and non-Western painting tradition.

I would like to turn now to Hodges's paintings and his views of India as we come to know them in his *Travels in India*. Commenting on "The Pass of Sicri Gully from Bengal, entering in the Province of Bahar" , he felt that the "whole scene appeared to me highly picturesque [... and] this view [...] marks the general character of this part of the country."[18] Calling the scene picturesque is of relevance because this term relates to the discourse on landscape and landscape painting discussed in the 1790s, as is documented in Sir Uvedale Price's (1747–1829) book, *Essay on the Picturesque, as Compared with the Sublime and the Beautiful* (1796). Among modern art critics the New Zealand art historian Francis Pound detailed elements composing the picturesque and referred to a ruined building, broken water, an old battered tree, and gypsies or beggars, in short: ragged irregularities.[19] Interestingly, in Hodges's painting we discover a ruined castle on top of a ragged hill suggesting age (and decay). Further, a dense forest at its foot, a single tree that appears out of place at the centre, a group of people dressed in — to the European viewer — unfamiliar clothes, and a lone animal create an impression of sudden variation — to quote Pound — all of which constitute the picturesque quality of this painting. It is a kind of artistic representation that points at Hodges's place in the European landscape painting tradition of the seventeenth and eighteenth century, as much as it directs the European viewer's eyes at a foreign country's landscape, which does not present itself as all that unfamiliar. On the contrary, it possesses

18 Hodges, *op.cit.*, 23
19 Pound, *op.cit.*, 25

The Pass of Sicri Gully from Bengal, Entering into the Province of Bahar

a certain familiarity and thus suggests that the painter's conception of the truth of a landscape remains essentially European.

Right behind the solitary tree we discover a house with a gabled roof, certainly an exceptional building considering the prevalence of flat terrace-roofed living-quarters typical of India. It obviously belongs to the village of Gully Sicri that is more clearly foregrounded in another oil painting Hodges must have done after his return to England, and which is based on the original aquatint. This feature — apart from calling up a familiar sight for the painter as well as for his European viewers — confronts us with the idea of a landscape as being an inhabited place, a distinct characteristic of Hodges's paintings generally. His landscapes are not desolate, not merely natural or even untouched, but have been taken possession of by humans. We could even go as far as to argue that it is one of his motifs for landscape painting to document the relationship between nature and mankind, and thus human history and progress as well as decay: a notion very much of the Age of Reason. A notion, furthermore bolstered by the painter's eye for the manufactured object, for example a boat as testimony of man's practical nature, or intricate architectural features of a building as proof of his artistic creativity.[20]

Yet, to confine Hodges's conception and representation of Indian scenery to the picturesque does not do him justice, as passages in *Travels*

20 See NOTE

A View of the Pass of Sicri Gully

in India illustrate:

> After returning to Sicri Gully, I continued my route across the pass of Terriagully, from the top of which a beautiful scene opens itself to the view, namely, the meandering of the river Ganges through the flat country, and glittering through an immense plain, highly cultivated, as far as the extent of the horizon, where the eye is almost at a loss to discriminate the termination of sky and land. (24)

Adding further details of the landscape, the traveller comes to the general conclusion that the

> country about Colgong is, I think, the most beautiful I have seen in India. The waving appearance of the land, its fine turf and detached woods, backed by the extensive forests on the hills [...] and its overlooking the Ganges, which has more the appearance of an ocean at this place than of a river, gives the prospect inexpressible grandeur. (25)

Expressing his experience of the land as beautiful and of "inexpressible grandeur", Hodges falls back on the contemporary discourse on the picturesque, relating it to the beautiful and the sublime. This means that he sets his aesthetic experience apart from his artistic representation of the Indian scenery: the attentive and sensitive beholder differs from the reflective painter. Furthermore, the eighteenth century traveller and writer does not only respond positively to the scenery of India[21] (24–28, 70–71), but also to its people (31–34, 60, 88), towns (60, 111), streets (9), houses (9, 125), temples (10), and monuments, like the "'Taje Mahel': a work of art [...that] far surpasses any thing I ever beheld." (124) Besides, Hodges often compares such views and impressions favourably with those experienced in his own country. (25, 26, 28, 33, 134–135) But he is also a discriminating observer of features of India or Indian life less amenable to his taste or judgement. Among them are several attitudes, the conduct of the 'Mahomedans' (62), or 'Mussulmans' (110) as well as what he calls indecent art objects (11) or customs (79, 93, 103–4, 132). Here the traveller proves the child of his time, as he does of course in his positive estimate of British attitudes and actions in India (. . .). Though he holds that "it is not my business to enter into the question respecting the rights of the government in different countries and those of the governed [because] facts are my object" (48), he does not distance himself from his country's policy — or rather the East India Company's: a politico-economic association that after all had paid for his expenses and exploits.

Nonetheless, my understanding of Hodges's paintings and my reading of his travel account appraise him as belonging to the beginning of British

The Taj Mahal

21 All further page references to Hodges, *op.cit.*

colonial expansion and domination in India, a period of political activities I would not readily subsume under the category of a "negative coding of others."[22] Hodges's positive emotional responses to India (2, 25, 128) do not only confirm this, but his often expressed melancholic mood at the sight of deprivation, neglect, decline or loss of past beauty and human achievements (106, 117, 120–1), and the many paintings of ruined fortresses or tombs also make us encounter a compassionate commentator on the passage of a grander age. Such emotional immersion anticipates the Orientalists' more prevalent conviction as to India's glorious past but dismal state of affairs in the nineteenth century.[23] However, this mood also points forward to an emotional state characteristic of the Romantic period and reveals itself here as a subtext to the Age of Reason, to which Hodges had felt himself akin.[24]

Works cited

Non-fiction books

DALRYMPLE, William, *White Mughals: Love & Betrayal in Eighteenth-Century India*, New York: Harper Collins 2000

HODGES, William, *Travels in India during the Years 1780, 1781, 1782, and 1783*, (London) 1793

—, *A Collection of Views in India, Drawn on the Spot, in the Years 178, 1781, 1782, and 1783, and Executed in Aquatinta, in Imitation of the Original Drawings*, London: printed for the author, n.d.

—, *Selected Views of India Drawn on the Spot, in the Years 1780, 1781, 1782 and 1783 and Extended in Aqua Tinta*, London 1785–88

Critical Studies

AHLUWALIA, Roda, *Rajput Painting: Romantic, Divine and Courtly Art from India*, London: The British Museum Press 2008

BLACKLEY, Roger, *Two Centuries of New Zealand Landscape Art*, Auckland: Auckland City Art Gallery 1990

BONEHILL, John, "Hodges and Cook's second voyage," eds. Geoff Quilley and John Bonehill, *William Hodges, 1744–1897: The Art of Exploration*, Catalogue to the Exhibition at the National Maritime Museum, Greenwich, 5 July–21 November 2004 and the Yale Center for British Art, New Haven, 27 January–24 April 2005, New Haven and London: Yale University Press 2004, 74–108

DELUE, Rachael Ziade and James Elkins, eds. *Landscape Theory*, London and New York: Routlege 2008

EATON, Natasha, "Hodges's Visual Genealogy for Colonial India, 1780–95", Quilley and Bonehill, *op.cit.*, 35–42

22 Gupta, *op.cit.*, 31

23 Tobin (see note 12) locates Hodges's "portraying of Mughal architecture as picturesque ruins" as part of the "ongoing construction of the British Orientalist doctrine of [...quoting Homi Bhabha] 'India as a primordial fixity [...] that satisfies the self-fulfilling prophecy of Western progress'." (46) This may be a pertinent interpretation in so far as it limits our attention to the painter's portraiture of Mughal buildings, but it is certainly not applicable to his total work.

24 It makes one wonder to what extent these landscape paintings relate to the judgement that Caspar David Friedrich's romantic landscapes "are not so much representations of landscape as of consciousness, or of consciousness *as* landscape." See DeLue and Elkins, *op.cit.* , 146

GUPTA, Jayati, "The Poetics and Politics of Travel Writing", ed. Somdatta Mandal, *Indian Travel Narratives,* Jaipur: Rawat Publications 2010, 26–36

POUND, Francis, *Frames on the Land: Early Landscape Painting in New Zealand*, Auckland: Collins 1983

PRICE, Sir Uvedale, *Essay on the Picturesque, As Compared with the Sublime and Beautiful*, London: J. Robson 1796

ROGERS, J. M., *Mughal Miniatures*, London: The British Museum Press 2006

TILLOTSON, Giles, *The Artificial Empire: The Indian Landscapes of William Hodges*, Richmond, Surrey: Curzo 2000

—, "Hodges and Indian Architecture", Quilley and Bonehill, *op.cit.*, 49–60

TOBIN, Beth Fowkes, "The artist's 'I' in Hodges's *Travels in India*", Quilley and Bonehill, *op.cit.*, 43–48

WAMBERG, Jacob, *Landscape as World Picture: Tracing Cultural Evolution in Images*, vol. 1, "Early Modernity", Aarhus: Aarhus University Press 2009

Picture credits

NOTE: A number of Hodges's Indian paintings can be seen at <http://www.racollection.org.uk> [accessed 14 March 2011]. See also Geoff Quilley and John Bonehill, *William Hodges 1744–1797: The Art of Exploration*, London: National Maritime Museum 2004, DVD; PAL, © Illuminations 2004 <http://www.illumin.co.uk/Hodges>

p. 168 "The North Entrance to Dusky Bay, New Zealand", Mitchell Library, State Library of New South Wales, Australia <http://www.sl.nsw.gov.au> (used by permission); also in Blackley, *op.cit.*, 12 (see note 1)

p. 170 "View in Pickersgill Harbour, Dusky Bay, New Zealand", National Maritime Museum, London <http://www.nmm.ac.uk/visit.exhibitions/past/william hodges> [accessed 5 August 2010]; also in Blackley, *op.cit.*, 14 (see note 1), and John Bonehill, "Hodges and Cook's second voyage", ed. Quilley and Bonehill, *op.cit.*, 83 (see note 2)

p. 172 "Bhimbetka Cave Painting" (c. 2000–1500 BC) <http://www.wikipedia.org/Wiki:/File:Bhimbetka Cave Paintings.jpg> Acknowledgement: Flickr upload bot by Ekabhishek (talk) (used by permission)

p. 173 "Shakuntala Looking Back to Glimpse Dushyanta" <http://www.commons.wikimedia.org/wiki/FileRavi Varma Shakuntala stops to look back.jpg> [accessed 22 March 2011]

p. 174 "Hilly Terrain, Udaka Mandal" <http://www.kamat.com/picturehouse/bharat/13200.htm> [accessed 1 September 2010]

p. 175 "The Pass of Sicri Gully from Bengal, Entering into the Province of Bahar." Hodges, *op.cit.*, after page 22; also in Tillotson, *op.cit*, 44 (used by permission)

p. 176 "A View of the Pass of Sicri Gully" <http://www.racollection.org.uk> ; also in William Hodges, 1785–88. *Select Views in India*, 1785–88, vol. 2, no.22 [accessed 22 March 2011]

p. 177 "The Taj Mahal" <http://www.ngmaindia.gov.in> ; also in Tillotson , 2004, 55 (used by permission)

Retrieving Human Rights

Indra Sinha's Novel *Animal's People* and Critical Cosmopolitanism

> *The biggest problem for a novelist dealing with important historical events, especially an event as devastating as the gas disaster in Bhopal, is to find a way to present exegetical commentary naturally through the lives of the characters. In my own novel inspired by the Bhopal survivors, I tried to avoid the problem by setting the story in an imaginary city, presenting the history and politics as a hazy backdrop and focusing on the foreground characters.*[1]

Indra Sinha's novel *Animal's People* (2008)[2] is not merely a fascinating, indeed a disturbing literary work about the aftermath of the Bhopal gas tragedy that occurred on December 3, 1984, but it also calls upon readers to engage themselves with a number of questions, such as informing themselves about the event, its politico-economic background and its long-lasting after-effects on people's minds, bodies and psyche. Besides, it raises the question of the novel's place within the literary tradition of the Indian novel in English, especially of works thematizing the fate of the poor, the weak and suppressed sections of Indian society. Finally, it asks the reader to analyse the author's chosen narrative strategy of "present[ing] exegetical commentary" on a horrible historical event and to judge its achievement from an aesthetic, a literary-historical and a moral point of view.

Information on the Bhopal disaster is widely available on the net, first

1 Indra Sinha, "The Justice Leak", *Tehelka*, 9, 27 (July 7, 2012) http://archive.tehelka.com/story main53.asp?filename=hubo

2 Indra Sinha, *Animal's People*, Simon & Schuster Pocket Books 2008 [2007]

and foremost under www.bhopal.org; further, in reports and analyses in "India's National Magazine from the publisher of *The Hindu*", *Frontline* (www.frontline.in). Similarly "Tehelka — India's Independent Weekly News Magazine" (www.tehelka.com), contains regular contributions to this day about the struggle for justice, while national and international newspapers like *The Guardian* or *The Economic Times* can also be consulted. Finally, Suroopa Mukherjee's study *Surviving Bhopal: Dancing Bodies, Written Texts, and Oral Testimonials of Women in the Wake of an Industrial Disaster* (2010)[3] offers a most comprehensive critical enquiry into the causes of the Bhopal tragedy, its horrifying dimensions, but it also testifies to peoples' demonstrations and their political and legal activities directed at obtaining medical treatment and receiving compensation; in short, at retrieving their rights as human beings.

Apart from presenting a survey, Mukherjee problematizes her account as far as it relies on oral testimonials collected by her and meant to capture the victims' suffering and protest. She asks herself: "What kind of history do we need to write to tell the story of the people who are brutally neglected by society?", and concludes that "in the ultimate analysis, we need to understand that oral history like any other form of history is a double-edged sword that remembers and forgets simultaneously."[4]

The scholar's skepticism about retrieving and retelling the truth reflects modernity's doubt in the master story and the power of language and in the very narration of personal experience. Implicitly, Sinha's words, as quoted above, point in the same direction. However, the novelist's strategy to convey 'the truth' by fictionalizing the historical event and its after-effects is less concerned with the problem of veracity than with the story's performative function. He seems to ask, should readers of *Animal's People* merely read or listen to the first-person narrator's presentation or shouldn't they also feel called upon to actively engage with the victims' and their supporters' political and legal struggle for justice and human rights against powerful state and corporate business institutions. It is a vexed question that takes us back to the function of literature, of poetry, as, for instance, discussed by the philosopher Theodor W. Adorno after the experience of the Holocaust. Is it not barbaric, he asked in 1951,[5] to write a poem after Auschwitz? To dare recreate verbally a reality that lies beyond language? Adorno's question invited criticism, and he responded, that

3 Suroopa Mukherjee, *Surviving Bhopal — Dancing Bodies, Written Texts, and Oral Testimonials of Women in the Wake of an Industrial Disaster*, New York: Palgrave Macmillan 2010

4 Ibid., 125

5 Theodor Wiesengrund Adorno, "Jene Zwanziger Jahre" ["Those Twenties"], ed. Petra Kiedaisch, *Lyrik nach Auschwitz* [*Poetry After Auschwitz*], Stuttgart: Reclam 1995, 4

authentic artists in the present age are those whose works' utmost horror trembles ever after;[6] which suggests an answer less from an aesthetic than a moral perspective — and, I would like to add here, also from the view of the performative function of an artist's work.

To understand Sinha's achievement of fictionally "present[ing[exegetical commentary" on an historical event, of configuring, indeed transfiguring it aesthetically, a comparison with Indian novels written in English and in an Indian language will be useful. At the same time, it will relate *Animal's People* to the literary tradition that thematizes the fate of the downtrodden in Indian society. From the post-First World War period onward, Indian authors invited their readers' attention to their fictionalized stories about socially and economically little-favoured individuals and communities. Among them we have K.S. Venkataramani's *Murugan the Tiller* (1927); Mulk Raj Anand's *Untouchable* (1935), *Coolie* (1936) and *Two Leaves and a Bud* (1937); and Raja Rao's *Kanthapura*. In the following decades these works were joined by Bhabhani Bhattacharya's *So Many Hungers* (1947) and *He Who Rides a Tiger* (1954), Kamala Markandaya's *Nectar in a Sieve* (1954) and *A Handful of Rice* (1967), and Khushwant Singh's *Train to Pakistan* (1956). Finally, Arun Joshi's *The City and the River* (1991), R.K. Jha's *Fireproof* (2006/07), Meher Pestonji's *Sadak Chhaap* (2005), Amitav Ghosh's *Sea of Poppies* (2008) and Arvind Adiga's *The White Tiger* (2008) could be added.

By sharing several of their characteristics, *Animal's People* represents an impressive contribution to this narrative tradition. The story is told realistically and with a strong naturalistic undertone and focuses on the daily lives of some of the people belonging to more than half the Indian population, people who live below the poverty line.[7] Similarly, Sinha's characters are aware of being discriminated against for social, religious or political reasons, but by contrast they are also made to act while Anand's or Markandaya's protagonists are not even listened to[8] or supported by other victims[9] and eventually prevented from empowering themselves. Among the few exceptions I can think of are the workers' combined actions during the Bombay trade union strike in Anand's *Coolie* or the women and the coolies' satyagraha and picketing on the Skeffington Coffee Plantation in Rao's *Kanthapura*.

---

6 Ibid., 53

7 In 2007, 55.4% or 645 million people lived below the poverty line, having less than US $1.25 or fifty Rupees per day at their disposal

8 Bakha in *Untouchable*

9 Cf.. *Two Leaves and a Bud*, or *Nectar in a Sieve*

Novels written after India's political independence, on the other hand, reflect gradual changes of sociospace, of social formations of identity 'below' those of state and nation,[10] as technical modernization, improved educational opportunities, increased mobilization and urbanization begin to cause a diversification of the labour market and the emergence of new social networks. Among others, this led to what sociologists refer to as processes of disembedding and embedding which would affect existing individual and social relations. For example, the impoverished villagers in Bhattacharya's *He Who Rides a Tiger* or Markandaya's *A Handful of Rice* leave their villages and hope to find work in a big city, but eventually they fail, though for different reasons.[11] Transplanted from their original places of living, they are unable to embed in unfamiliar socioscapes — unless they employ questionable if not criminal methods of adaptation or join "the systemic embedding of the criminals in their social surroundings"[12]: a path followed by several characters in Suketu Mehta's docu-fictional tome *Maximum City: Bombay Lost and Found* (2004) and Vikram Chandra's 900 page novel *Sacred Games* (2006) — where this process is acted out between the gangster Ganesh Gaitonde and his opponent, policeman Sartaj Singh. Similarly, Balram, the White Tiger, quickly adopts his 'new' community's questionable socio-moral attitudes after he has embedded himself in the socioscape of international technology that has sprung up in Bangalore.[13] By contrast, Markandaya's Ravi in *A Handful of Rice*, Biju in Kiran Desai's *The Inheritance of Loss* (2006), or Ammu and Velutha in Arundhati Roy's *The God of Small Things* (1997) are temporarily included in pre-existing socioscapes, but eventually rejected and excluded. The one novel I can think of, where a strong social network of a marginalized group, viz. street kids, empowers its members to some degree to run their lives independently, is Pestonji's *Sadak Chhaap*, though in the end ten-year old Rahul's struggle 'to belong' also proves futile.

10 See M. Albrow, J. Eade, J. Durrschmidt and N. Washburne, "The impact of globalization on sociological concepts: community, culture and milieu", ed. J. Eade, *Living the Global City: Globalization as Local Process*, London and New York: Routledge 1997, 20–36

11 After having assumed the role of the Brahmin priest Mandal Adhikari, or 'riding a tiger', Kalo admits his low-caste origin and voluntarily forfeits the social and economic benefits that had accrued to him from his faked status. Ravi, first successful as a tailor in his father-in-law's shop, loses customers after the old man's death, can hardly grasp 'a handful of rice' to feed his family any longer and ends in resignation

12 Bernd-Peter Lange, "Crime and the Mega City", *museindia* 24 (March–April 2009), www.museindia.com

13 A course of action ambiguously recommended by Neil Mukherjee who in his review does not only suggest that "Adiga is going to go places", but that "[w]e'd do well to follow him." (Adiga 2008, book jacket) Would we?

Novels originally written in an Indian language, including works by Dalit and Adivasi authors, suggest parallels.[14] Merely verbal protest by individuals against social oppression and their wish to be accepted as members of the human community can be found in Daya Pawar's autobiography *Balute* (original in Marathi, 1974) and in Omprakash Valmiki's *Joothan — A Dalit's Life* (English translation, 2003). Krishna Baldev Vaid's *Ek naukarani ki diary* (original in Hindi, 2007) takes its protagonist, a housemaid, a step further, by making her assert her individuality both by leaving her workplace in spite of her precarious economic situation and by condemning her middle-class employer's world. Finally, Uday Prakash's novella *Mohandas* (original in Hindi, 2006) tells the story of a well-educated low-caste person who fights for a job that he had been promised. He is outmanoeuvered by a social network — a specific sociospace — of corruptible and corrupted bureaucrats, engineers, politicians, lawyers, policemen and upper-caste members who deny him his individuality and literally divest him of his identity.

Such parallels between novels in English and in Indian languages are not coincidental — quite apart from running counter to the often raised argument that Indian English writing ipso facto represents an outsider's, if not an exotic point of view. On the contrary: these literary configurations represent humanitarian concerns about the living conditions of the underprivileged vis-à-vis the 'new' middle class across linguistic barriers and reflect Indian macro-politics: viz. a fundamental shift in Indian economic and financial politics that set in with Rajiv Gandhi's premiership in 1984 and began to affect all social layers of the population,[15] though in a vastly different manner. "In the two decades following the gas disaster", Mukherjee comments, "India began its forward march toward greater progress and development in an increasingly global scenario." Nonetheless, "the forces of globalization and corporatization, with their models of development rendered communities as expendable by distancing them from the forward march of progress."[16] Thus, the establishment of a global scenario in India and an increasingly deregulated and privatized economy — of which Union Carbide India Ltd. with its factory in Bhopal is one instance — has further harmed the socio-economic situation of the underprivileged and has created new socio-political formations within the asymmetry of power. On the one hand, a group of "high net worth [Indian]

14 Overviews of Dalit literature can be found in *museindia* 10 (2006), www.museindia.com; and in Sheoraj Singh 'Bechan', "Voices of Awakening", *The Hindu* (August 3, 2008)

15 S. Mukherjee, *op.cit.*, 39

16 Ibid.

individuals" (HNWI) has grown fastest in the world, with more 'crime' money banked by them abroad than by the rest of the world. Besides, there is "pervasive corruption in the lower bureaucracy";[17] politicians and members of parliament face criminal cases and entrepreneurs have "to bribe twenty to forty functionaries if [they are] to be serious about doing business."[18] As regards the growth of the 'new' middle class, termed 'consuming class' by the National Council of Applied Economic Research (NCAER), Gurcharan Das holds that

> [this class] is pushing the politicians to liberalize and globalize [and is] too busy thinking of money and [is] not unduly exercised by politics. [...] It has no clear ethos beyond money and the here and now.[19]

On the other hand,

> half a century after Independence the Dalits and some of the backward castes are still the most wretchedly poor, the most illiterate, the most exploited, and the most disadvantaged in India."[20]

A fact confirmed by Amartya Sen who rejects the belief "that India has managed the challenge of hunger very well since independence [, but] has done worse than nearly any other country in the world [...,] with endemic undernourishment and hunger."[21] And yet, the 'Argumentative Indian' also observes that

> [t]he possibilities of public agitation [I'd like to underline the term 'public'] on issues of social inequality and deprivation are now beginning to be more utilized than before. There has been much more action recently in organized movements based broadly on demands for human rights, such as the right to school education, the right to food [...], the entitlement to basic health care, guarantees of environmental preservation, and the right of employment guarantee.[22]

With reference to the "disaster scenes" in Orissa in 1992 and Gujarat in

---

17 Gurcharan Das, *India Unbound. From Independence to the Global Information Age*, New Delhi: Penguin Books ^{2}2002 [2000], 324

18 Ibid., 202

19 Ibid., 287–288

20 Ibid., 146

21 Amartya Sen, *The Argumentative Indian*, London: Penguin Books 2005, 213

22 Ibid., 202

2001, Shiv Visvanathan specifies Sen's "more action [...] in organized movements", by pointing out

> the emergence of a new civil society group, cultural and fundamentalist groups, sometimes just religious groups that provide new styles of rescue and competence."[23]

Indeed, the vast documentation of public agitation in Bhopal over three decades since 1984[24] testifies to the emergence of local civil society and its continued and continuing activities. Here, we encounter new types of local allegiances and new collective identities of active political subjects, which, I propose, have formed a public movement steered by *critical cosmopolitanism,*

> as an alternative view [my emphasis] of globalization that is founded on the recognition of the struggles of individuals and groups for justice worldwide.[25]

Fuyuki Kurasawa draws our attention to the inherent dynamic power of critical cosmopolitanism, its

> dedication to the advancement [my emphasis] of global justice in all its dimensions, [for example of] domestic socio-economic redistribution [and] the pluralistic recognition of marginalized subjectivities, (463)

while Ulrich Beck and Edgar Grande contextualize the term cosmopolitanism in their essay "Beyond methodological nationalism: Non-European and European variations of the Second Modernity",[26] by proposing a theory of cosmopolitan modernities. The authors advocate a "cosmopolitical turn-around in sociological and political theory and research", undergirded by the deconstruction of the (earlier) Eurocentric model of western modernization, or First Modernity. National institutions, they maintain, cannot any longer regulate the globalization of capital and risk, nor can they successfully challenge global conflicts, which in turn raise questions of social justice. Further, a theory of cosmopolitan modernities presupposes the existence of multiple [my emphasis] modern societies,

---

23 Shiv Visvanathan, "The Tsunamis of the Mind", *Tehelka* 8, 14 (April 9, 2011); www.tehelka.com-the-tsunamis-of-the-mind

24 See S. Mukherjee's bibliography, *op.cit.*, 197–208, as well as regular news and comments in *Frontline*

25 Adam De Luca, "Review Essay — Fuyuki Kurasawa's, *The Work of Global Justice*", *German Law Journal* 11, 4 (2012), 457-468; here 463

their plurality, and their dynamic entanglement and mutual interaction, all of which result from different paths of modernisation having been taken by different societies. To challenge global risks these societies are facing requires awareness on their part of cosmopolitical responsibility beyond nation-state borders and towards humanity within "imagined cosmopolitan communities"[27]: a process of cosmopolitanization that

> connects individuals, groups and societies and relates them across existing boundaries and dualisms in a new kind of way so that the status and function of 'self' and 'other' undergo a change.[28]

Coalitions formed in the process of cosmopolitanization are heterogeneous and fluctuating but bound to each other "to represent the universal and to define the parameters of social life." More recently, Beck has pointed out a further characteristic aspect of cosmopolitanization, viz. a process of acting upon cosmopolitical imperatives; in other words, embodying group cooperation across national boundaries in their effort to meet global risks and crises of an ecological, a technical, a financial or a humanitarian nature. Crossings, I'd like to add, also of social, ethnic, gender and religious boundaries.[29]

To return to the novel, I propose that *Animal's People* is an example of aesthetically representing a scenario of cosmopolitan modernities and that its main characters act as the kind of coalition outlined by Beck and Grande: agents inspired by critical cosmopolitanism and involved in the process of cosmopolitanization who, with their story, present documentary evidence of cosmopolitan modernities. Here, people from different social and socio-religious backgrounds join the victims' struggle and create a socioscape, a web of social relations, that radically differs from those in earlier novels about the lives of landless labourers, poor peasants and villagers, about discrimination against untouchables and women and about the bleak prospects of unskilled urban workers to find a living. *Animal's People* also comes across more authentically than earlier novels like *Coolie, Train to*

26 Ulrich Beck und Edward Grande, "Jenseits des methodologischen Nationalismus — Außereuropäische und europäische Variationen der Zweiten Moderne" ["Beyond methodological nationalism — Non-European and European variations of Second Modernity"], *Soziale Welt* 61 (2010), 187-216

27 Ibid., 187

28 Ibid, 195

29 Ulrich Beck, "Weltbürger. Das Zeitalter der Kosmopolitisierung" ["Cosmopolitan. The Age of Cosmopolitanization"], *Frankfurter Allgemeine Zeitung* (8. September 2013)

Pakistan or *So Many Hungers* because well-documented actual events of a real place like Bhopal are integrated into the story's fictionalized scenario of Khaufpur — which, in turn, enhances the performative function of this docu-fictional text. Finally, the "foreground[ing of] characters" transforms hitherto passively suffering people into actively engaged agents. Their struggle for justice and human rights empowers Animal and his people to act as cosmopolitans in the globalized world of the 21st century.

From a narratological perspective, this effect is achieved by Sinha's choice of a first-person narrator who wants to tell his story. Initially sceptical of the "Kakadu Jarnalis […] from Ostrali" (*Animal's People*, 3), who asks him to tell his story to people in the world, Animal initially responds, "what can I say that they will understand?'" (7), but in the end yields to the journalist's request because

> here's a lot to tell, it wants to come out. Like rejoicing, the world's unspoken languages are rushing into my head. Unusual meanings are making themselves known to me. Secrets are shouting themselves into my ear, seems there is nothing I cannot know [since] this story has been locked up in me [and] it's struggling to be free. (11–12)

Unlike an autobiographer, Animal perceives himself not as the teller of his own story but as a mediator. His thoughts about himself and his role preceding his story acquaint the reader with the narrator's psyche (3-12) — and draw attention to the fact that Sinha dedicated his book to Sunil Kumar, a boy who at the age of thirteen lost his parents and five siblings in Bhopal on the day when forty-two tons of toxic gas escaped from a storage tank on "the premises of Union Carbide India Limited (UCIL), a subsidiary of Union Carbide Corporation (UCC), United States."[30] Sunil brought up a younger sister and brother, became involved with activists' groups who fought for restitution and did health work for the disaster's survivors. He campaigned against Union Carbide at home and abroad, fell mentally ill and heard voices plotting to kill him.[31] Eventually, he was treated for schizophrenia and, in July 2006, committed suicide at the age of thirty-five.

No doubt, Sunil who was interviewed by the author in 2004 impacted on Sinha and influenced his authentic portrayal of the seventeen-year old, orphaned, impoverished, physically handicapped, mentally traumatized and semi-literate narrator. However, we must bear in mind that Animal's

30 *Frontline* 29 (August 2012), 16

31 S. Mukherjee, *op.cit.*, 51

creator is an educated member of the middle-class, an intellectual who chose a subaltern living on the fringes of society; a young man who was "not part of the country's development plans,"[32] and whose access to the hegemonic part of society — who, in their own eyes, represent the state — remains closed. Who then controls the story? Could Sinha be called an organic intellectual who through Animal articulates what his narrator cannot really express? Here, the discourse on the subaltern's voice raises its head again, cannot be shunned, but must be kept in mind in the following analysis.

The personal interaction in Animal's richly textured[33] story of about a dozen major and minor characters and their communal struggle to alleviate the fate of the Khaufpuri gas victims and fight for compensation and justice can be subsumed under the category of cosmopolitanization: a process which has already set in when Animal begins the story and which is pushed forward during the course of events covering more than two years between 2001 and 2003.[34] Metaphorically speaking, the characters' interaction resembles the movement of concentric waves spreading from a centre where a stone has hit the water. Animal is the centre and connects with the innermost circle of activists: Zafar bhai, Somraj, Nisha, Farouq and Elli Barber. In turn, they connect outward with 'Zafar's gang' (27), Faqri and Ma Franci and, still further outward, the small family of Hanif, Huriya and Aliya as well as with Pyaré Bai: all of whom represent the large group of severely affected gas victims, a group later joined by Anjali, who had been sold by her poor family to work as a prostitute. Again, further outward they connect with Baju, Bhoora, Chunaram, Dr. Misra, Shastri, Khan, Uttamchand, Chaurilal Babu, and journalists of the Khaufpur Gazette: all of them Khaufpuri citizens less immediately affected by the disaster, yet on occasion supportive of the activists. Finally and on the widest and outermost concentric wave, we have the nameless crowd of victims and their supporters. Their demonstration against the conspiratorial meeting of American lawyers and Indian politicians, whom

32 Ibid., 59

33 The rich nature of the novel's texture is largely nourished by Animal's language which testifies to his entertaining, humorous and not infrequently cynical ways of expressing himself and foregrounding his bravado in its directness and outspokenness. Its main linguistic elements are a mix of English (143, 194), Hindi (122, 167, 209, 284), and French (100-101, 276); frequent vulgar and abusive expressions (45); at times, by way of illustrating a point, quoting made-up poems and rhymed statements in Hindi (66) and English (45, 75, 348); or Hindi songs either from films or made up..

34 The "Editor's Note" preceding Animal's story refers to him as "a nineteen-year-old boy", obviously pointing at the narrator's age at the time of recording his story. Born "before a few days before that night" (1) in 1984, he would be between seventeen and eighteen years old in the story told.

they suspect to secretly arrange a financial settlement before the court has taken a decision on the lawsuit for compensation, lead to the dramatic climax of the story in front of the court building: violent clashes with the police that involve even peace-loving Somraj who slaps a policeman and, like Animal who bites another one's arm, is beaten up and has to be rescued by the demonstrators.

As their names tell, among the activists we find Indian Muslims — Zafar and Farouq, a member of the Yar-yilkai community, Uzbegs, who had arrived from Samarkand generations ago — , as well as Boora and Faqri. There are Hindus like Somraj and Nisha; the French Christian nun Mère Ambrosine called Ma Franci; and the American doctor Elli Barber. We meet older — Pyaré Bai, Dr. Misra — and younger — Nisha — women; older — Boora, Shastri, Khan — and younger — Farouq — men; intellectuals and artists like Zafar and Somraj and the semi-literates Farouq and Faqri; lawyers, students, a tabla player, shopkeepers, bureaucrats and auto-rikshaw drivers. It is, indeed, a local alliance of campaigners across religious, caste, gender, social, generational and national boundaries who constitute a cosmopolitan community in a nutshell, together with Animal, who doggedly rejects to be classified as either a Hindu, a Muslim or perhaps an "Isayi" (14). Instead, he insists on being called Animal, the name once forced upon him by the orphanage kids he grew up with, "who started calling me Animal one day […] 'Jaanvar, jungli Jaanvar'. Animal, wild Animal." (15)

Were we to follow his individual story here, we would quickly realize the weight he carries on his crippled body and in his mind in spite of his daredevil attitude. A profoundly ambivalent attitude both towards himself and others controls his inner and outer world: his thoughts and hopes, and the despair that overwhelms him over and again on the one hand, and the various roles he has to play vis-à-vis his fellow beings on the other. Looked at from a narratological angle, Sinha could hardly have created a more authentic narrator, because it is precisely Animal's ambivalence that distances the reader from his story, and challenges us to weigh Animal's judgments of his own feelings and his behaviour as well as of those of the group members he describes. We ask ourselves, should we believe or doubt his words? Here I return to Adorno's revised view and suggest that our estimate of the *aesthetic* achievement or failure of the story takes second place against its claim of authentically conveying the *moral* nature of the activists' resentment against the US company and Indian politicians and their deep empathy for and practical engagement with the victims.

Of course, Animal's ambivalence feeding into his story is also rooted in the multiple roles he is made to play: a second narrative device. Having turned into a smart street kid ever since he became crippled at the age of six, and having adopted the 'language of the street' and become a master of the lashing tongue as well as of survival strategies, Jaanvar, "'one who lives'" (35) in a hole on the contaminated factory site, which he calls "my kingdom" (30), appears to be the perfect go-between to connect his own with Zafar's world; the world of the group's intellectual leader, who has given up everything in life and dedicated it to the poor (22); the leader who has won over Animal to work with his group — and earn a small income. Zafar's faith in life, his "sensible view" (207) and deep belief in "humanity, [and] that deep down people are good" (207) impress Animal as much as his Gandhian-like non-violent pursuit of justice. (202) At the same time, he cannot help but call Zafar — as well as Pandit Somraj, known as *Aawaaz-e-Khaufpur* "until that night took away his wife and baby son and fucked up his lungs" (33) — and other members of 'Zafar's gang' "just a bunch of fucking do-gooders." (27) Nonetheless, he accepts his role of go-between by, for instance, delivering money collected by the do-gooders to the needy, and he is the one who reports "to Zafar if anything unusual was going on in the bastis [and what he has found] out what the government, munisipal etc were up to, because those buggers are always up to no good." (27)

The campaigners' activities are manifold, varied, and by no means always agreed upon, apart from being obstructed by those in power. They range from Zafar organizing the protest against the "Kampani", addressing the demonstrators, arguing legal points with local politicians and judges, and generally acting as the victims' spokesman; Somraj running a poison-relief committee for the poorest people; his daughter Nisha participating in street marches — and teaching Animal how to read and write; Ma Franci attending sick and injured people; Farouq acting as Zafar's right hand man and, of course, Animal carrying, for example, 20 000 Rupees to a woman so she can pay back her debts to the money lender. He also sees to it that the sick little girl Aliya is given medical help by Elli Barber, the American doctor, who sets up a clinic and offers free health service: a step deeply distrusted by members of the group since they assume the Kampani behind her, which they suspect of using the Free Clinic as a ruse not to pay the victims. In his role of "Namispond Jamispond" (110) Animal acts on Zafar's request to find out who she is, but he is unable to establish her identity. Zafar's subsequent call to boycott the clinic is followed by the people, but not really shared by Somraj and Animal who convinces the Pandit to meet Elli because he trusts her humanity.

Though Zafar eventually relents and the clinic starts functioning, tension within the group is heightened again by his decision, taken against Somraj and Nisha's entreaty, to go on a hunger strike during 'nantap', the height of summer, together with two women and Farouq; a fast to last till the day of the court hearing. Though watched by "hundreds of women [...] in a mass of bright saris and black burkhas [...] always women who support" (288), dissent prevails about Zafar's strategy within the group. It testifies to individual differences but also reflects the story-teller's ambivalent feelings toward single group members and, more importantly, indicates the author's narrative strategy to avoid creating a flawless "bunch of do-gooders": yet one more narrative device to bolster up the story's authenticity.[35]

Animal's story seems to close on a note of apotheosis: "'So, after all, we've won", he says; and quoting Zafar's earlier words that "we are left with nothing. Having nothing means we have nothing to lose [... and] with the power of nothing we are invincible, we are bound to win'" (54), he exclaims: "The power of nothing rose up and destroyed our enemies'" (358): Elli, clad in a burkha, had smuggled herself into the hotel conference hall and "emptied a bottle of stink bomb juice into the air conditioner" (361), which led to the break-up of the meeting.

In the group's common struggle for the retrieval of human rights, boundaries have been successfully crossed: the American Elli and Pandit Somraj marry, and so do forty-year old Muslim Zafar and the young Hindu woman Nisha. Animal continues to have his lunch with them every day, but he is back in his old place, and preparations are underway for him to travel to the States and be operated upon. The process of cosmopolitanization, the activists' struggle in Khaufpur against economic, financial, health and ecological risks, across religious, social and national boundaries, has been pushed forward and is firmly anchored in the here and now of cosmopolitan modernities — but has not quite achieved its aims. The Kampani will continue to evade its responsibility, supported by politicians and lawyers, and "there is still sickness all over Khaufpur, hundreds come daily to Elli doctress's clinic." (365)

Towards the end of their essay, Beck and Grande ask whether there exists a chance for establishing cosmopolitanism in the sense they propose and draw up several scenarios: an optimistic one based on the belief that cosmopolitical responsibility will grow and transform humanity into

35 In Anjali Deshpande's novel *Impeachment* (2012) we come across a very similar constellation of increasingly differing voices within the group of the Friends of Bhopal (FOB) in New Delhi. Finally, it leads to its break-up in spite of the members' preparedness to actively support the legal case of Bhopal victims for compensation.

a political subject; a realistic one that doubts a solution will be worked out between the producers and the recipients/victims of global risks; or a negative one of a vicious circle caused by climate catastrophes, ensuing global migratory movements, fundamentalist counter movements, violence and climate wars.[36] I propose that the cosmopolitanization process at the centre of *Animal's Story* is located at the intersection of the alternative trends towards the optimistic and the realistic scenario. The novel places its hope for cosmopolitanism on the allegiance of professionals — intellectuals, lawyers, doctors, teachers, artists motivated by their humanitarian commitment — and the socially, economically and educationally deprived; an allegiance metonymically encapsulated in the interaction and cooperation of Zafar, Somraj, Nisha and Elli with Animal and his impoverished and sick Khaufpuri friends.

Looking back at Indian English narratives about the country's marginalized humans, Sinha's novel represents the first example I know of which literally configures the manifold conflicts between the powerless and the power-wielders from the angle of critical cosmopolitanism. An emerging local group acts upon the cosmopolitical imperative of cooperation and establishes agency and empowerment across subnational and national boundaries. Though Animal does not really end his story on an optimistic note when he reaffirms his view that "the poor remain. [… and] tomorrow there will be more of us" (366), his admiration for Zafar's confidence that "we'll get them in the end" (365) lingers on in him — and in the readers' minds. As do Zafar's words, "*Jahaañ jaan hai, jahaan hai.* While we have life, we have the world", which, as Animal admits, sent "thrills up and down my crooked back, they want to make me weep. 'Wah. wah,' I say, before I can stop myself." (284)

Works cited

Novels

Adiga, Aravind, *The White Tiger*, New Delhi: Harper Collins 2008

Anand, Mulk Raj, *Untouchable*, London: Lawrence & Wishart 1935 [Bombay: Kutub-Popular n.d.]

—, *The Coolie*, London: Lawrence & Wishart 1936 [Bombay: Kutub-Popular n.d.]

—, *Two Leaves and a Bud*, London: Lawrence & Wishart 1937 [Bombay: Kutub-Popular ^{2}1951]

—, *The Old Woman and the Cow*, Bombay: Kutub-Popular 1960

Bhattacharya, Bhabani, *So Many Hungers!* London: Victor Gollancz 1947

—, *He Who Rides a Tiger*, New York: Crown 1954

Chandra, Vikram, *Sacred Games*, New Delhi: Penguin Books India 2006

36 Beck/Grande, *op.cit.*, 206–207

DESAI, Anita, *Cry, the Peacock*, London: Peter Owen 1963
DESAI, Kiran, *The Inheritance of Loss*, New Delhi: Penguin Books India 2006
DESHPANDE, Anjali, *Impeachment*, Gurgaon: Hachette 2012
GHOSH, Amitav, *Sea of Poppies*, New Delhi: Penguin Books India 2008
JHA, Raj Kamal, *Fireproof*, London: Picador 2006
JOSHI, Arun, *The City and the River*, New Delhi: Orient Paperbacks 1994
MARKANDAYA, Kamala, *Nectar in a Sieve*, New York: Signet Classic 1954
—, *A Handful of Rice*, New York: The John Day Company 1966
MEHTA, Suketu, *Maximum City — Bombay Lost and Found*, New Delhi: Penguin Books India 2004
PESTONJI, Meher, *Sadak Chhaap*, New Delhi: Penguin Books 2005
PRAKASH, Udai, *Mohandas*, in: *Hans*, New Delhi: Akshar Prakashan 2005
RAO, Raja, *Kanthapura*, London: George Allen and Unwin 1938
ROY, Arundhati, *The God of Small Things*, London: Harper Collins 1997
SINGH, Kushwant, *Train to Pakistan*, London: Chatto and Windus 1956
SINHA, Indra, *Animal's People*, London: Simon & Schuster Pocket Books 2008 [2007]
VAID, Krishna Baldev, *Ek naukarani ki diary*, New Delhi: Rajpal and Sons 2000
VALMIKI, Omprakash, *Joothan — A Dalit's Life*, trs. from the Hindi by Arun Prabha Mukherjee, Kolkata: Bhatkla and Sen 2003
VENKATARAMANI, K.S., *Murugan the Tiller*, 1927

Critical Studies

ADORNO, Theodor Wiesengrund, "Jene Zwanziger Jahre" ["Those Twenties"], ed. Petra Kiedaisch, *Lyrik nach Auschwitz [Poetry After Auschwitz]*, Stuttgart: Reclam 1995
ALBROW, M., J. Eade, J.Durrschmidt and N. Washburne, "The impact of globalization on sociological concepts: community, culture and milieu", ed. J. Eade, *Living the Global City: Globalization as Local Process*, London and New York: Routledge 1997, 20–36
BECK, Ulrich und Edgar Grande, "Jenseits des methodologischen Nationalismus — Aussereuropäische und europäische Variationen der Zweiten Moderne" ["Beyond Methodological Nationalism — Non-European and European Variations of Second Modernity"], *Soziale Welt* 61 (2010), 187–216
BECK, Ulrich, "Weltbürger. Das Zeitalter der Kosmopolitisierung" ["Cosmopolitan. The Age of Cosmopolitization"], *Frankfurter Allgemeine Zeitung* (8. September 2013)
DAS, Gurcharan, *India Unbound. From Independence to the Global Information Age*, New Delhi: Penguin Books ²2002 [2000]
DE LUCA, Adam, "Review Essay — Fuyuki Kurasawa's, *The Work of Global Justice*", *German Law Journal* 11, 4 (2012), 457–468
LANGE, Bernd-Peter, "Crime and the Mega City", *museindia* 24 (March–April 2009), www.museindia.com
MUKHERJEE, Suropa, *Surviving Bhopal — Dancing Bodies, Written Texts, and Oral Testimonials of Women in the Wake of an Industrial Disaster*, New York: Palgrave Macmillan 2010
SEN, Amartya, *The Argumentative Indian*, London: Penguin Books 2005
SHEORAJ SINGH 'Bechan', "Voices of Awakening", *The Hindu* (August 3, 2008)
VISVANATHAN, Shiv, "The Tsunamis of the Mind", *Tehelka* 8, 14 (2011, April 9)

Sources

"Critical Studies of Indo-English Literature", *Kritikon Litterarum* III, 1 (1974), 61–66

"The Function of Labour in Mulk Raj Anand's Novels", *The Journal of the School of Languages* (Monsoon 1976), 1–20

"Modern Indo-English Poetry and P. Lal's 'New Poets Manifesto'", *Commonwealth Quarterly* I, 5 (1977), 3–16

"History and the Individual in Anita Desai's *Clear Light of Day* and Salman Rushdie's *Midnight's Children*", *World Literature Written in English* 23, 1 (Winter 1984), 196–207

"Indian Women Writing in English in the 1970s", *World Literature Written in English* 25, 1 (1985), 312–318

"Marginalizing the Centre — Centring the Periphery: The Reception of Indian Literature in English", eds. Günter Blaicher and Brigitte Glaser, *Anglistentag Eichstätt: Proceedings*, Tübingen: Max Niemeyer 1994, 193–204

"'... in the days when the Love Laws were made': Arundhati Roy's *The God of Small Things*", ed. R.K. Dhawan, *Arundhati Roy: The Novelist Extraordinary*, New Delhi: Prestige 1999, 120-131

"Global Fantasy — Glocal Imagination: The New Literatures in English and their Fantastic Imagi-Nations", *Journal of Postcolonial Writing* 41, 1 (2005), 14–25

"The Indian Novel in English: A National Literature?", *Muse India* Issue 7 (2006)

"Nature and Landscape in Raja Rao's Writing — An Evolutionary Psychological Analysis", unpublished 2008

"'The Train Has Moved On' — R.K. Narayan's *The Guide* and Literary History", *Asiatic* vol. 3, 2 (December 2009), 88–100, www.asiatic.iiu.ed.my

"The New English Language Literatures and the Globalization of Tertiary Education", ed. Sumanyu Satpathy, *Southern Postcolonialisms: The Global South and the 'New' Literary Representations*, London/New York/New Delhi: Routledge 2009, 97–110

"The Persistence and Creation of Internal Borders: Indians in Aotearoa/New Zealand", ed. Cynthia vanden Driesen and T. Vijay Kumar, *Globalisation: Australian–Asian Perspectives*, Delhi: Atlantic Publishers 2014, 181–196

"Translating Cultures: Pictorial and Literary Representation of India in William Hodges's Paintings and Travel Book", ed. Stella Borg Barthet, *Imbatti — Crosscurrents in Postcolonial Memory and Literature: Festschrift for Daniel Massa*, University of Malta [in print]

"The Postcolonial Agenda: Literary Configurations of Retrieving Human Rights in Indra Sinha's Novel *Animal's People*" ["Retrieving Human Rights: Indra Sinha's *Animal's People* and Critical Cosmopolitanism"], *The IACLALS Journal* vol. 1 (2015), 11–28

Photo Credits

Page	
ix	Humped Indian Bull, Mohenjo-Daro, 3rd mill B.C. — own copy cast DR 1965
1	Campus with Gandhi Bhavan, Punjab University, Chandigarh — DR 2014
6	Kochi scene, Kerala — DR 2008
26	P. Lal's poetry collection *The Parrot's Death* — own copy DR 1965
37	Srinagar picture postcard of the 1960s, Kashmir — DR 1966
51	Poster in Thiruvananthapuram, Kerala — DR 2008
59	Dhvanyaloka library and reading room, Mysore — DR 1993
61	Diagram N(ew) English Language Literatures (NELL) — DR 1993
76	Village near Balaram-puram, Kerala — DR 2008
92	Diagram Calcutta chromosome — DR 2015
106	Post-1990 Indian English Novels — own copies Jan Kemp 2015
114	Kardamom Hills towards Periyar National Park, Kerala — DR 2008
125	Sadhu in Varanasi, Uttar Pradesh — DR 2004
138	Lake Palace Hotel, Udaipur, Rajasthan — Konstanze Streese 2004
153	Book cover *Indian Ink* — Victoria UP, New Zealand 2005 — own copy DR
166	William Hodges, 'Great Pagoda at Tanjore'; *Travels in India* — own copy DR
179	Animal Sculpture — Artist Eleanor Stride: www. eleanorstride.blogspot.com (2015); and Indra Sinha: www.indrasinha.com (2015)
88	Mulk Raj Anand in Kandala, Maharashtra — Jan Kemp 2002
89	Book cover *Untouchable* — own copy DR
88	R.K. Narayan in Madras/Chennai, Tamil Nadu — DR 1993
89	Book cover *The Guide* — own copy DR
90	Raja Rao in Singapore — Jan Kemp 1986
91	Book cover *The Serpent and the Rope* — own copy
90	P. Lal in his library in Calcutta — www.writerswork-shopindia.com
91	*Modern Indian Poetry in English — An Anthology & a Credo* — own copy DR

Author's Publications

BOOKS

Der moderne englischsprachige Roman Indiens, Darmstadt: Thesen Verlag 1974, 161pp [Ph.D. thesis]

Ed., *Shiva tanzt. Das indische Kulturlesebuch*, Zürich: Unionsverlag 1986; repr.1987 & rev. ed.1999, 285pp

Ed., *Im Schatten des Banyanbaumes. Geschichten aus Indien*, Frauenfeld: Verlag im Waldgut 1990, 208pp

The Indian Novel in English: Its Critical Discourse 1934–2004, Jaipur/Delhi: Rawat Publications 2005, 386pp

Ed., *Reise nach Indien: Kulturkompass fürs Handgepäck*, Zürich: Unionsverlag 2008, UT 423 (rev. & updated edition of *Shiva tanzt*), 256pp

MONOGRAPHS

An Ideal of Man in Mulk Raj Anand's Novels, Bombay: Kutub Popular 1967, 25pp

Studies in Indian Fiction in English, Dharwad: Karnataka University 1983, 32pp

Mulk Raj Anand, München: *edition text und kritik* 1984, 17pp; rev. in: *Kritisches Lexikon zur fremdsprachigen Gegenwartsliteratur*, 69. Nlfg. (2006), 1–11, A1–3, D1–2

R.K. Narayan, München: *edition text und kritik* 1985, 14pp; rev. in *Kritisches Lexikon zur fremdsprachigen Gegenwartsliteratur*, 69. Nlfg. (2006), 1–13, A1–2, B1–2, D1–2

Raja Rao, München: *Kritisches Lexikon zur fremdsprachigen Gegenwartsliteratur*, 70. Nlfg. (2006), 8–9, A1, B1, D1–2

ARTICLES IN JOURNALS AND BOOKS

"An Ideal of Man in Mulk Raj Anand's Novels", *Indian Literature* 10, 1 (1967), 29-51; repr. as "Alienation in the Novels of Mulk Raj Anand", ed. K.K. Sharma, *Perspectives on Mulk Raj Anand*, Ghaziabad: Vimal Prakashan 1978, 94-114

"Critical Studies of Indo-English Literature", *Kritikon Litterarum* III, 1 (1974), 61-66

"Literary Criticism in India: M. Mukherjee's Study *The Twice Born Fiction: Themes and Techniques of the Indian Novel in English*", *The Journal of the School of Languages* (Winter 1974-75), 13-33

"The Function of Labour in Mulk Raj Anand's Novels", *The Journal of the School of Languages* (Monsoon 1976), 1-20; repr. in: eds. M.S.N. Eakambaram and A. Natarajan Nagarajan, *Essays in Criticism on Indian Literature in English*, New Delhi: S Chand & Company 1991, 67-83

"Die indo-englische Literatur", Hg. Heinz Kosock und Horst Prießnitz, *Literaturen in englischer Sprache*, Bonn: Bouvier Verlag 1977, 219-238

"Modern Indo-English Poetry and P. Lal's 'New Poets Manifesto'", *Commonwealth Quarterly* I, 5 (1977), 3-16; repr. in: *Commonwealth Newsletter* 12 (1977), 40-47

"British Characters in Indo-English Fiction", ed. M.K. Naik, *Aspects of Indian Writing in English*, Madras: Macmillan 1979, 137-149

"The Indo-English Novel", *Indian Literature* 26, 5 (1983), 27-39; repr. in: *Commonwealth Fiction*, vol. I, ed. R.K. Dhawan, New Delhi: Classical Publishing Company 1988, 49–61

"History and the Individual in Anita Desai's *Clear Light of Day* and Salman Rushdie's *Midnight's Children*", *WLWE* 23, 1 (Winter 1984), 196-207: repr. in: *Kunapipi* VI, 2 (1984), 53-66

"Indian Women Writing in English in the 1970s", *WLWE* 25, 1 (1985), 312-318; repr. as "Indian Women Writing in English: The Short Story", ed. Peter Stummer, *The Story Must Be Told*, Würzburg: Koenigshausen und Neumann 1986, 171-178

"The Search for Cultural Identity: G.V. Desani's *All About H.Hatterr*", *The Literary Criterion* XX, 2 (1985), 23-35

"Marginalizing the Centre — Centring the Periphery: The Reception of Indian Literature in English", Hg. Günther Blaicher und Brigitte Glaser, *Anglistentag Eichstätt: Proceedings*, Tübingen: Max Niemeyer 1994, 193–204; repr. in: *Littcrit* 21, 1 (June 1995), 52–76; repr. in: ed. P.K. Rajan, *Indian Literary Criticism in English: Critics, Texts, Issues*, Jaipur/Delhi: Rawat Publishers 2004, 171–193

". . . in the days when the Love Laws were made", ed. R.K. Dhawan, *Arundhati Roy: The Novelist Extraordinary*, New Delhi: Prestige 1999, 120–131; repr. as "In the days when the Love Laws were made", eds. Richard Corballis and André Viola, *Postcolonial Knitting: The Art of Jaqueline Bardolphe*, Palmerston North/Nice: Massey University/Université de Nice-Sophia Antipolis 2000, 124–134

"Global Fantasy — Glocal Imagination: The New Literatures in English and their Fantastic ImagiNations", *Journal of Postcolonial Writing* 41, 1 (2005), 14–25

"Contemporary Indian Literature in English: Its Impact and Relevance in Germany", eds. Bernd-Peter Lange, Mala Pandurang, *Mediating Indian Writing in English: German Responses*, Berlin: LIT Verlag 2006, 19–40; repr. in: *Mediating Indian Writing in English: German Responses* , Jaipur/ Delhi: Rawat Publishing 2006

"Mulk Raj Anand: A diffused and continuous narrative, a story of dauntless search for truth", *The Journal of Indian Writing in English* 33, 1 (2005), 44–58

"Glocality and its (Dis)contents: The Future of English Language Studies", *Zeitschrift für Anglistik und Amerikanistik* LIII, 4 (2005), 385–396

"Die Migrantenliteratur Indiens", Hg. Gisela Febel u.a., *Kontakt und Konflikt: Perspektiven der Postkolonialismus-Forschung*, Trier: Wissenschaftlicher Verlag Trier 2006, 177–188

"Doppelperspektiven: Die englischsprachige Literatur Indiens", Hg. Helmuth A. Niederle, *Literatur und Migration — Indien: Migranten aus Südindien und der westliche Kontext*, Wien: Edition Milo im Verlag Lehner 2007, 175–197

"The Persistance and Creation of Internal Borders: Indians in Aotearoa/New Zealand", eds. Cynthia vanden Driesen and T. Vijay Kumar, *Globalisation: Australian-Asian Perspectives*, Delhi: Atlantic Publishers 2014, 181–196

"The Postcolonial Agenda: Literary Configurations of Retrieving Human Rights in Indra Sinha's Novel *Animal's People*", *The IACLALS Journal*, vol. 1 (2015), 11–28

"Translating Cultures: Pictorial and Literary Representation of India in William Hodges's Paintings and Travel Book"; ed. Stella Borg Barthet, *Imbatti — Crosscurrents in Postcolonial Memory and Literature: Festschrift for Daniel Massa*, Malta: University of Malta, in print

NEWSLETTERS AND OTHER PRINTED ARTICLES

"Der englischsprachige Roman Indiens", *Lektorenforum* 2 (September 1968), 41–49

"Keki N. Daruwalla — ein indischer Dichter", *Literaturnachrichten* 19 (September 1988), 8–10

"Die Unzeit des Imam. Zu Salman Rushdies Satanischen Versen", *Literaturnachrichten* 21 (Mai 1989), 1–5

"Jayanta Mahapatra, Der indische Weg", *Literaturnachrichten* 89 (2006), 8–11

ELECTRONIC PUBLICATIONS

"The Indian Novel in English", *Muse India — the literary ejournal* Issue 7 (2006) www.museindia.com

Ed. and "Introduction: Indian Fiction in English: German Responses", *Muse India — the literary ejournal* Issue 24 (March/April 2009), www.museindia.com

"Tarun J. Tejpal, *The Alchemy of Desire*", *Muse India — the literary ejournal* Issue 24 (March/ April2009), www.museindia.com

"'The Train Has Moved On' — R.K. Narayan's *The Guide* and Literary History", *Asiatic* vol. 3, 2 (December 2009), 88–100 www.asiatic.iiu.ed.my

"India in New Zealand: Local identities, global relations", ed. Sekhar Bandyopadhyay, Dunedin: Otago UP 2012", *Landfall*, www.landfallreviewonline.com (February 2012)

BOOK REVIEWS

"Mulk Raj Anand: *Confession of a Lover*", *WLWE* XVI, 1 (1977), 105-109

"Saros Cowasjee, *So Many Freedoms. A Study of the Major Fiction of Mulk Raj Anand*", *The Journal of the School of Languages* 1&2 (1978/79), 150-155

"Monika Fludernik (ed.), *Hybridity and Postcolonialism: Twentieth Century Indian Literature*", *ZAA* 47, 4 (1999), 408–410; repr. in: *Canadian Literature* 174 (2002), 160–162

"*Genres of modernity: contemporary Indian novels in English*, by Dirk Wiemann, Amsterdam and New York, Rodopi, 2008, 334pp., €69.00, ISBN 978 9 420 2493 9", *Journal of Postcolonial Writing* 46, 3/4 (2010), 428–30

"Elleke Boehmer and Rosinka Chaudhuri (eds.), *The Indian Postcolonial — A Critical Reader*, London and New York: Routledge, 2011, pp.366", *Journal of Postcolonial Writing* 47, 5 (December 2011), 571–573

CONTRIBUTIONS TO DICTIONARIES / HAND-BOOKS OF LITERATURE

"Mulk Raj Anand; Anita Desai; G.V.Desani; P.Lal; Kamala Markandaya; R.K.Narayan; Raja Rao; Salman Rushdie; Khushwant Singh," *Lexikon der Weltliteratur*, Dortmund: Harenberg Kommunikation 1989

"Arun Joshi, *The Strange Case of Billy Biswas*; *The Last Labyrinth*", *Kindlers Literaturlexikon* Bd.8 (1990), 884–6

"Raja Rao, *Kanthapura*", *Kindlers Literaturlexikon*, Bd.13 (1991), 949–950

"Salman Rushdie, *Midnight's Children*; *Shame*; *The Satanic Verses*", *Kindlers Literaturlexikon* Bd.14 (1991), 478–485

"Vikram Seth, *A Suitable Boy*", ibid., 463–464

"Bapsi Sidhwa, *Ice-Candy-Man*", ibid., 477–479

[19 texts by and biograms on Indian English authors, *Kindlers Literaturlexikon* 3, Stuttgart: Metzler 2009]

CO/EDITORSHIP

Co-ed. with Pavan Malreddy, "Special Issue: Arun Joshi: Avant-Garde, Existentialism and the West", *Zeitschrift für Anglistik und Amerikanistik* vol. 62, 1 (2014), 3–76

RADIOFEATURES/REVIEWS

"Indian Poetry by Nirmal Varma, Ajneya, Sitakant Mahapatra, Kamala Das, A.K. Ramanujam", Hessischer Rundfunk, 2. Progr., 22.-26.8.1986

"Shashi Deshpande, *The Dark Holds no Terror*", Hessischer Rundfunk, 2.Progr., 9.12.1987

"Salman Rushdie, *The Satanic Verses*", Radio New Zealand, Concert Programme, 3 May 1990